Karl Marx

The Critique Of The Political Economy

OK Publishing 2021

Karl Marx
The Critique Of The Political Economy

Published by
MUSAICUM
Books

- Advanced Digital Solutions & High-Quality book Formatting -

musaicumbooks@okpublishing.info

2021 OK Publishing

ISBN 978-80-272-7308-9

Contents

Author's Preface   11

BOOK I. Capital in general   15

Chapter I. Commodities   16

A. Notes on the History of the Theory of Commodities   28

Chapter II. Money or Simple Circulation   32

B. Theories of the Unit of Measure of Money   37

C. Theories of the Medium of Circulation and of Money   74

Introduction to the Critique of Political Economy155   89

1.   Production in General   90

2.   The General Relation of Production to Distribution, Exchange, and Consump-
     tion   92

3.   The Method of Political Economy   99

4.   Production, Means of Production, and Conditions of Production, the Relations
     of Production and Distribution.164 The Connection Between Form of State and
     Property on the One Hand and Relations of Production and Distribution(1) on
     the Other. Legal Relations. Family Relations.   103

Footnotes   107

Author's Preface

I consider the system of bourgeois economy in the following order: *Capital, landed property, wage labor; state, foreign trade, world market.* Under the first three heads I examine the conditions of the economic existence of the three great classes, which make up modern bourgeois society; the connection of the three remaining heads is self evident. The first part of the first book, treating of capital, consists of the following chapters: 1. Commodity; 2. Money, or simple circulation; 3. Capital in general. The first two chapters form the contents of the present work. The entire material lies before me in the form of monographs, written at long intervals not for publication, but for the purpose of clearing up those questions to myself, and their systematic elaboration on the plan outlined above will depend upon circumstances.

I omit a general introduction which I had prepared, as on second thought any anticipation of results that are still to be proven, seemed to me objectionable, and the reader who wishes to follow me at all, must make up his mind to pass from the special to the general. On the other hand, some remarks as to the course of my own politico-economic studies may be in place here.

The subject of my professional studies was jurisprudence, which I pursued, however, in connection with and as secondary to the studies of philosophy and history. In 1842-43, as editor of the "Rheinische Zeitung," I found myself embarrassed at first when I had to take part in discussions concerning so-called material interests. The proceedings of the Rhine Diet in connection with forest thefts and the extreme subdivision of landed property; the official controversy about the condition of the Mosel peasants into which Herr von Schaper, at that time president of the Rhine Province, entered with the "Rheinische Zeitung;" finally, the debates on free trade and protection, gave me the first impulse to take up the study of economic questions. At the same time a weak, quasi-philosophic echo of French socialism and communism made itself heard in the "Rheinische Zeitung" in those days when the good intentions "to go ahead" greatly outweighed knowledge of facts. I declared myself against such botching, but had to admit at once in a controversy with the "Allgemeine Augsburger Zeitung" that my previous studies did not allow me to hazard an independent judgment as to the merits of the French schools. When, therefore, the publishers of the "Rheinische Zeitung" conceived the illusion that by a less aggressive policy the paper could be saved from the death sentence pronounced upon it, I was glad to grasp that opportunity to retire to my study room from public life.

The first work undertaken for the solution of the question that troubled me, was a critical revision of Hegel's "Philosophy of Law"; the introduction to that work appeared in the "Deutsch-Französische Jahrbücher," published in Paris in 1844. I was led by my studies to the conclusion that legal relations as well as forms of state could neither be understood by themselves, nor explained by the so-called general progress of the human mind, but that they are rooted in the material conditions of life, which are summed up by Hegel after the fashion of the English and French of the eighteenth century under the name "civic society;" the anatomy of that civic society is to be sought in political economy. The study of the latter which I had taken up in Paris, I continued at Brussels whither I emigrated on account of an order of expulsion issued by Mr. Guizot. The general conclusion at which I arrived and which, once reached, continued to serve as the leading thread in my studies, may be briefly summed up as follows: In the social production which men carry on they enter into definite relations that are indispensable and independent of their will; these relations of production correspond to a definite stage of development of their material powers of production. The sum total of these relations of production constitutes the economic structure of society-the real foundation, on which rise legal and political superstructures and to which correspond definite forms of social consciousness. The mode of production in material life determines the general character of the social, political and spiritual processes of life. It is not the consciousness of men that determines their existence, but, on the contrary, their social existence determines their consciousness. At a certain stage of their development, the material forces of production in society come in conflict with the existing relations of production, or-what is but a legal expression for the same thing-with the property relations within which they had been at work before. From forms of development of the forces of production these relations turn into their fetters. Then comes the period of social revolution. With the change of the economic foundation the entire immense superstructure is more or less rapidly transformed. In considering such transformations the distinction should always be made between the material transformation of the economic conditions of production which can be determined with the precision of natural science, and the legal, political, religious, aesthetic or philosophic-in short ideological forms in which men become conscious of this conflict and fight it out. Just as our opinion of an individual is not based on what he thinks of himself, so can we not judge of such a period of transformation by its own consciousness; on the contrary, this consciousness must rather be explained from the contradictions of material life, from the existing conflict between the social forces of production and the relations of production. No social order ever disappears before all the productive forces, for which there is room in it, have been developed; and new higher relations of production never appear before the material conditions of their existence have matured in the womb of the old society. Therefore, mankind always takes up only such problems as it can solve; since, looking at the matter more closely, we will always find that the problem itself arises only when the material conditions necessary for its solution already exist or are at least in the process of formation. In broad outlines we can designate the Asiatic, the ancient, the feudal, and the modern bourgeois methods of production as so many epochs in the progress of the economic formation of society. The bourgeois relations of production are the last antagonistic form of the social process of production-antagonistic not in the sense of individual antagonism, but of one arising from conditions surrounding the life of individuals in society; at the same time the productive forces developing in the womb of bourgeois society create the material conditions for the solution of that antagonism. This social formation constitutes, therefore, the closing chapter of the prehistoric stage of human society.

Frederick Engels, with whom I was continually corresponding and exchanging ideas since the appearance of his ingenious critical essay on economic categories (in the "Deutsch-Französische Jahrbücher"), came by a different road to the same conclusions as myself (see his "Condition of the Working Classes in England"). When he, too, settled in Brussels in the spring of 1845, we decided to work out together the contrast between our view and the idealism of the German philosophy, in fact to settle our accounts with our former philosophic conscience. The plan was carried out in the form of a criticism of the post-Hegelian philosophy. The manuscript in two solid octavo volumes had long reached the publisher in Westphalia, when we received information that conditions had so changed as not to allow of its publication. We abandoned the manuscript to the stinging criticism of the mice the more readily since we had accomplished our main purpose-the clearing up of the question to ourselves. Of the scattered writings on various subjects in which we presented our views to the public at that time, I recall only the "Manifesto of the Communist Party" written by Engels and myself, and the "Discourse on Free Trade" written by myself. The leading points of our theory were first presented scientifically, though in a polemic form, in my "Misère de la Philosophie, etc." directed against Proudhon and published in 1847. An essay on "Wage Labor," written by me in German, and in which I put together my lectures on the subject delivered before the German Workmen's Club at Brussels, was prevented from leaving the hands of the printer by the February revolution and my expulsion from Belgium which followed it as a consequence.

The publication of the "Neue Rheinische Zeitung" in 1848 and 1849, and the events which took place later on, interrupted my economic studies which I could not resume before 1850 in London. The enormous material on the history of political economy which is accumulated in the British Museum; the favorable view which London offers for the observation of bourgeois society; finally, the new stage of development upon which the latter seemed to have entered with the discovery of gold in California and Australia, led me to the decision to resume my studies from the very beginning and work up critically the new material. These studies partly led to what might seem side questions, over which I nevertheless had to stop for longer or shorter periods of time. Especially was the time at my disposal cut down by the imperative necessity of working for a living. My work as contributor on the leading Anglo-American newspaper, the "New York Tribune," at which I have now been engaged for eight years, has caused very great interruption in my studies, since I engage in newspaper work proper only occasionally. Yet articles on important economic events in England and on the continent have formed so large a part of my contributions that I have been obliged to make myself familiar with practical details which lie outside the proper sphere of political economy.

This account of the course of my studies in political economy is simply to prove that my views, whatever one may think of them, and no matter how little they agree with the interested prejudices of the ruling classes, are the result of many years of conscientious research. At the entrance to science, however, the same requirement must be put as at the entrance to hell:

Qui si convien lasciare ogni sospetto
Ogni viltà convien che qui sia morta.

Karl Marx.

London, January, 1859.

BOOK I. Capital in general

Chapter I
Commodities

At first sight the wealth of society under the capitalist system presents itself as an immense accumulation of commodities, its unit being a single commodity. But every commodity has a twofold aspect, that of *use value* and *exchange value.*[1]

A commodity is first of all, in the language of English economists, "any thing necessary, useful or pleasant in life," an object of human wants, a means of existence in the broadest sense of the word. This property of commodities to serve as use-values coincides with their natural palpable existence. Wheat e. g. is a distinct use-value differing from the use-values cotton, glass, paper, etc. Use-value has a value only in use and is realized only in the process of consumption. The same use-value may be utilized in various ways. But the extent of its possible applications is circumscribed by its distinct properties. Furthermore, it is thus limited not only qualitatively but also quantitatively. According to their natural properties the various use-values have different measures, such as a bushel of wheat, a quire of paper, a yard of linen, etc.

Whatever the social form of wealth may be, use-values always have a substance of their own, independent of that form. One can not tell by the taste of wheat whether it has been raised by a Russian serf, a French peasant, or an English capitalist. Although the object of social wants and, therefore, mutually connected in society, use-values do not bear any marks of the relations of social production. Suppose, we have a commodity whose use-value is that of a diamond. We can not tell by looking at the diamond that it is a commodity. When it serves as a use-value, aesthetic or mechanical, on the breast of a harlot, or in the hand of a glasscutter, it is a diamond and not a commodity. It is the necessary pre-requisite of a commodity to be a use-value, but it is immaterial to the use-value whether it is a commodity or not. Use-value in this indifference to the nature of its economic destination, i. e. use-value as such lies outside the sphere of investigation of political economy.[2] It falls within the sphere of the latter only in so far as it forms its own economic destination. It forms the material basis which directly underlies a definite economic relation called *exchange value.*

Exchange-value appears at first sight as a *quantitative relation*, as a proportion in which use-values are exchanged for one another. In such a relation they constitute equal exchangeable quantities. Thus, a volume of Propercius and eight ounces of snuff may represent the same exchange value, in spite of the dissimilar use-values of tobacco and elegy. As exchange-value, one kind of use-value is worth as much as another kind, if only taken in right proportion. The exchange value of a palace can be expressed in a certain number of boxes of shoe-blacking. On the contrary, London manufacturers of shoe-blacking have expressed the exchange value of their many boxes of blacking, in palaces. Thus, entirely apart from their natural forms and without regard to the specific kind of wants for which they serve as use-values, commodities in certain quantities equal each other, take each other's place in exchange, pass as equivalents, and in spite of their variegated appearance, represent the same entity.

Use-values are primarily means of existence. These means of existence, however, are themselves products of social life, the result of expended human vital power, *materialized labor.* As the embodiment of social labor, all commodities are the crystallization of the same substance. Let us now consider the nature of this substance, i. e., of labor, which is expressed in exchange value.

Let one ounce of gold, one ton of iron, one quarter of wheat and twenty yards of silk represent equal exchange values. As equivalents, in which the qualitative difference between their use-values has been eliminated, they represent equal volumes of the same kind of labor. The labor which is equally embodied in all of them must be uniform, homogeneous, simple labor. It matters as little in the case of labor whether it be embodied in gold, iron, wheat, or silk, as it does in the case of oxygen, whether it appears in the rust of iron, in the atmosphere, in the juice of a grape, or in the blood of a human being. But the digging of gold, the extraction of iron from a mine, the raising of wheat and the weaving of silk are so many kinds of labor, differing in quality. As a matter of fact, what in reality appears as a difference in use-values, is in the process of production, a difference in the work creating those use-values. Just as labor, which creates exchange value, is indifferent to the material of use-values, so it is to the special form of labor itself. Furthermore, the different use-values are the products of the work of different individuals, consequently the result of various kinds of labor differing individually from one another. But as exchange values, they represent the same homogeneous labor, i. e., labor from which the individuality of the workers is eliminated. Labor creating exchange value is, therefore, *abstract general labor*.

If one ounce of gold, one ton of iron, one quarter of wheat, and twenty yards of silk are exchange values of equal magnitude or equivalents; then one ounce of gold, half a ton of iron, three bushels of wheat and five yards of silk are exchange values of different magnitudes, and this quantitative difference is the only difference of which they are capable as exchange values. As exchange values of different magnitudes, they represent greater or smaller quantities of that simple, homogeneous, abstract, general labor, which forms the substance of exchange value. The question arises, how are these quantities to be measured? Or, rather what constitutes the substance of labor, which makes it capable of quantitative measurement, since the quantitative differences of commodities in their capacity of exchange values are but quantitative differences of labor embodied in them. Just as motion is measured by time, so is labor measured by *labor-time*. Given the quality of labor, the difference in its duration is the only property by which it can be distinguished. As labor-time, labor has the same standard of measurement as the natural time measures, viz., hours, days, weeks, etc. Labor-time is the vital substance of labor, independent of its form, composition, individuality; it is its vital substance quantitatively, having at the same time its own inherent measure. Labor-time embodied in the use-values of commodities is the substance which makes exchange values and, therefore, commodities of them and at the same time serves to measure definite quantities of their value. Corresponding quantities of different use-values, in which the same quantity of labor-time is embodied, are equivalents; or, to put it in another form, all use-values are equivalents when taken in proportions containing the same quantity of expended, materialized labor-time. As exchange values, all commodities are but definite measures of *congealed labor-time*.

To understand how exchange value is determined by labor-time, the following main points must be kept in mind: The reduction of labor to simple labor, devoid of any quality, so to speak; the specific ways and means by which exchange-value-creating, i. e., commodity producing labor becomes *social labor*; finally, the difference between labor as the producer of use-values, and labor as the creator of exchange values.

In order to measure commodities by the labor-time contained in them, the different kinds of labor must be reduced to uniform, homogeneous, simple labor, in short, to labor which is qualitatively the same, and, therefore, differs only in quantity.

This reduction appears to be an abstraction; but it is an abstraction which takes place daily in the social process of production. The conversion of all commodities into labor-time is no greater abstraction nor a less real process than the chemical reduction of all organic bodies to air. Labor, thus measured by time, does not appear in reality as the labor of different individuals. but on the contrary, the various working individuals rather appear as mere organs of labor; or, in so far as labor is represented by exchange values, it may be defined as human labor in general. This abstraction of human labor in general virtually exists in the average labor which the average individual of a given society can perform —a certain productive expenditure of human muscles, nerves, brain, etc. It is unskilled labor to which the average individual can be put and which he has to perform in one way or another. The character of this average labor varies in different countries and at different stages of civilization, but appears fixed in a particular society. Unskilled labor constitutes the bulk of all labor performed in capitalist society, as may be seen from all statistics.

It is obvious that if A spends six hours in the production of iron and six hours on linen, and B also produces iron during six hours and linen during another six hours, it is but a different application of *the same* labor time that would be expended, if A produced iron during twelve hours, while B worked twelve hours on linen. But how about skilled labor which rises above the level of average labor by its higher intensity, by its greater specific gravity? This kind of labor resolves itself into unskilled labor composing it; it is simple labor of a higher intensity, so that one day of skilled labor, e. g., may equal three days of unskilled labor. This is not the place to consider the laws regulating this reduction. It is clear, however, that such reduction does take place, for, as exchange value, the product of the most skilled labor is, when taken in a certain proportion, equivalent to the product of unskilled average labor, or equal to a definite quantity of that unskilled labor.

The determination of exchange-value by means of labor-time implies, further, the fact that an equal quantity of labor is embodied in any given commodity, e. g., a ton of iron, no matter whether it is the work of A or B, that is to say, various individuals expend an equal amount of labor-time for the production of the same use-value of a given quality and quantity. It is thus assumed that the labor-time contained in a commodity is the labor-time *necessary* for its production, i. e., it is the labor-time which is required for the production of another specimen of the same commodity under the same general conditions of production.

The conditions of labor, which creates exchange value, as shown by the analysis of the latter, are *social conditions* of labor or conditions of *social labor*. Social, not in the ordinary, but in a special sense. It is a specific form of the social process. The homogeneous simplicity of labor means first of all *equality* of the labors of various individuals, a reciprocal relation of equality of their labors determined by the actual reduction of all kinds of labor to uniform labor. The labor of every individual, as far as it is expressed in exchange value possesses this social character of equality and finds expression in exchange value only in so far as it is a relation of equality with the labor of all other individuals.

Furthermore, the labor-time of a single individual is directly expressed in exchange value as *universal labor-time*, and this *universal character* of individual labor is the manifestation of its *social character*. The labor-time represented by exchange value is the labor-time of an individual, but of an individual undistinguished from other individuals in so far as they perform the same labor; therefore, the time required by one individual for the production of a certain commodity is the *necessary* labor-time which any other individual would have to spend on the production of the same commodity. It is the labor-time of an individual, *his* labor-time, but only as labor-time common to all, regardless as to which particular individual's labor-time it is. As universal labor-time it is represented in a universal product, in a *universal equivalent*, in a definite quantity of materialized labor-time: the latter is indifferent as to the particular form of use-value in which it appears directly as the product of an individual, and may be turned at will into any other form of use-value to represent the product of any other individual. Only as such a *universal* quantity, is it a *social* quantity. In order to result in exchange value, the labor of an individual must be turned into a *universal equivalent*, i. e., the labor-time of an individual must be expressed as universal labor-time, or universal labor-time as that of an individual. It is the same as though different individuals had put together their labor-time and contributed the different quantities of labor-time at their common disposal in the form of different use-values. The labor-time of the individual is thus, in fact, the labor time which society requires for the production of a certain use-value, i. e., for the satisfaction of a certain want. But the question that interests us here is as to the specific form in which labor acquires a social character. Let us suppose that a certain quantity of labor-time of a spinner is realized in 100 lbs. of yarn. Suppose 100 yards of linen, the product of the weaver, represent the same quantity of labor-time. Inasmuch as these two products represent equal quantities of universal labor-time and, hence, are equivalents of *every* use-value which contains the same amount of labor-time, they are also equivalent to each other. Only because the labor-time of the spinner and that of the weaver take the form of universal labor-time and their products appear as universal equivalents, is the labor of the weaver realized for the spinner, and that of the spinner, for the weaver, the labor of one takes the place of the labor of the other, i. e., the social character of their labors is realized for both.

Quite different it was under the patriarchal system of production, when spinner and weaver lived under the same roof, when the female members of the family did the spinning, and the male members did the weaving to supply the wants of their own family; then yarn and linen were *social* products, spinning and weaving were *social* labor within the limits of the family. But their social character did not manifest itself in the fact that yarn, as a universal equivalent, could be exchanged for linen as a universal equivalent, or that one was exchanged for another, as identical and equivalent expressions of the same universal labor-time. It was rather the family organization with its natural division of labor that impressed its peculiar social stamp on the product of labor. Or, let us take the services and payments in kind of the Middle Ages. It was the specific kind of labor performed by each individual in its natural form, the particular and not the universal aspect of labor, that constituted then the social tie. Or, let us finally take labor carried on in common in its primitive natural form, as we find it at the dawn of history of all civilized races.[3] It is clear that in this case labor does not acquire its social character from the fact that the labor of the individual takes on the abstract form of universal labor or that his product assumes the form of a universal equivalent. The very nature of production under a communal system makes it impossible for the labor of the individual to be private labor and his product to be a private product; on the contrary, it makes individual labor appear as the direct function of a member of a social organism. On the contrary, labor, which is expressed in exchange value, at once appears as the labor of a separate individual. It becomes social labor only by taking on the form of its direct opposite, the form of abstract universal labor.

Labor, which creates exchange value, is, finally, characterized by the fact that even the social relations of men appear in the reversed form of a social relation of things. Only in so far as two use-values are in a mutual relation of exchange values does the labor of different persons possess the common property of being identical universal labor. Hence, if it be correct to say that exchange value is a relation between persons,[4] it must be added that it is a relation disguised under a material cover. Just as a pound of iron and a pound of gold represent the *same* weight in spite of their different physical and chemical properties, so do two use-values, as commodities containing the same quantity of labor-time, represent the *same exchange value*. Exchange value thus appears as the natural social destination of use-values, a property which they possess by virtue of being things and in consequence of which they are exchanged for one another in definite proportions, or form equivalents, just as chemical elements combine in certain proportions, forming chemical equivalents. It is only through the habit of everyday life that we come to think it perfectly plain and commonplace, that a social relation of production should take on the form of a thing, so that the relation of persons in their work appears in the form of a mutual relation between things, and between things and persons.

In commodities this mystification is as yet very simple. It is more or less plain to everybody that a relation of commodities as exchange values is nothing but a mutual relation between persons in their productive activity. This semblance of simplicity disappears in higher productive relations. All the illusions in regard to the monetary system are due to the fact that money is not regarded as something representing a social relation of production, but as a product of nature endowed with certain properties. The modern economists who sneer at the illusions of the monetary system, betray the same illusion as soon as they have to deal with higher economic forms, as, e. g., capital.[5] It breaks forth in their confession of naive surprise, when what they have just thought to have defined with great difficulty as a thing suddenly appears as a social relation and then reappears to tease them again as a thing, before they have barely managed to define it as a social relation.

Since the exchange value of commodities is, in fact, nothing but a mutual relation of the labors of individuals-labors which are similar and universal-nothing but a material expression of a specific social form of labor, it is a tautology to say that labor is the *only* source of exchange value and consequently of wealth, in so far as the latter consists of exchange values. Similarly, it is a tautology to say that matter in its natural state has no exchange value, because it does not contain any labor, and that exchange value as such does not contain matter. But when

William Petty calls "labor the father and earth the mother of wealth," or when Bishop Berkeley asks "whether the four elements and man's labour therein, be not the true source of wealth,"[6] or when the American, Thomas Cooper puts it popularly: "Take away from a piece of bread the labour bestowed by the baker on the flour, by the miller on the grain brought to him, by the farmer in ploughing, sowing, tending, gathering, threshing, cleaning and transporting the seed, and what will remain? A few grains of grass, growing wild in the woods, and unfit for any human purpose"[7] —then all these views do not refer to abstract labor as the source of exchange value, but to concrete labor as the source of material wealth; in short, to labor in so far as it produces use-values. In assuming that a commodity has use-value we assume the special usefulness and distinct fitness of the labor absorbed by it, but that is all there is to the view of labor as useful labor from the standpoint of commodity. Considering bread as a use-value, we are interested in its properties as an article of food and not at all in the different kinds of labor of the farmer, miller, baker, etc. If by some invention nineteen-twentieths of this labor could be saved, the loaf of bread would still render the same service as before. If it fell ready-made from the sky it would not lose a single atom of its use-value. While labor which creates exchange value is realized in the equality of commodities as universal equivalents, labor as a productive activity with a useful purpose is realized in the endless variety of use-values created by it. While labor which creates exchange values is *abstract, universal* and *homogeneous*, labor which produces use-values is concrete and special and is made up of an endless variety of kinds of labor according to the way in which and the material to which it is applied.

It is wrong to speak of labor in so far as it is applied to the production of use-values as of *the only* source of wealth, namely, the material wealth produced by it. Being an activity intended to adapt materials to this or that purpose, it requires matter as a pre-requisite. In different use-values the proportion between labor and raw material varies greatly, but use-value always has a natural substratum. Labor, as an activity, directed to the adaptation of raw material in one form or another, is a natural condition of human existence, a condition of exchange of matter between man and nature, independent of all social forms. On the contrary, labor producing exchange value is a specifically social form of labor. Tailoring, e. g., in its material manifestation as a distinct productive activity, produces a coat, but not the exchange value of the coat. The latter is produced not by the labor of the tailor as such, but by abstract universal labor, and that belongs to a certain organization of society which has not been brought about by the tailor. Thus, the women under the ancient system of house industry made coats without producing the exchange value of the coats. Labor as a source of material wealth was known to Moses, the legislator, as well as to Adam Smith, the customs official.[8]

Let us consider now some propositions which follow from the determination of exchange value by labor-time.

As a use-value, every commodity owes its usefulness to itself. Wheat, e. g., serves as an article of food. A machine saves labor to a certain extent. This function of a commodity by virtue of which it serves only as use-value, as an article of consumption, may be called its service, the service which it renders as use-value. But as an exchange value, a commodity is always regarded as a result; the question in this case is not as to the service which it renders, but as to the service[9] which it has been rendered in its production. Thus, the exchange value of a machine is determined not by the quantity of labor-time which it saves, but by the quantity of labor-time which has been expended on its own production and which is, therefore, required to produce a new machine of the same kind.

If, therefore, the quantity of labor-time required for the production of commodities remained constant, their exchange value would remain the same. But the ease and the difficulty of production are constantly changing. If the productivity of labor increases, the same use-value will be produced in less time. If the productivity of labor declines, more time will be required for the production of the same use-value. Thus, the labor-time contained in a commodity or its exchange-value is a variable quantity, increasing or diminishing in an inverse ratio to the rise and fall of the productivity of labor. The productive power of labor which is applied in the manufacturing industry on a predetermined scale depends in the agricultural and extractive industries also on natural conditions which are beyond human control. *The same labor* will yield a greater or less output of various metals, according to their more or less close occurrence in the earth's crust. *The same labor* may be embodied in two bushels of wheat in a favorable season, and only in one in an unfavorable season. In this case, scarcity or abundance, as natural conditions, seem to determine the exchange value of commodities, because they determine the productivity of certain kinds of labor which depend upon natural conditions.

Unequal volumes of different use-value contain the same quantity of labor-time or the same exchange value. The smaller the volume of a use-value containing a certain quantity of labor-time as compared with other use-values, the greater its *specific exchange-value*. If we find that certain use-values, such as, e. g., gold, silver, copper and iron, or wheat, rye, barley and oats, form a series of specific exchange values which, though not retaining exactly the same numerical ratio, still retain through widely remote epochs of civilization the same rough proportion of relatively larger and smaller quantities, we may draw the conclusion that the progressive development of the productive powers of society has equally, or approximately so, affected the labor-time necessary for the production of the various commodities.

The exchange value of a commodity is not revealed in its own use-value. But, as the embodiment universal social labor-time, the use-value of one commodity bears a certain ratio to the use-values of other commodities. Thus, the exchange value of one commodity is manifested in the use-values of other commodities. An equivalent is, in fact, the exchange value of one commodity expressed in the use-value of another commodity. If I say, e. g., that one yard of linen is worth two pounds of coffee, then the exchange value of linen is expressed in terms of the use-value of coffee, viz., in a certain quantity of that use-value. This ratio being given, I can express the value of any quantity of linen in coffee. It is clear that the exchange value of one commodity, say linen, is not confined to the ratio of any one commodity, e. g. coffee, as its equivalent. The quantity of universal labor-time which is represented in one yard of linen is at the same time embodied in an endless variety of volumes of use-values of all other commodities. The use-value of any other commodity forms the equivalent of one yard of linen, in the proportion in which it represents the same quantity of labor-time as that yard of linen. The exchange value of *this single commodity* is, therefore, fully expressed in the endless number of equations in which the use-values of all other commodities form its equivalents. Not until the exchange value of a commodity is expressed in the sum total of these equations or of the different proportions in which one commodity is exchanged for every other commodity, does it find an exhaustive expression as a *universal equivalent*; e. g., the series of equations:

1 yard of linen	=	1/2 lb. of tea,
1 yard of linen	=	2 lbs. of coffee,
1 yard of linen	=	8 lbs. of bread,
1 yard of linen	=	6 yards of calico,

may be represented as follows:

1 yard of linen = 1/8 lb. of tea + 1/2 lb. of coffee + 2 lbs. of bread + 1 1/2 yards of calico.

Therefore, if we had before us the sum total of the equations, in which the value of a yard of linen is exhaustively expressed, we could represent its exchange value in the form of a series. As a matter of fact, the series is an endless one, since the circle of commodities, constantly expanding, can never be closed up. But while the exchange value of one commodity is thus measured by the use-values of all other commodities, the exchange values of all the other commodities are, in their turn, measured by the use-value of this one commodity.[10]

If the exchange value of one yard of linen is expressed in 1/2 lb. of tea, or 2 lbs. of coffee, or 6 yards of calico, or 8 lbs. of bread, etc., it follows that coffee, tea, calico, bread, etc., are equal to each other if taken in the same proportion in which they are equal to the third article, linen; consequently, linen serves as the common measure of their exchange values. Every commodity, as the embodiment of universal labor-time, i. e., as a certain quantity of universal labor-time, expresses in turn its exchange value in definite quantities of the use-values of all other commodities, and the exchange values of all the other commodities are, on the other hand, measured by the use-value of this one exclusive commodity. But as an exchange value, every commodity is at the same time the one exclusive commodity that serves as a common measure of the exchange values of all other commodities; and, on the other hand, it is but one of the many commodities in the entire series of which every commodity expresses directly its exchange value.

The value of a commodity is not affected by the number of commodities of other kinds. But the length of the series of equations in which its exchange value is realized does depend upon the greater or less variety of other commodities. The series of equations in which the value of coffee, e. g., is represented, indicates the extent to which it is exchangeable, the limits within which it performs the function of an exchange value. The exchange value of a commodity as an embodiment of universal social labor-time is expressed in its equivalence to an endless variety of use-values.

We have seen that the exchange value of a commodity varies with the quantity of labor-time directly contained in it. Its realized exchange value, i. e., its exchange value expressed in the use-values of other commodities, must also depend on the proportion in which the labor-time spent on the production of all other commodities is changing. If, e. g., the labor-time required for the production of a bushel of wheat remained constant, while that required for the production of all other commodities doubled, the exchange value of a bushel of wheat expressed in its equivalents would become half as large as before. The result would be practically the same as if the amount of time necessary for the production of one bushel of wheat had been reduced by one-half, and that required for all other commodities had remained unchanged. The value of commodities is determined by the proportion in which they can be produced in the same labor-time. In order to see what possible changes this proportion may undergo, let us take two commodities, A and B.

First case. Let the labor-time required for the production of commodity B remain unchanged. In that case the exchange value of A, expressed in terms of B, rises and falls with the rise and fall of the labor-time required for the production of A.

Second case. Let the labor-time required for the production of commodity A remain constant. Then the exchange value of A, expressed in terms of B, falls and rises in an inverse ratio with the rise and fall of the labor-time required for the production of B.

Third case. Let the labor-time required for the production of commodities A and B rise and fall in equal proportion. Then the expression of equivalence of A and B remains unchanged. If through some cause the productivity of all kinds of labor were to decline uniformly, so that the production of all commodities would require an equally increased quantity of labor-time, then the value of all commodities would rise, though the expression of their exchange values would remain unchanged, and the actual wealth of society would decrease, because it would have to expend more labor-time on the production of the same stock of use-values.

Fourth case. Let the labor-time required for the production of A and B rise and fall, but not uniformly; that is to say, the labor-time required for the production of A may rise, while that required for B may fall, or vice versa. All of which can be reduced to the simple case where the labor-time required for the production of one commodity remains unchanged, while that required for the other rises or falls.

The exchange value of any commodity is expressed in the use-value of any other commodity, be it in integral units or in fractions thereof. As exchange value, every commodity is capable of subdivision, like the labor-time embodied in it. The equivalence of commodities is independent of their physical divisibility as use-values, just as the sum of the exchange values of commodities is indifferent to the change of form which use-values have to undergo when converted into a *single* new commodity.

So far we have considered commodities from a two-fold point of view, as use-values and exchange values alternately. But a commodity as such is a direct combination of use-value and exchange value; and it is a commodity only in relation to other commodities. The *actual* relation between commodities constitutes the *process of their exchange*. It is a social process participated in by individuals independent of each other but the part they take in it is that of owners of commodities only. Their mutual relations are those of their commodities, and thus they really appear as conscious factors of the process of exchange.

A commodity *is* a use-value, wheat, linen, a diamond, a machine, etc., but as a commodity it is, at the same time, *not* a use-value. If it were a use-value for its owner, i. e., a direct means for the satisfaction of his own wants, then it would not be a commodity. To him it is rather *a non-use-value*; it is merely the material depository of exchange-value, or simply a *means of exchange*; as an active bearer of exchange value, use-value becomes a means of exchange. To the owner it is a use-value only in so far as it constitutes exchange value.[11]

It has yet *to become* a use-value, viz., to others. Not being a use-value to its owner, it is a use-value to the owners of other commodities. If it is not, then the labor expended on it was useless labor, and the result of that labor is not a commodity. On the other hand, the commodity must become a use-value *to the owner himself*, because his means of existence lie outside of it in the use-values of commodities not belonging to him. In order to become a use-value, the commodity must meet the particular want of which it is the means of satisfaction. Use-values of commodities are thus *realized* use-values through a universal change of hands by passing from the hands in which they were held as means of exchange into those where they become use values. Only through this universal transfer of commodities does the labor contained in them become useful labor. In this process of their mutual interchange as use-values, commodities do not acquire any new economic forms. On the contrary, even the form which marked them as commodities disappears. Bread, e. g., by changing hands from the baker to the consumer does not change its identity as bread. On the contrary, it is only the consumer that begins to regard it as a use-value, as a certain article of food, while in the hands of the baker it was only the bearer of an economic relation, a palpable yet transcendental object. Thus, the only change of form that commodities undergo while becoming use-values, consists in the fact that they cease to be, as a matter of form, non-use-values to their owners, and use-values to those who do not own them. To become use-values commodities must be universally alienated; they must enter the sphere of exchange; but they are subject to exchange in their capacity of exchange values. Hence, in order to be realized as use-values, they must be realized as exchange values.

While the single commodity appeared from the standpoint of use-value as something independent, as exchange value it was regarded first of all in its relation to all other commodities. This relation was, however, merely theoretical, imaginary. It becomes real only in the process of exchange. On the other hand, a commodity *is* an exchange value in so far as a certain quantity of labor-time has been expended on it, and it consequently represents *materialized labor-time*. But of itself it is only materialized individual labor-time of a particular kind, and not *universal* labor-time. Therefore, it *is not* directly an exchange value, but must first *become* such. First of all, it is an embodiment of universal labor-time only in so far as it represents labor-time applied to a definite useful purpose, i. e., when it represents a use-value. This was the material condition under which alone labor-time contained in commodities was regarded as universal social labor. Thus, while a commodity can become a use-value only after it has been realized as an exchange value, it can, on the other hand, be realized as an exchange value only if it proves to be a use-value in the process of alienation.

A commodity can be alienated as a use-value only to one whom it serves as a use-value, i. e., as a means of satisfying a certain want. On the other hand, it is exchanged for another commodity, or, if we put ourselves on the side of the owner of the other commodity, it, too, can be alienated, i. e., be realized, only if brought in contact with that particular want of which it is the object. In the universal exchange of commodities as *use-values* the basis for their mutual relations is in their material difference as distinct objects which satisfy different wants by their specific properties. But as mere use-values, they are indifferent to each other, and are incommensurable. As use-values they can be exchanged only with reference to certain wants. They are exchangeable only as equivalents, and they are equivalents only as equal quantities of materialized labor-time, so that all regard to their natural properties as use-values and therefore to the relation of the commodities to particular wants is eliminated. On the contrary, a commodity is realized as an exchange value by replacing as an equivalent any definite quantity of any other commodity, regardless of whether it is a use-value for the owner of the other commodity or not. But to the owner of the other commodity it is a commodity only in so far as it is a use-value to him, and it becomes an exchange value to its owner only in so far as it is a commodity to that other person. Thus, the same relation appears as a proportion between commodities as magnitudes of the same denomination, but differing qualitatively; or, as an expression of their equivalence as embodiments of universal labor-time, and, at the same time, as a relation of qualitatively different objects, of use-values intended for the satisfaction of particular wants, in short, a relation in which they are distinguished as actual use-values. But this equivalence and non-equivalence mutually exclude each other. Thus we have before us not only a vicious circle of problems in which the solution of one implies that of the other, but a combination of contradicting claims, since the fulfillment of one is directly connected with that of its opposite.

The process of exchange of commodities must result both in the unfolding and in the solution of these contradictions, neither of which, however, can appear in that process in this simple way. We have only observed how commodities are mutually related to each other as use-values, i. e., how they appear as use-values *within* the process of exchange. The exchange-value, on the contrary, as we have considered it so far, appeared as an abstraction formed in our own minds, or-if we may so put it-in the mind of the individual owner of commodities, which lie stored in his warehouse as use-values, and weigh upon his conscience as exchange values. In the process of exchange, however, commodities must be not only use-values, but also exchange values to one another, and that should appear as their own mutual relation. The difficulty which we first encountered was that a commodity must be first alienated and delivered to its purchasers as a use-value, in order to appear as an exchange value, as materialized labor, while on the other hand its alienation as use-value implies its being an exchange value. But let us assume that this difficulty has been overcome. Suppose the commodity has divested itself of its use-value, and has thereby fulfilled the material condition of being socially useful labor, instead of a particular labor of an individual. In that case, the commodity must become an exchange value, a universal equivalent, an embodiment of universal labor-time for all other commodities in the process of exchange, and thus, leaving behind its limited role of a particular use-value, acquire the ability to be directly represented in all use-values as its equivalents. But every commodity is *just such* a commodity, appearing as a direct incarnation of universal labor-time by divesting itself of its particular use-value. On the other hand, however, commodities confront each other in the process of exchange as particular commodities, as the labor of private individuals embodied in particular use-values. Universal labor-time is itself an abstraction, which, as such, does not exist for commodities.

Let us examine the series of equations in which the exchange value of a commodity finds its concrete expression, e. g.:

1 yard of linen	=	2 lbs. of coffee.
1 yard of linen	=	1/2 lb. of tea.
1 yard of linen	=	8 lbs. of bread, etc.

These equations simply signify that equal quantities of universal social labor-time are embodied in one yard of linen, two pounds of coffee, half a pound of tea, etc. But as a matter of fact the individual labors which are represented in these particular use-values, become universal, and, in that form, also social labor, only when they are actually exchanged for one another in proportion to the labor-time contained in them. Social labor-time exists in these commodities in a latent state, so to say, and is first revealed in the process of exchange. We do not proceed from the labor of individuals as social labor, but, on the contrary, from special labor of private individuals which appears as universal social labor only by divesting itself of its original character in the process of exchange. Universal social labor is, therefore, no ready-made assumption, but a growing result. And thus we are confronted with a new difficulty, that on the one hand commodities must enter the process of exchange as embodiments of universal labor-time, while, on the other hand, this embodiment of the labor-time of individuals as social labor-time is itself a result of the process of exchange.

Every commodity becomes an exchange value by divesting itself of its use-value, or of its original nature. The commodity must therefore assume a double capacity in the process of exchange. But that second capacity of exchange value can appear only in the shape of another commodity, because only commodities confront each other in the process of exchange. How is a particular commodity to represent directly *materialized universal* labor-time, or-to put it differently-how is individual labor-time, which is embodied in a particular commodity to be made directly universal in character? The concrete expression of the exchange value of a commodity, i. e., of every commodity as a universal equivalent, is represented in an endless series of equations, such as:

1 yard of linen	=	2 lbs. of coffee.
1 yard of linen	=	1/2 lb. of tea.
1 yard of linen	=	8 lbs. of bread.
1 yard of linen	=	6 yards of calico.
1 yard of linen	=	etc.

The above form is theoretical in so far as commodities are only *thought of* as definite quantities of materialized universal labor-time. But the capacity of a particular commodity to serve as a universal equivalent from a mere abstraction becomes a *social* result of the process of exchange by a simple inversion of the above series of equations, viz.:

2 lbs. of coffee	=	1 yard of linen.
1/2 lb. of tea	=	1 yard of linen.
8 lbs. of bread	=	1 yard of linen.
6 yards of calico	=	1 yard of linen.

While coffee, tea, bread, calico, in short, all commodities express in linen the labor-time contained in them, the exchange value of linen, on the other hand, unfolds itself in all other commodities as its equivalents, and the labor-time embodied in it becomes direct universal labor-time, which is equally expressed in different volumes of all other commodities. Linen thus becomes the *universal equivalent* through the *universal action* of all other commodities upon it. As exchange value, every commodity served as a measure of value of all other commodities. Now, on the contrary, since all commodities measure their exchange values by means of a particular commodity, this excluded commodity becomes the special expression of exchange value, as a universal equivalent. At the same time, the endless series of equations in which the exchange value of every commodity was expressed, is reduced to one single equation consisting of two members. The equation 2 lbs. of coffee = 1 yard of linen now fully expresses the exchange value of coffee, for in this expression a yard of linen appears as the direct equivalent of a definite quantity of every other commodity. Thus, within the sphere of exchange all commodities are or appear to each other as exchange values in the form of linen. The proposition that commodities, as exchange values, are to each other as different quantities of materialized universal labor-time, may now be worded to the effect that commodities, as exchange values, represent nothing but different quantities of *the same* article, linen. Universal labor-time thus assumes the aspect of a distinct thing, as a commodity existing along with and outside of all other commodities. At the same time the equation 2 lbs. of coffee = 1 yard of linen, in which one commodity appears as the exchange value of another, is yet to be realized. Only by being alienated as use-value —which depends upon whether it proves to be in the process of exchange the object of a certain want-does the commodity actually transform its existence as coffee into the existence as linen and thus takes on the form of a universal equivalent and becomes, indeed, an exchange value for all other commodities. Conversely, since all commodities are turned into linen by being alienated as use-values, linen becomes the converted form of all other commodities, and only as a result of this transformation of all other commodities into it, it becomes the direct *embodiment of universal labor-time*, i. e., the product of universal exchange and of the elimination of individual labor. If commodities thus assume a twofold character in order to appear as exchange values to each other, the commodity which has been singled out as the universal equivalent becomes, on the other hand, a use-value in two ways. Besides its special use-value as a particular commodity, it assumes a universal use-value. This latter kind of use-value constitutes its special feature, emanating as it does, from the specific part which the commodity plays as a result of the universal relation which all other commodities bear toward it in the process of exchange. The use-value of every commodity as an object of a particular want, has a different value in different hands, e. g., it has a different value in the hands of the one who disposes of it, than in those of the one who acquires it. But the commodity singled out as the universal equivalent, is now an object of a universal want arising from the very process of exchange, and it has the same use-value to everybody, viz., that of serving as the depository of exchange value, of being a universal means of exchange. Thus we find in one commodity the solution of the contradiction which is inherent in commodity as such, namely, of being at one and the same time a particular use-value and a universal equivalent, and, therefore, a use-value for everybody or universal use-value. Thus, while all other commodities express their exchange value in the form of an ideal equation with the excluded commodity-an equation yet to be realized-the use-value of the special commodity, although real, appears in the process itself as a mere form which is yet to be realized through transformation into actual use-values. Originally the commodity appeared simply as commodity, as universal labor-time embodied in a particular use-value. In the process of exchange, all commodities are related to the one excluded commodity as to a simple commodity, one which appears as the embodiment of universal labor-time in a particular use-value. Thus, *particular* commodities become related to one particular commodity as a universal commodity.[12] In that manner the mutual relations of possessors of commodities based on the fact that they regard their labor as universal social labor, takes on the aspect of their relations to commodities as exchange values; and the mutual relation of commodities as exchange values appears in the process of exchange as the relation of all of them to one particular commodity as to a specially adopted means of expression of their exchange value; again, from the point of view of that particular commodity the above relation appears as its specific relation to all other commodities, and, therefore, as its own definite, spontaneous, social character. The particular commodity which thus appears as the specially adopted expression of the exchange value of all other commodities, or the exchange value of commodities as a particular exclusive commodity, is *money*. Money is a crystallization of the exchange value of commodities which they themselves form in the process of exchange. Thus, while commodities become *use-values* to each other in the process of exchange by casting off all definite forms and entering into mutual relations in their direct material shape, they must assume a new form, viz., proceed to the formation of money in order to appear as *exchange values* to each other. Money is not a symbol, no more than the commodity aspect of a use-value is a symbol. That a social relation of production takes the form of an object existing outside of individuals, and that the definite relations into which individuals enter in the process of production carried on in society, assume the form of specific properties of a thing, is a perversion and by no means imaginary, but prosaically real, mystification marking all social forms of labor which creates exchange value. In money this mystification appears only more strikingly than in commodities.

The necessary physical properties of the particular commodity in which the money form of all other commodities is to be crystallized-as far as they are directly determined by the nature of exchange value-are: divisibility to any desired extent, homogeneity of its parts, and uniformity of all the specimens of the commodity. As an embodiment of universal labor-time it must be homogeneous in its structure and capable of representing only quantitative differences. Another necessary property is durability of its use-value, as it must last through the process of exchange. The precious metals excel in these qualities. Money not being a result of a scheme or agreement, but having been produced instinctively in the process of exchange, a great variety of more or less unsuited commodities had successively performed its functions. At a certain stage of development of the process of exchange, the necessity arises for a polar distribution of the functions of exchange value and use-value among commodities, so that one commodity e. g. should act as a medium of exchange, while another is being alienated as a use-value. This necessity brings it about that one or even several commodities possessing the most generally accepted use-value, begin, incidentally at first, to play the part of money. Even if not direct means of satisfying existing wants, their being the most considerable material constituent part of wealth, insures to them a more general character than to the other use-values.

Direct barter, the original natural form of exchange, represents rather the beginning of the transformation of use-values into commodities, than that of commodities into money. Exchange value has as yet no form of its own, but is still directly bound up with use-value. This is manifested in two ways. Production, in its entire organization, aims at the creation of use-values and not of exchange values, and it is only when their supply exceeds the measure of consumption that use-values cease to be use-values, and become means of exchange, i. e., commodities. At the same time, they become commodities only within the limits of being direct use-values distributed at opposite poles, so that the commodities to be exchanged by their possessors must be use-values to both, —each commodity to its non-possessor. As a matter of fact, the exchange of commodities originates not within the primitive communities,[13] but where they end, on their borders at the few points, where they come in contact with other communities. That is where barter begins, and from here it strikes back into the interior of the community, decomposing it. The various use-values which first become commodities in the barter between different communities, such as slaves, cattle, metals, constitute therefore in most cases the first money within those communities themselves. We have seen how the exchange value of a commodity is manifested the more perfectly as exchange value, the longer the series of its equivalents or the *greater* the sphere of exchange of that commodity. With the gradual expansion of barter, the increase in the number of exchanges, and the growing diversification of the commodities drawn into exchange, commodities develop into exchange values, which leads to the formation of money and has a destructive effect on direct barter. The economists are in the habit of ascribing the origin of money to the difficulties which are encountered in the way of extensive barter, but they forget that these difficulties arise from the development of exchange value and from the fact that social labor becomes universal labor. E. g., commodities as use-values can not be subdivided at will, a property which they should possess as exchange values. Or, a commodity belonging to A may be a use-value to B, while the commodity belonging to B may not have any use-value to A. Or the owners of the commodities may need each other's indivisible goods in unequal proportions. In other words, under the pretence of analyzing simple barter, economists bring out certain aspects of the contradiction which is inherent in commodities as entities simultaneously embodying both use-value and exchange value. On the other hand, they consistently cling to the idea that barter is the natural form of exchange, which suffers only from certain technical difficulties, for which money is a cunningly devised expedient. Arguing from this perfectly superficial view, an ingenious English economist has rightly maintained that money is merely a material instrument like a ship or a steam-engine, but not an expression of a social relation in the field of production and consequently not an economic category; and that it is, therefore, wrong to treat the subject in political economy, which really has nothing in common with technology.[14]

The world of commodities implies the existence of a highly developed division of labor; this division is manifested directly in the great variety of use-values, which confront each other as particular commodities and which embody as many different kinds of labor. The division of labor embracing all the particular kinds of productive occupations, is the complete expression of social labor in its material aspect viewed as labor creating use-values. But from the standpoint of commodities and within the process of exchange, it exists only in its results, in the variety of the commodities themselves.

The exchange of commodities constitutes the social metabolic process, i. e. the process in which the exchange of the special products of private individuals is the result of certain social relations of production into which the individuals enter in this interchange of matter. As they develop, the mutual relations of commodities crystalize into various aspects of the universal equivalent and thus the process of exchange becomes at the same time the process of the formation of money. The whole of this process which takes the form of a succession of processes, constitutes circulation.

A. Notes on the History of the Theory of Commodities

The analysis of commodities according to their twofold aspect of use-value and exchange value by which the former is reduced to work or deliberate productive activity; and the latter, to labor time or homogeneous social labor, is the result of a century and a half of critical study by the classical school of political economy which dates from William Petty in England and Boisguillebert in France[15] and closes with Ricardo in the former country and Sismondi in the latter.

Petty reduces use-value to labor, without deceiving himself as to the natural limitation of its creative power. As regards concrete labor, he sizes it up in the magnitude of its social aspect, as *the division of labor*.[16] This view of the source of material wealth does not remain more or less fruitless as in the case of his contemporary, Hobbes, but leads up to his *Political Arithmetic*, the first form in which Political Economy is differentiated as an independent science.

He defines exchange value, however, just as it *appears* in the process of exchange of commodities, viz. as money; and money he defines as an existing commodity, gold and silver. Laboring under the ideas of the monetary system, he declares the special branch of labor which is devoted to the production of gold and silver as the labor which determines exchange value. What he really means is that the labor of members of society must produce not direct use-values, but commodities or use-values which by means of exchange are capable of assuming the form of gold and silver, i. e. of money, i. e. of exchange value, i. e. of embodiments of universal labor. His example, however, shows strikingly that the recognition of labor as the source of material wealth by no means excludes the misconception of the particular social form in which labor constitutes the source of exchange value.

In his turn, Boisguillebert, if not consciously, at any rate actually reduces the exchange value of a commodity to labor-time, since he determines "true value" (la juste valeur) by the right proportion in which the labor-time of individuals is distributed among the several branches of industry, and defines free competition as the social process which determines these correct proportions. At the same time, however, and in contrast with Petty he wages a fanatical war against money which, by its interference, disturbs the natural equilibrium or harmony of exchange of commodities and, like a wanton Moloch, demands all natural wealth as sacrifice. It is true that this assault on money was called forth by certain historic conditions. Since Boisguillebert attacked[17] the blind destructive lust after gold which possessed the court of Louis

XIV, his tax collectors, and his nobility; on the other hand, Petty extolled in the greed of gold the mighty impulse which spurred on the nation in her industrial development and in her conquest of the world-market; still, there asserts itself here a deeper antagonism of principles which constantly recurs between true English and true French[18] Political Economy. Boisguillebert sees, in fact, only the material substance of wealth, its use-value, the enjoyment[19] of it, and considers the capitalistic form of labor, i. e. the production of use-values as commodities and the exchange of those commodities, as the natural social form in which individual labor attains its end. When he is, therefore, confronted with the specific character of capitalistic wealth as in the case of money, he sees in it the usurping interference of extraneous elements and gets into a rage about the capitalist system of labor in one form while utopian-like he praises it in another.[20] Boisguillebert furnishes us with proof that one may treat labor-time as the measure of value of commodities, and at the same time confound labor embodied in the exchange value of commodities and measured by time, with the direct natural activity of individuals.

The first sensible analysis of exchange value as labor-time, made so clear as to seem almost commonplace, is to be found in the work of a man of the New World where the bourgeois relations of production imported together with their representatives sprouted rapidly in a soil which made up its lack of historical traditions with a surplus of humus. That man was Benjamin Franklin, who formulated the fundamental law of modern political economy[21] in his first work which he wrote when a mere youth and published in 1721.

He declares it necessary to look for another measure of value than precious metals. That measure is labor. "By labor may the value of silver be measured as well as other things. As, suppose one man employed to raise corn, while another is digging and refining silver; at the year's end, or at any other period of time, the complete produce of corn, and that of silver, are the natural price of each other; and if one be twenty bushels, and the other twenty ounces, then an ounce of that silver is worth the labor of raising a bushel of that corn. Now if by the discovery of some nearer, more easy or plentiful mines, a man may get forty ounces of silver as easily as formerly he did twenty, and the same labor is still required to raise twenty bushels of corn, then two ounces of silver will be worth no more than the same labor of raising one bushel of corn, and that bushel of corn will be as cheap at two ounces, as it was before at one, *ceteris paribus*. Thus the riches of a country are to be valued by the quantity of labor its inhabitants are able to purchase."[22] Thus Franklin regards labor-time from the one-sided economic point of view, as the measure of value. The transformation of actual products into exchange values is self-evident with him and the only question is as to finding a quantitative measure of value. "Trade," says he, "in general being nothing else but the exchange of labour for labour, the value of all things is, as I have said before, most justly measured by labour."[23] Substitute the word "work" for "labor" in the above statement, and the confusion of labor in one form and labor in another form becomes at once apparent. Since trade consists e. g. in the exchange of the respective labors of the shoemaker, miner, spinner, painter, etc., does it follow that the value of shoes is most justly measured by the work of a painter? On the contrary, Franklin meant that the value of shoes, mining products, yarn, paintings, etc., is determined by abstract labor which possesses no particular qualities and can, therefore, be measured only quantitatively.[24] But since he does not develop the idea that labor contained in exchange value is abstract universal labor which assumes the form of social labor as a result of the universal alienation of the products of individual labor, he necessarily fails to recognize in money the direct embodiment of this alienated labor. For that reason he sees no inner connection between money and labor which creates exchange value, and considers money merely as an instrument introduced from outside into the sphere of exchange for purposes of technical convenience.[25] Franklin's analysis of exchange value did not exert any direct influence on the general trend of science, because he discussed only special questions of political economy whenever there was a definite practical occasion for it.

The contrast between useful work and labor which creates exchange value agitated all Europe during the eighteenth century in the form of this question: what particular kind of labor constitutes the source of bourgeois wealth? It was thus assumed that not every kind of labor which is realized in use-values or yields certain products does thereby directly create wealth. With the physiocrats, however, as well as with their opponents, the burning question was not, what kind of labor creates *value*, but which is it that creates *surplus value*. They approached the problem in its complicated form before they had solved it in its elementary form; such is the historical course of all sciences leading them by a labyrinth of intersecting paths to the real starting points. Unlike other builders, science not only erects castles in the air, but constructs separate stories of the building, before it has laid the foundation. Without dwelling any longer on the physiocrats and omitting quite a number of Italian economists who in some more or less ingenious ideas came close to a correct analysis of the nature of commodity,[26] we pass at once to the first Briton who elaborated the general system of bourgeois economics, Sir James Steuart.[27] His idea of exchange value as well as all the abstract categories of political economy still seem to be with him in the process of differentiation from the material elements they represent and therefore appear quite vague and unsettled. In one place he determines *real value by labor-time* ("what a workman can perform in a day"), but immediately creates confusion by introducing the elements of wages and raw material.[28] In another place his struggle with the material substance of the subject he treats of is revealed even more strikingly. He calls the material of nature contained in a commodity, such as the silver in a silver plate, its "intrinsic worth," while the labor-time contained in it he calls "useful value." The former, he says "is ... something real in itself," while "the value of the second must be estimated according to the labour it has cost to produce it....The labour employed in the modification [of the substance] represents a portion of a man's time."[29]

What distinguishes Steuart from his predecessors and followers is his keen differentiation between specifically social labor which is represented in exchange value, and concrete labor which produces use-values. Labor, he says, which through its alienation creates a universal equivalent, I call *industry*. Labor as industry he distinguishes not only from concrete labor, but from all other social forms of labor.[30] It is to him the capitalistic form of labor in contrast to its antique and mediaeval forms. He is especially interested in the difference between capitalistic and feudal labor, of which he had observed the latter in its decaying forms both in Scotland and on his extensive travels over the continent. Steuart knew, of course, very well that products took on the form of commodities and commodities, the form of money in pre-capitalistic epochs as well; but he proves conclusively that it is only in the capitalistic period of production that the commodity becomes the elementary and fundamental form of wealth, and alienation [of commodities], the ruling form of acquisition and that consequently labor creating exchange value is specifically capitalistic in its character.[31]

After different forms of concrete labor, such as agriculture, manufacture, navigation, trade, etc., had each in turn been declared the true source of wealth, Adam Smith proclaimed labor in general, and namely in its general social form of *division of labor*, to be the only source of material wealth or use-values. While ignoring in connection with the latter the part played by nature, he is troubled by it when he comes to deal with purely social wealth i. e. exchange value. To be sure, Adam determines the value of a commodity by the labor-time contained in it, but relegates the actual application of the principle to pre-Adamic times. In other words, what seems to him true from the standpoint of simple commodity, ceases to be clear as soon as the higher and more complex forms of capital, wage-labor, rent, etc. take its place. This he expresses by saying, that the value of commodities used to be measured by labor-time in the paradise lost of bourgeois society, in which men dealt with each other not as capitalists, wage-workers, landlords, tenants, usurers, etc., but merely as plain producers of commodities which they exchanged. He constantly confuses the determination of the value of commodities by the labor-time contained in them with the determination of their value by the value of labor. He becomes confused in working out the details and fails to see the objective equalization of different kinds of labor which the social process forcibly carries out, mistaking it for the subjective equality of the labors of individuals.[32] The transition from concrete labor to labor creating exchange value, i. e. to labor in its fundamental capitalistic form he tries to derive from the *division of labor*. Yet, while it is true that private exchange implies the division of labor, it is false to maintain that division of labor implies private exchange. Among the Peruvians, e. g., labor was divided to an extraordinary extent, although there was no private exchange, no exchange of products, as commodities.

Contrary to Adam Smith, David Ricardo elaborated with great clearness the determination of the value of a commodity by labor-time and showed that this law governs also such relations of capitalistic production which seem to contradict it most. Ricardo confines his investigations exclusively to the *quantitative determination of value* and as regards the latter he is at least conscious of the fact that the realization of the law depends upon certain historical conditions. He says, namely, that the determination of value by labor-time holds good for commodities "only as can be increased in quantity by the exertion of human industry, and on the production of which competition operates without restraint."[33] What he really means is that the law of value presupposes for its full development an industrial society in which production is carried on a large scale and free competition prevails, i. e. the modern capitalist society. In all other respects, Ricardo considers the capitalist form of labor as the eternal natural form of social labor. He makes the primitive fisherman and the primitive hunter straightway exchange their fish and game as owners of commodities, in proportion to the labor-time embodied in these exchange values. On this occasion he commits the anachronism of making the primitive fisherman and primitive hunter consult the annuity tables in current use on the London Exchange in the year 1817 in the calculation relating to their instruments. The "parallelograms of Mr. Owen" seem to be the only form of society outside of the bourgeois form with which he was acquainted. Although confined within this bourgeois horizon, Ricardo analyzes the bourgeois economy-which looks quite different to deeper insight than it does on the surface-with such keen power of theoretical penetration that Lord Brougham could say of him: "Mr. Ricardo seemed as if he had dropped from another planet."

In a direct controversy with Ricardo, Sismondi lays stress upon the specifically social character of labor which creates exchange value,[34] and says it is "characteristic of our economic progress" to reduce the magnitude of value to the *necessary* labor-time, to the relation between the demand of society as a whole and the quantity of labor which is sufficient to satisfy this demand.[35] Sismondi is no more laboring under Boisguillebert's idea, that labor which creates exchange value is adulterated by money; but just as Boisguillebert denounced money, so does Sismondi denounce large industrial capital. In Ricardo political economy reached its climax, after recklessly drawing its ultimate conclusions, while Sismondi supplemented it by impersonating its doubts.

Since Ricardo gave to classical political economy its final shape, having formulated and elaborated with the greatest clearness the law of the determination of exchange value by labor-time, it is natural that all the polemics among economists should center about him. Stripped of its puerile[36] form this controversy comes down to the following points:

First: Labor itself has exchange value, and different kinds of labor have different exchange values. We get into a vicious circle by making exchange value the measure of exchange value, because the measuring exchange value needs a measure itself. This objection may be reduced to the following problem: Given labor-time as the intrinsic measure of exchange value, develop from that the determination of wages. The theory of wages gives the answer to that.

Second: If the exchange value of a product is equal to the labor-time contained in it, then the exchange value of one day of labor is equal to the product of that labor. In other words, wages must be equal to the product of labor.[37] But the very opposite is actually the case. Ergo. this objection comes down to the following problem: How does production, based on the determination of exchange value by labor-time only, lead to the result that the exchange value of labor is less than the exchange value of its product? This problem is solved by us in the discussion of capital.

Third: The market price of commodities either falls below or rises above its exchange value with the changing relations of supply and demand. *Therefore*, the exchange value of commodities is determined by the relation of supply and demand and not by the labor-time contained in them. As a matter of fact, this queer conclusion merely amounts to the question, how a market price based on exchange value can deviate from that exchange value; or, better still, how does the law of exchange value assert itself only in its antithesis? This problem is solved in the theory of competition.

Fourth: The last and apparently the most striking objection, if not raised in the usual form of queer examples: If exchange value is nothing but mere labor-time time contained in commodities, how can commodities which contain no labor possess exchange-value, or in other words, whence the exchange value of mere forces of nature? This problem is solved in the theory of rent.

Chapter II
Money or Simple Circulation

In a parliamentary debate on Sir Robert Peel's Bank Act of 1844 and 1845, Gladstone remarked that not even love has made so many fools of men as the pondering over the nature of money. He spoke of Britons to Britons. The Dutch, on the contrary, who, from times of yore, have had, Petty's doubts notwithstanding, "angelical wits" for money speculation have never lost their wits in speculations about money.

The main difficulty in the analysis of money is overcome as soon as the evolution of money from commodity is understood. This point once granted, it only remains to comprehend clearly the particular forms of money, which is to some extent made difficult by the fact that all bourgeois relations, being gilt or silver plated, have the appearance of money relations, and money, therefore, seems to possess an endless variety of forms, which have nothing in common with it.

In the following investigation only those forms of money are treated of which directly grow out of the exchange of commodities; the forms which belong to a higher stage of production, as e. g., credit money will not be discussed here. For the sake of simplicity gold is assumed throughout as the money commodity.

1. THE MEASURE OF VALUE.

The first process of circulation constitutes, so to say, the theoretical preparatory process to actual circulation. To begin with, commodities which are use-values by nature, acquire a form in which they *appear* in idea to each other as exchange values, as definite quantities of incorporated *universal* labor-time. The first necessary step in this process is, as we have seen, the setting apart by the commodities of a specific commodity, say *gold*, as the direct incarnation of universal labor-time, or the universal equivalent. Let us go back for a moment to the form in which commodities turn gold into money.

> 1 ton of iron = 2 ounces of gold
> 1 quarter of wheat = 1 ounce of gold
> 1 hundred weight of Mocca coffee = 1-1/4 ounce of gold
> 1 hundred weight of potash = 1/2 ounce of gold
> 1 ton of Brazil timber = 1-1/2 ounces of gold
> Y commodities = X ounces of gold

In the above series of equations iron, wheat, coffee, potash, etc. appear to each other as embodiments, of homogeneous labor, namely, as labor materialized in money, from which all the peculiarities of the different kinds of concrete labor represented in the different use-values are completely eliminated. As value they are all identical, they are the incarnation of *the same* labor, or *the same* incarnation of labor, viz., gold. As uniform embodiments of the same labor they display only *one* difference, a quantitative one, by appearing as different quantities of value, because *unequal* quantities of labor-time are contained in their use-values. The mutual relation of these separate commodities is that of embodiments of universal labor-time, since they are related to universal labor-time as to an excluded commodity, viz., gold. The same relation the development of which causes commodities to appear to each other as exchange values, causes the labor time contained in gold to appear as universal labor-time, a given quantity of which is expressed in different quantities of iron, wheat, coffee, etc, —in short, in the use-values of all commodities, or is directly unfolded in the endless series of commodity-equivalents. While all commodities express their exchange values in gold, gold expresses its exchange value directly in all commodities. While commodities assume the form of exchange value in relation to each other, they lend to gold the form of the universal equivalent, or of money.

Gold becomes the *measure of value*, because *all* commodities measure their exchange values in gold, in proportion as a certain quantity of gold and a certain quantity of the commodity contain the same amount of labor-time; and it is only by virtue of this function of being a measure of value, in which capacity its own value is measured directly in the entire series of commodity equivalents, that gold becomes a universal equivalent or money. On the other hand, the exchange value of all commodities is expressed in gold. In this expression, the qualitative aspect is to be distinguished from the quantitative: there is the exchange value of the commodity as the embodiment of the same uniform labor-time; while the magnitude of value is exhaustively expressed, since in the same proportion in which commodities are equated to gold they are equated to one another. On the one hand the *universal* character of the labor-time contained in them is revealed; on the other, its quantity is expressed in its golden equivalent. The exchange value of commodities thus expressed in the form of a universal equivalent and, moreover, as a numerical proportion of this equivalent, in terms of one specific commodity, or represented in the form of a series of commodities equated to one specific commodity, is PRICE. Price is the form into which the exchange value of commodities is converted when it *appears* within the sphere of circulation.

By the same process by which commodities express their values in gold prices, they turn gold into a measure of value i. e. into money. If all of them were to measure their values in silver, wheat, or copper, and therefore express them in the form of silver, wheat or copper prices, then silver, wheat or copper would be measures of value and consequently universal equivalents. In order to appear as prices in circulation, commodities must be exchange values before they enter circulation. Gold becomes the measure of value only because all commodities estimate their exchange value in it.

The universality of this relation which is the result of evolution and from which alone springs the function of gold as the measure of value, implies however, that every single commodity is measured in gold, in proportion to the labor-time contained in both; that the actual common measure of the commodity and of gold is labor; or that commodity and gold are passed for each other in direct barter as equal exchange values. How this equalization actually takes place, can not be discussed here when treating of simple circulation. So much, however, is clear, that in countries producing gold and silver, certain quantities of labor-time are directly embodied in definite quantities of gold and silver, while in countries which do not produce gold and silver the same result is reached in a round-about way, by direct or indirect exchange of the commodities of those countries; i. e. a definite portion of average national labor is given for a definite quantity of labor-time, embodied in the gold and silver of the mine-owning countries. In order to be able to serve as a measure of value, gold must be as far as possible a *variable* value, because it can become the equivalent of other commodities only as an incarnation of labor-time, and the same labor-time is realized in unequal volumes of use-values with the change in the productive power of concrete labor. In estimating all commodities in gold it is only assumed that gold represents a given quantity of labor at a given moment, as was done when the exchange value of any commodity was expressed in terms of the use-value of any other commodity. As for the variations of the value of gold, the law of exchange value formulated above holds good in its case as well. If the exchange value of commodities remains unchanged, then a general rise in their gold prices is possible only in the case of a fall in the exchange value of gold. If the exchange value of gold remains unchanged, a general rise of gold prices is possible only when the exchange value of all commodities rises. The reverse is true in case of a general fall in the prices of commodities. If the value of an ounce of gold falls or rises in consequence of a change in the labor-time required for its production, then the values of all other commodities fall or rise to an equal extent. Thus, the ounce of gold represents after the change, as it did before, a *given* quantity of labor-time with regard to all commodities. The same exchange values are now estimated in greater or smaller quantities of gold than before, but they are estimated in proportion to the magnitude of their values, and consequently retain the same proportion to each other. The ratio $2 \div 4 \div 8$ remains the same when expressed as $1 \div 2 \div 4$ or as $4 \div 8 \div 16$. The change in the quantity of gold in which exchange values are estimated with a variation in the value of gold, interferes as little with the function of gold as a measure of value, as the fifteen times smaller value of silver as compared with that of gold interferes with the performance of that function by the latter. Since labor-time is the common measure of gold and commodities, and since gold figures as the measure of value only in so far as all commodities are measured by it, the idea that money makes commodities commensurable, is therefore a mere fiction of the process of circulation.[38] It is rather the commensurability of commodities as incorporated labor-time, that turns gold into money.

Commodities enter the process of exchange in the concrete form of use-values. They are yet to be turned into the real universal equivalent through their alienation. The determination of their prices merely amounts to their ideal transformation into the universal equivalent, a process of equation to gold which is yet to be realized. But since commodities are, in their prices, transformed into gold only in imagination, or are converted only into imaginary gold, and since their money form is not differentiated as yet from their concrete selves, it follows that gold has also been turned into money only in imagination; it appears so far but as a measure of value, and in fact definite quantities of gold serve merely as names for certain quantities of labor-time. The form in which gold is crystallized in money always depends upon the way in which commodities express their own exchange value to each other.

Commodities now confront one another in a double capacity: actually as use-values, ideally as exchange values. The twofold aspect of labor contained in them is reflected in their mutual relations; the special concrete labor being virtually present as their use-value, while universal abstract labor-time is ideally represented in their price in which commodities appear as commensurable embodiments of the same value-substance differing merely in quantity.

The difference between exchange value and price appears to be merely nominal or, as Adam Smith says, labor is the real price, and money the nominal price of commodities. Instead of estimating the value of one quarter of wheat in thirty days of labor, it is estimated in one ounce of gold if one ounce of gold is the product of thirty days 'labor. However, far from this difference being merely nominal, all the storms which threaten commodities in the actual process of circulation center about it. Thirty days of labor are contained in a quarter of wheat and it need not, therefore, be expressed in terms of labor-time. But gold is a commodity distinct from wheat, and only in circulation it can be ascertained, whether the quarter of wheat can be actually turned into an ounce of gold as is anticipated in its price. That will depend on whether or not it proves to be a use-value, whether or not the quantity of labor-time contained in it is the quantity necessarily required by society for the production of a quarter of wheat. The commodity as such *is* an exchange value, it *has* a price. In this difference between exchange value and price lies the demonstration of the fact that the particular individual labor contained in a commodity has first to be expressed through the process of alienation in terms of its counterpart, i. e. as impersonal, abstract, universal and, only in that form, social labor, viz. money. Whether it can be so expressed seems to be a matter of chance. Thus, although the exchange value of a commodity finds only ideally a distinct expression in price, and the twofold character of labor contained in the commodity exists as yet merely as two distinct forms of expression, and, although in consequence thereof, the embodiment of universal labor-time, gold, confronts actual commodities only as an imaginary measure of value, yet the fact that exchange value exists as price, or that gold exists as a measure of value implies the necessity of the alienation of commodities for hard cash and the possibility of their non-alienation. In short, here lies latent the entire contradiction which is inherent in the fact that products are commodities or that the particular work of a private individual can be of no account in society until it has taken the very opposite form of abstract universal labor. For that reason, the utopians, who want to have commodities but not money, who want a system of production based on private exchange without the necessary conditions underlying such a system, are consistent when they "destroy" money not in its tangible form but in its nebulous illusory form of a measure of value. Under the invisible measure of value there lurks the hard cash.

The process by which gold has become the measure of value and exchange value has been turned into price, being once assumed, all commodities express in their prices but imagined quantities of gold of various magnitudes. As such various quantities of the same thing, gold, they are equated, compared and measured with each other, and thus arises the technical necessity of referring them to a definite quantity of gold as a unit of measure, a unit which develops into a standard measure by virtue of its divisibility into aliquot parts, which in their turn can be sub-divided into aliquot parts.[39] But quantities of gold as such are measured by weight.

The standard of measure is thus found ready in the general measures of weight of metals and, therefore, where-ever metallic circulation is in vogue, these measures serve originally as standards of price. Since commodities no more relate to each other as exchange values to be measured by labor-time, but as magnitudes of the same denomination measured in gold, the latter is transformed from a *measure of value* into a *standard of price*. The comparison of prices with each other as different quantities of gold is thus crystallized in figures which correspond to an assumed quantity of gold and represent it as a standard of aliquot parts. Gold as measure of value and as standard of price has entirely different forms of manifestation and the confusing of the two has resulted in the wildest of theories. Gold is a measure of value as incorporated labor-time; it is the standard of price as certain weight of metal. Gold becomes the measure of value by virtue of its relation as exchange value to commodities as exchange values; as standard of price, a definite quantity of gold serves as a unit for other quantities of gold. Gold is the measure of value, because its value is variable; it is the standard of price, because it is fixed as a constant unit of weight. In this case, as in all cases of measuring quantities of the same denomination, the establishment of a definite and unvarying unit of measure is all-important. The necessity of settling upon a quantity of gold as a unit of measure and upon its aliquot parts as subdivisions of that unit, has given rise to the notion that a certain quantity of gold which has naturally a variable value had been assigned a fixed ratio of value to the exchange values of all commodities; the fact is overlooked that exchange values of commodities are transformed into prices, i. e. into quantities of gold, before gold develops as a standard of price. No matter how the value of gold may vary, the ratios between the values of different quantities of gold remain constant. Let the fall in the value of gold amount to 1000 per cent., still twelve ounces of gold will have a twelve times greater value than one ounce of gold; and in prices the only thing considered is the ratio between different quantities of gold. Since, on the other hand, no rise or fall in the value of an ounce of gold can alter its weight, no alteration can take place in the weight of its aliquot parts. Thus gold always renders the same service as an invariable standard of price, no matter how much its value may vary.[40]

An historical process which, as we shall explain later, was determined by the nature of metallic circulation, led to the result that the same denomination of weight was retained for a constantly changing and decreasing weight of precious metals in their function of a standard of price. Thus the English pound sterling denotes less than one-third of its original weight; the pound Scot, before the Union, only 1-36; the French livre, 1-74; the Spanish Maravedi, less than 1-1000; the Portuguese Rei, a still smaller fraction. Such was the historical origin of the discrepancy between the current money names of various weights of metals and their weight denominations.[41] Since the determination of the unit of measure, of its aliquot parts, and of their names is purely conventional, and since they should possess within the sphere of circulation the character of universality and compulsion, they had to be settled *by law*. The purely formal operation thus devolved upon the government.[42] The metal which was to serve as the money material, was found already adopted in the community. In different countries the legal standard of price is naturally different. In England e. g. the ounce as a weight of metal is divided into pennyweights, grains and carats Troy, but the ounce of gold as the unit of money is divided into 3 7-8 sovereigns, the sovereign into 20 shillings, the shilling into 12 pence, so that 100 pounds of 22 carat gold (1200 ounces) = 4672 sovereigns and 10 shillings. In the world market, however, where national boundaries disappear, these national characteristics of the measure of money also disappear and give place to the general measures of weight of metals.

The price of a commodity or the quantity of gold into which it is ideally transformed, is, therefore, now expressed in the names of coins of the gold standard. Thus, instead of saying: a quarter of wheat is worth an ounce of gold, it is said in England to be worth 3£ 17s. 10-1/2d. All prices are thus expressed in the same denominations. The peculiar form which commodities lend to their exchange values is transformed into a *money-denomination* by which commodities tell each other how much they are worth. Money in its turn becomes *money of account*.[43]

We transform commodities into money of account, in our mind, on paper, in conversation, whenever it is a question of expressing any kind of wealth in terms of exchange value.[44] For that transformation we need the gold substance, but only in imagination. In order to estimate the value of a thousand bales of cotton in a certain number of ounces of gold and then to express this number of ounces in the denominations of the ounce, £. s. d., not a single atom of gold is required. Thus, not a single ounce of gold was in circulation in Scotland before Robert Peel's Bank Act of 1845, although the gold ounce, expressed in its English standard of account, 3£ 17s. 10-1/2d., served as the legal standard of price. In a similar manner silver serves as standard of price in the trade between Siberia and China, although that trade virtually amounts to barter. It is, therefore, immaterial to money, as money of account, whether or not its entire unit of measure or the fractions thereof are really coined. In England, at the time of William the Conqueror, 1£, then a pound of pure silver, and the shilling, 1-20 of a pound, existed only as money of account, while the penny, 1-240 of a pound of silver, was the largest silver coin in existence. On the other hand, there are no shillings and pence in England to-day, although they are legal denominations for certain parts of an ounce of gold. Money as money of account may exist exclusively in idea, while the money in actual existence may be coined according to an entirely different standard. Thus the money in circulation in many English colonies of North America consisted until late in the eighteenth century of Spanish and Portuguese coins, although the money of account was throughout the same as in England.[45]

Owing to the fact that money, when serving as the standard of price, appears under the same reckoning names as do the prices of commodities, and that, therefore, the sum of 3£ 17s. 10-1/2d. may signify, on the one hand, an ounce weight of gold, and on the other, the value of a ton of iron, this reckoning name of money has been called its *mint-price*. Hence, there sprang up the extraordinary notion that the value of gold is estimated in its own material, and that, in contradistinction to all other commodities, its price is *fixed* by the State. It was erroneously thought that the giving of reckoning names to definite weights of gold is the same thing as fixing the value of those weights.[46] In so far as gold serves as one of the elements in determining price, i. e., where it performs the function of money of account, it not only has no *fixed* price, but has *no* price whatever. In order to have a price, i. e., in order to express itself in a *specific* commodity as a *universal* equivalent that other commodity would have to play the same exclusive role in the process of circulation as gold. But two commodities excluding all other commodities mutually exclude each other. Therefore, wherever gold and silver have by law been made to perform side by side the function of money or of a measure of value it has always been tried, but in vain, to treat them as one and the same material. To assume that there is an invariable ratio between the quantities of gold and silver in which a given quantity of labor-time is incorporated, is to assume, in fact, that gold and silver are of one and the same material, and that a given mass of the less valuable metal, silver, is a constant fraction of a given mass of gold. From the reign of Edward III to the time of George II, the history of money in England consists of one long series of perturbations caused by the clashing of the legally fixed ratio between the values of gold and silver, with the fluctuations in their real values. At one time gold was too high; at another, silver. The metal that for the time being was estimated below its value was withdrawn from circulation, melted and exported. The ratio between the two metals was then again altered by law, but the new nominal ratio soon came into conflict again with the real one. In our own times, the slight and transient fall in the value of gold compared with silver, which was a consequence of the Indo-Chinese demand for silver, produced on a far more extended scale in France the same phenomena, export of silver, and its expulsion from circulation by gold. During the years 1855, 1856 and 1857, the excess in France of gold imports over gold exports amounted to £41,580,000, while the excess of silver exports over silver imports was £14,704,000. In fact, in those countries in which both metals are legally measures of value, and therefore both legal tender, so that every one has the option of paying in either metal, the metal that rises in value is at a premium, and, like every other commodity, measures its price in the over-estimated metal which alone serves in reality as the standard of value. The result of all experience and history with regard to this question is simply that, where two commodities perform by law the functions of a measure of value, in practice one alone maintains that position.[47]

B. Theories of the Unit of Measure of Money

The circumstance that commodities are converted into gold only in ideas as prices and that gold is therefore turned into money only in idea, gave rise to the theory of the *ideal unit of measure of money*. Since, in the determination of prices, gold and silver serve only ideally as money of account, it was asserted that the names pound, shilling, pence, thaler, franc, etc., instead of denoting certain weights of gold and silver or labor incorporated in some way, stood rather for ideal atoms of value. Thus, if, e. g., the value of an ounce of silver should rise it would contain more such atoms and would therefore have to be estimated and coined in a greater number of shillings. This doctrine, revived again during the last commercial crisis in England and even voiced in Parliament in two separate reports attached to the report of the select Committee on the Bank Acts sitting in July, 1858, dates from the end of the seventeenth century.

At the time of the accession of William III., the English mint-price of an ounce of silver was 5s. 2d., or 1-62 of an ounce of silver was equal to a penny; 12 of these pence were called a shilling. According to that standard, a piece of silver weighing, say, 6 ounces, would be coined into thirty-one coins, each called a shilling. But the *market price* of an ounce of silver rose above its *mint price*, from 5s. 2d. to 6s. 3d., or, in order to buy an ounce of silver bullion 6s. 3d. had to be paid. How could the market price of an ounce of silver rise above its mint price, when the mint price is merely a reckoning name for aliquot parts of an ounce of silver? The riddle was easily solved. Out of £5,600,000 of silver money which was in circulation at that time, four millions were worn out, clipped and debased. A trial disclosed that £57,000 of silver which were supposed to weigh 220,000 ounces, weighed only 141,000 ounces. The mint went on coining according to the same standard, but light-weighted shillings in actual circulation represented smaller parts of an ounce than their name implied. Hence, a greater quantity of these light-weighted shillings had to be paid in the market for an ounce of silver bullion. When a general recoinage was decided upon in consequence of the derangement that had been produced, LOWNDES, the Secretary of the Treasury, declared that the value of an ounce of silver had risen and therefore it must henceforth be coined into 6s. 3d. instead of into 5s. 2d. as heretofore. His argument practically amounted to the assertion that the rise in the value of the ounce caused a fall in the value of its aliquot parts. His false theory, however, served merely as an embellishment for a just, practical purpose. The government debts were contracted in light shillings, were they to be paid in heavy ones? Instead of saying pay back four ounces of silver, when you had received nominally five ounces but virtually only four, he said pay back nominally five ounces but reduce the metallic contents to four ounces and call a shilling what you had called four-fifths of a shilling heretofore. Thus Lowndes practically adhered to the metallic weight while theoretically he clung to the reckoning name. His adversaries who clung only to the name and therefore declared the 25 to 50 per cent. lighter shilling to be identical with the full-weight shilling maintained on the contrary that they adhered to the metallic weight.

JOHN LOCKE, who was an advocate of the new bourgeoisie in all forms, the manufacturers against the working classes and paupers, the commercial class against the old fashioned usurers, the financial aristocracy against the state debtors, and who went so far as to prove in his own work that the bourgeois reason is the normal human reason, also took up the challenge against Lowndes. John Locke carried the day and money borrowed at ten or fourteen shillings to a guinea was repaid in guineas of twenty shillings.[48] SIR JAMES STEUART sums up the entire transaction as follows: " ... the state gained considerably upon the score of taxes, as well as the creditors upon their capitals and interest; and the nation, which was the principal loser, was pleased; because their *standard* (The standard of their own value) was not debased."[49] Steuart thought that the nation would prove more alert with the further development of commerce. He was mistaken. About 120 years later the same *quid pro quo* was repeated.

It was just in the order of things that Bishop BERKELEY, the representative of a mystical idealism in English philosophy, should have given a theoretical turn to the doctrine of the ideal unit of measure of money, something which the practical "Secretary to the Treasury" had failed to do. He asks: "Whether the terms Crown, Livre, Pound Sterling, etc., are not to be considered as Exponents or Denominations of such Proportion? [namely proportions of abstract value as such.] And whether Gold, Silver, and Paper are not Tickets or Counters for Reckoning, Recording and Transferring thereof? (of the proportion of value). Whether *Power* to command the Industry of others be not real Wealth? And whether Money be not in Truth, Tickets or Tokens for conveying and recording such Power, and whether it be of great consequence what Materials the Tickets are made of?"[50] Here we find a confusion, first of the measure of value and the standard of price, and secondly of gold and silver as measures on the one hand and mediums of circulation on the other. Because precious metals can be replaced by tokens in the process of circulation Berkeley comes to the conclusion that these tokens represent nothing, i. e., only the abstract idea of value.

SIR JAMES STEUART had so fully developed the theory of the ideal unit of measure of money, that his successors-unconscious successors since they do not know him-have added to it neither a new version nor even a new example. "Money, which I call of account, is no more than an arbitrary scale of equal parts, invented for measuring the respective value of things vendible. Money of account, therefore, is quite a different thing from money coin, which is price[51] and might exist, although there was no such thing in the world as any substance which could become an adequate and proportional equivalent, for every commodity....Money of account ... performs the same office with regard to the value of things, that degrees, minutes, seconds, etc., do with regard to angles, or as scales do to geographical maps, or to plans of any kind. In all these inventions, there is constantly some denomination taken for the unit. ... The usefulness of all those inventions being solely confined to the marking of proportion. Just so the unit in money can have no invariable determinate proportion to any part of value, that is to say, it cannot be fixed to any particular quantity of gold, silver, or any other commodity whatsoever. The unit once fixed, we can, by multiplying it, ascend to the greatest value....The value of commodities, therefore, depending upon a general combination of circumstances relative to themselves and to the fancies of men, their value ought to be considered as changing only with respect to one another; consequently, anything which troubles or perplexes the ascertaining those changes of proportion by the means of a general, determinate and invariable scale, must be hurtful to trade....Money ...is an ideal scale of equal parts. If it be demanded what ought to be the standard value of one part? I answer by putting another question: What is the standard length of a degree, a minute, a second? It has none ...but so soon as one part becomes determined by the nature of a scale, all the rest must follow in proportion. Of this kind of money ...we have two examples. The bank of Amsterdam presents us with the one, the coast of Angola with the other."[52]

Steuart speaks here simply of the part money plays in circulation as the *standard of price* and *money of account*. If different commodities are marked in the price-list at 15s., 20s., 36s., respectively, then I care, in fact, neither for the silver substance, nor for the name of the shilling when comparing the magnitudes of their values. The ratios between the numbers 15, 20, 36, tell everything, and the number 1 has become the only unit of measure. Only the abstract proportion of numbers can at all serve as a purely abstract expression of proportion. In order to be consistent, Steuart should have dropped not only gold and silver, but their legal baptismal names as well. Since he does not understand the nature of the transformation of the measure of value into a standard of price, he naturally believes that the definite quantity of gold which serves as a unit of measure relates as a measure not to other quantities of gold, but to values as such. Since commodities appear as quantities of the same denomination through the conversion of their exchange values into prices, he denies that property of the measure which reduces them to one denomination; and since in this comparison of different quantities of gold the quantity of gold which serves as a unit of measure is conventional, he does not see the necessity of fixing it at all. Instead of calling 1-360 part of a circle degree, he might give that name to 1-180th part; the right angle would then be measured by 45 degrees instead of 90, and acute and obtuse angles would be measured accordingly. Nevertheless, the measure of the angle would remain, then, as before, first a qualitatively definite mathematical figure, the circle, and second a quantitatively definite part of the circle. As for Steuart's economic illustrations, he refutes his own argument with one and does not prove anything with the other. The bank money of Amsterdam was, in fact, merely the reckoning name for Spanish doubloons, which retained their full weight by lying idly in the bank vaults, while the circulating coins became thinner from hard rubbing against the outer world. And as for the African idealists we have to abandon them to their fate until critical travelers will tell us more about them.[53] The French assignat could be called an almost ideal money in Steuart's sense: *"National property. Assignation of 100 francs."* To be sure, the use-value which the assignation was supposed to represent, namely, the confiscated land, was indicated here, but the quantitative definition of the unit of measure was forgotten and "the franc" became a meaningless word. How much or how little land the assignation franc represented depended on the results of the public auctions. In practice, however, the assignation franc circulated as a token of value of silver money and its depreciation was, therefore, measured by this silver standard.

The period of the suspension of cash payments by the Bank of England was hardly more fruitful of war-bulletins than of money theories. The depreciation of bank notes and the rise of the market price of gold above its mint price called forth again the doctrine of the ideal unit of money on the part of some of the advocates of the Bank. Lord Castlereagh found the classical confused expression for the confused idea by speaking of the unit of measure of money as "a sense of value in reference to currency as compared with commodities." When a few years after the peace of Paris conditions permitted the resumption of cash payments, the same question which had been stirred up by Lowndes under William III., came up, hardly changed in form. An enormous government debt, as well as a mass of private debts, accumulated in twenty years, fixed obligations, etc., had been contracted on the basis of depreciated bank notes. Were they to be paid back in bank notes of which £4672, 10s. nominal, actually represented 100 pounds of 22 carat gold? THOMAS ATTWOOD, a banker of Birmingham, came forth as *Lowndes redivivus*. The creditors were to receive nominally as many shillings as had been nominally borrowed, but if about 1-78 of an ounce of gold constituted a shilling according to the old standard of coinage, then say 1-90 of an ounce should now be christened a shilling. Attwood's adherents are known as the Birmingham school of "little shillingmen." The controversy over the ideal money unit, which had started in 1819, still went on in 1845 between Sir Robert Peel and Attwood, whose own wisdom, as far as the function of money as a measure is concerned, is exhaustively summed up in the following passage, in which, referring to Sir Robert Peel's controversy with the Birmingham Chamber of Commerce, he says: "The substance of your queries is ... in what sense is the word pound to be used?... To what will the sum one pound be equivalent?... Before I venture a reply I must enquire what constitutes a standard of value?... Is £3 17s. 10-1/2d. an *ounce* of gold, or is it only of the *value* of an ounce of gold? If £3 17s. 10-1/2d. be an ounce of gold, why not call things by their proper names, and, dropping the terms pounds, shillings and pence, say ounces, pennyweights and grains?... If we adopt the terms ounces, pennyweights and grains of gold, as our monetary system, we should pursue a direct system of barter.... But if gold be estimated as of the *value* of £3 17s. 10-1/2d. per ounce ... how is this ... that much difficulty has been experienced at different periods to check gold from rising to £5 4s. per ounce, and we now notice that gold is quoted at £3 17s. 9d. per ounce?... The expression *pound* has reference to value, but not a fixed standard value.... The term pound is the *ideal unit*.... Labour is the parent of cost and gives the relative value to gold or iron. *Whatever denomination of words are used to express the daily or weekly labour of a man*, such words express the cost of the commodity produced."[54]

In the last words the hazy conception of the ideal money measure melts away and its real meaning breaks through. The reckoning names of gold, pound sterling, shilling, etc., should be names for definite quantities of labor-time. Since labor-time constitutes the substance and the intrinsic measure of values, these names would then actually represent definite proportions of value. In other words, labor-time is maintained to be the true unit of measure of money. With this we leave the Birmingham school, but should add in passing that the doctrine of the ideal measure of money acquired new importance in the controversy over the question of the convertibility or non-convertibility of bank notes. If paper receives its name from gold or silver, then the convertibility of a note or its exchangeability for gold or silver remains an economic law, no matter what the civil law may be. Thus a Prussian paper thaler, although legally inconvertible, would immediately depreciate if it were worth less than a silver thaler in ordinary trade, i. e., if it were not practically convertible. The consistent advocates of inconvertible paper money in England, therefore, sought refuge in the ideal measure of money. If the reckoning names of money, £, s., etc., are names of certain quantities of atoms of value, of which a commodity absorbs or loses now more, now less in exchange for other commodities, then an English £5 note, e. g., is just as independent of its relation to gold as of that to iron and cotton. Since its title would no more imply its theoretical equality with a certain quantity of gold or any other commodity, the demand for its convertibility, i. e., for its practical equality with a definite quantity of a specified thing would be excluded by the very conception of the note.

The theory of labor-time as the direct measure of money was first systematically developed by JOHN GRAY.[55] He makes a National Central Bank ascertain through its branches the labor-time consumed in the production of various commodities. The producer receives an official certificate of value in exchange for his commodity. i. e., he gets a receipt for as much labor-time as his commodity contains,[56] and these bank notes of one week's labor, one day's labor, one hour's labor, etc., serve at the same time as a check for an equivalent in all other commodities stored in the bank warehouses.[57] This is the fundamental principle carefully worked out in detail and based throughout on existing English institutions. Under this system, says Gray, "to sell for money may be rendered, at all times, precisely as easy as it now is to buy with money; ... production would become the uniform and never-failing cause of demand."[58] The precious metals would lose their "privilege" as against other commodities and "take their proper place in the market beside butter and eggs, and cloth and calico, and then the value of the precious metals will concern us just as little ... as the value of the diamond."[59] "Shall we retain our fictitious standard of value, gold, and thus keep the productive resources of the country in bondage? or, shall we resort to the natural standard of value, labour, and thereby set our productive resources free?"[60]

Labor-time being the intrinsic measure of value, why should there be another external measure side by side with it? Why does exchange value develop into price? Why do all commodities estimate their value in one exclusive commodity, which is thus converted into a special embodiment of exchange value into money? That was the problem which Gray had to solve. Instead of solving it, he imagined that commodities could be related directly to each other as products of social labor. But they can relate to each other only in their capacity of commodities. Commodities are the direct products of isolated independent private labors, which have to be realized as universal social labor through their alienation in the process of private exchange, that is to say, labor based on the production of commodities becomes social labor only through universal alienation of individual labors. But by assuming that the labor-time contained in commodities is *directly social* labor-time, Gray assumes it to be common labor-time or labor-time of directly associated individuals. Under such conditions a specific commodity like gold or silver could not confront other commodities as the incarnation of universal labor, and exchange value would not be turned into price; but, on the other hand, use-value would not become exchange value, products would not become commodities and thus the very foundation of the capitalistic system of production would be removed. But that is not what Gray has in mind. *Products are to be produced as commodities, but are not to be exchanged as commodities.* He entrusts a national bank with the carrying out of this pious wish. On the one hand, society, through the bank, makes individuals independent of the conditions of private exchange, and on the other, it allows them to go on producing on the basis of private exchange. The logic of things, however, compels Gray to do away with one condition of capitalistic production after another, although he wishes to "reform" only the money system which results from the exchange of commodities. Thus he transforms capital into national capital,[61] land into national property,[62] and if his bank is to be watched closely, it will be found that it not only receives commodities with one hand and issues certificates for work delivered with the other, but that it regulates production as well. In his last work, "Lectures on Money," in which Gray is anxious to demonstrate that his labor-money is a purely bourgeois reform, he gets tangled up in even more glaring contradictions.

Every commodity is directly money. That was Gray's theory deducted from his incomplete and, therefore, false analysis of commodities. The "organic" structure of "labor money," the "national bank" and the "ware-docks" are mere fantastic visions in which the dogma is made by a legerdemain to appear to us as a universal law. The dogma that a commodity is money or that the isolated labor of the individual contained in it is direct social labor, will of course not become true through the mere fact that a bank believes in it and carries on operations accordingly. It is more likely that bankruptcy would play in that case the part of the practical critic. What remains concealed in Gray's writings and hidden from himself as well, namely, that labor-money is a well-sounding economic phrase for the pious wish to get rid of money, and with money, of exchange value, and with exchange value, of commodities, and with commodities, of the capitalistic mode of production, was clearly expressed by some English socialists of whom a few preceded and others followed Gray.[63]

But it remained for Mr. Proudhon and his school to preach in all earnest the degradation of *money* and the exaltation of the *commodity* as the gist of socialism and thus to reduce socialism to an elementary misconception of the necessary connection between commodity and money.[64]

2. THE MEDIUM OF CIRCULATION.

After the commodity has received in the process of price determination the form in which it becomes capable of circulation, and after gold has acquired the character of money in the same process, circulation will both present and solve the contradictions which are inherent in the process of exchange of commodities. The actual exchange of commodities, i. e., the social interchange of matter consists of a change of form in which is unfolded the double character of the commodity as use-value and exchange value, and at the same time its own change of form is crystallized in distinct forms of money. To describe this change of form is to describe circulation. As we have seen, given a world of commodities and with it a system of division of labor, commodity is but a developed form of exchange value; in the same manner, circulation implies a steady stream of exchange transactions which are being continually renewed on all sides. The second assumption we make is that commodities enter the process of exchange with a *definite price* or that they appear to each other in that process in a double capacity, really as use-values, ideally-in price-as exchange values.

The liveliest streets of London are crowded with stores whose show windows are filled with the riches of the world, Indian shawls, American revolvers, Chinese porcelain, Parisian corsets, Russian furs and tropical spices, but all of these things of joy bear fatal white labels marked with Arabian figures with the laconic characters £, s., d. Such is the picture of the commodity appearing in circulation.

a. THE METAMORPHOSIS OF COMMODITIES.

On close examination the process of circulation is seen to consist of two distinct cycles. If we denote commodity by the letter C and money by the letter M we can express these two forms as follows:

$$C—M—C$$
$$M—C—M.$$

In this chapter we are interested exclusively in the first form, i. e., in the form which serves as the direct expression of the circulation of commodities.

The process C —M —C consists of the movement C —M, the exchange of the commodity for money, or *selling*; the opposite movement M —C, exchange of money for a commodity, or *buying*; and of the unity of the two movements C —M —C, exchange of the commodity for money in order to exchange the money for a commodity, or *selling* in order to *buy*. But the result which marks the end of the process is C —C, exchange of commodity for commodity, real interchange of matter.

If we look at it from the extreme end of the first commodity, C —M —C represents its transformation into gold and its retransformation from gold into a commodity; a movement in which the commodity exists first as a particular use-value, then divests itself of that character, acquires the character of exchange value or universal equivalent, in which capacity it has nothing in common with its natural form, then throws off the last form as well to remain finally an actual use-value for the satisfaction of particular wants. In this last form it falls out of the sphere of circulation into that of consumption. The entire process of circulation C —M —C thus includes the combined series of metamorphoses, which every single commodity undergoes in order to become a direct use-value to its possessor. The first metamorphosis is accomplished in the first phase of the circulation process, C —M; the second in the last phase, M —C; and the entire process constitutes the *curriculum vitae* of the commodity. But the process C —M —C represents the combined metamorphosis of a single commodity and constitutes at the same time the sum of certain one-sided metamorphoses of other commodities, since every metamorphosis of the first commodity constitutes its transformation into another commodity and therefore the transformation of the other commodity into it; hence it constitutes a twofold transformation which takes place at the same stage of circulation. We must then consider separately each of the two processes of exchange into which circulation C —M —C breaks up.

C —M or *sale*: commodity C enters the process of circulation not only as a particular use-value, e. g., a ton of iron, but as a use-value of a certain price, say, £3 17s. 10-1/2d., or an ounce of gold. While this price is on the one hand the exponent of the quantity of labor-time contained in a ton of iron, i. e., of the magnitude of its value, it at the same time expresses the pious wish of the iron to become gold, i. e., to give to the labor-time it contains the aspect of universal social labor-time. Unless this trans-substantiation takes place, the ton of iron not only ceases to be a commodity, but even a product, for it is a commodity only because it is a non-use-value to its owner; that is to say, his labor counts as actual labor only in so far as it is labor useful to others, and the thing is useful to him only as abstract universal labor. It is, therefore, the business of iron, or of its owner, to find that point in the world of commodities where iron attracts gold. But this difficulty, the *salto mortale* of the commodity, is overcome when the sale actually takes place, as is assumed here on the analysis of simple circulation. When the ton of iron is realized as a use-value through its alienation, i. e., by passing from the hands in which it is a non-use-value to hands in which it is a use-value, it at the same time realizes its price and from mere imaginary gold it becomes real gold. In place of the name one ounce of gold or £3 17s. 10-1/2d., an ounce of real gold has appeared, but the ton of iron has cleared that place. Not only does the commodity-which in its price had been ideally converted into gold-actually turn into gold through the sale C —M, but gold, which as a measure of value had been only ideal money and in fact figured merely as a money name of commodities-is now turned into actual money[65] by the same process. Just as gold became the ideal universal equivalent, because all commodities measured their values by it, so does it now become the absolutely alienable commodity, real money, because it is the product of the universal alienation of commodities for it-and the sale C —M is the process by means of which that universal alienation takes place. But gold becomes real money only through sale, because the exchange values of commodities were already ideal gold in their prices.

In the sale C —M, as well as in the purchase M —C, two commodities, entities of exchange value and use-value, confront each other, but the exchange value of the commodity exists only ideally as price; while as regards gold, although it is really a use-value, its use-value is confined only to its being the bearer of exchange value and is, therefore, merely a formal use-value, having no relation to a real individual want. The antithesis of use-value and exchange value is thus distributed at the two extreme poles of C —M, so that the commodity confronts gold as a use-value which has yet to realize in gold its exchange value or its price, while gold confronts the commodity as an exchange value, whose formal use-value is yet to be realized in the commodity. Only through this duplication of the commodity as commodity and gold, and, further, through the twofold and polar relation by virtue of which each extreme represents but ideally what its opposite is in reality and is in reality what its opposite is only ideally-in short, only through the appearance of commodities as two-sided polar opposites are the contradictions solved that are inherent in the process of exchange.

So far we have considered C —M as sale, as the conversion of commodity into money. But if we look at it from the other end, the same process will assume the form M —C, or purchase, i. e., the conversion of money into commodity. Sale is necessarily its opposite at the same time; it is the former if we look at the process from one end, and the latter if we regard the process from the other end. In practice this process differs only in that the initiative in C —M originates at the commodity end or with the seller, while in M —C it comes from the money end or the buyer. In describing the first metamorphosis of the commodity, its conversion into money as a result of the completion of the first phase of circulation C —M, we assume at the same time that another commodity has been converted into money and is now in its second phase of circulation, M —C. Thus we get into a vicious circle of assumptions. Circulation itself constitutes such a vicious circle. If we did not consider M in M —C as the result of a metamorphosis of another commodity, we would thereby take exchange out of the process of circulation. But outside of the latter the form C —M disappears and only two different Cs confront each other, say iron and gold, the exchange of which does not constitute a part of the process of circulation, being direct barter. Gold, at the source of its production, is a commodity like any other commodity. Its relative value and that of iron or of any other commodity is expressed here in quantities in which they are mutually exchanged. But in the process of circulation this operation is implied, the value of gold being already given in the prices of commodities. Nothing can, therefore, be more erroneous than the idea that gold and commodity enter into the relation of direct barter *within the process of circulation* and that their relative values are ascertained through their exchange as simple commodities. The illusion that gold is bartered as a simple commodity for other commodities in the process of circulation is due to the fact that prices represent equations in which certain quantities of commodities are made equal to certain quantities of gold, i. e., that the commodities are made to relate to gold in its capacity of money, as a universal equivalent, and, therefore, appear to be directly exchangeable for it. In so far as the price of a commodity is *realized* in gold, it is exchanged for gold as a commodity, as a particular embodiment of labor-time; but in so far as it is the *price* that is realized in gold, the commodity is exchanged for gold in its capacity of money and not of a commodity, i. e., it is exchanged for gold as a universal embodiment of labor-time. But in either case the quantity of gold for which the commodity is exchanged in the process of circulation is not determined by exchange, but the exchange is determined by the price of the commodity, i. e., by its exchange value estimated in gold.[66]

Within the process of circulation gold appears in everybody's hands as the result of sale C — M. But since C —M, sale, is at the same time M —C, purchase, it is apparent that while C, the commodity from which the process starts, is passing through its first metamorphosis, another commodity, which confronts it as the opposite pole M, is completing its second metamorphosis and is, therefore, passing through the second phase of circulation, while the first commodity is still in the first phase of its course.

As a result of the first phase of circulation, the sale, we get money which is the starting point of the second phase. In place of the commodity in its first form appears its golden equivalent. This result may now form a resting point, since the commodity in this second form possesses a lasting existence of its own. The commodity, a non-use-value in the hands of its possessor, is now on hand in an always useful, since always exchangeable, form, and it depends upon circumstances when and at what point of the surface of the commodity world it will again enter circulation. Its formation into a gold chrysalis constitutes an independent period in its life which may last a greater or less length of time. While in the case of barter the exchange of one particular use-value is directly bound up with the exchange of another particular use-value, the universal character of labor which creates exchange value is manifested in the separation and lack of coincidence of acts of purchase and sale.

M —C, purchase, is the inverted movement of C —M and at the same time the second or final metamorphosis of the commodity. As gold, i. e., in the form of the universal equivalent, the commodity can be directly represented in the use-values of all other commodities; the latter aspire to gold as their hereafter, but at the same time indicate in their prices the key in which it must sound in order that their bodies, their use-values, may take the place of money, while their souls, their exchange-values, may enter gold. The universal product of the alienation of commodities is the absolutely alienable commodity. There is no qualitative and only a quantitative limit to the transformation of gold into commodity, namely, the limit of its own quantity or magnitude of its value. "Everything is to be had for cash." While in the movement C —M, the commodity, through its alienation as a use-value, realizes its own price and the use-value of somebody else's money; it realizes in the movement M —C, through its alienation as an exchange value, its own use-value and the price of the other commodity. While through the realization of its price the commodity transforms gold into actual money, it turns gold into its merely fleeting money-form, through its own retransformation. Since the circulation of commodities implies an extensive division of labor and consequently a diversity of wants on the part of individuals, a diversity which bears an inverse ratio to the specialization of their own products, the purchase M —C may appear as an equation with one commodity equivalent or split up into a series of commodity-equivalents limited by the variety of the demands of the purchaser and by the amount of money in his possession. Just as a sale is a purchase, so is a purchase a sale. M —C is at the same time C —M, but the initiative belongs in this case to gold or the purchaser.

Coming back now to C —M —C, or to circulation as a whole, it is apparent that it contains the combined series of metamorphoses through which a commodity passes. But at the same time as one commodity enters the first phase of its circulation and completes its first metamorphosis, another commodity enters the second phase of circulation, completes its second metamorphosis and falls out of circulation; the first commodity enters at the same time the second phase of circulation completes its second metamorphosis and falls out of circulation, while a third commodity enters circulation, passes through the first phase of its course completing the first metamorphosis.

Thus, the combined circulation C —M —C, as a complete metamorphosis of a commodity always constitutes at the same time the end of the complete metamorphosis of another commodity and the beginning of a complete metamorphosis of a third commodity, i. e., a series without beginning or end. To illustrate this let us call C in either extreme C' and C" respectively, in order to distinguish the commodities, the series reading thus: C' —M —C". The first member, C' —M, presupposes in fact that M is the result of another transaction C —M, and is thus itself merely the last member of a series C —M —C', while the second part M —C" is merely a result of C" —M, or appears as the first part of C" —M —C'", and so on. Furthermore, although M is the result of only *one* sale, it appears that the last part M —C, may be represented as M —C' + M —C" + M —C'", etc., i. e., it may be split up into a number of purchases, and consequently a number of sales, or into a number of first members of new complete metamorphoses of commodities. Since the complete metamorphosis of a single commodity thus appears as a link not only of one endless chain of metamorphoses, but of many such chains, the process of circulation in the world of commodities presents a hopeless confusion of intertwined movements constantly ending and starting anew at a countless number of points. But every single sale or purchase stands as an independent isolated act, whose supplemental act may be separated from it in time and place, and therefore does not need to follow it directly as its continuation. Every separate process of circulation, C —M or M —C, as a transformation of one commodity into use-value and of another into money, i. e., as the first and second phases of circulation respectively forms an independent halting point from either direction; but, on the other hand, all commodities commence their second metamorphosis in the common form of the universal equivalent, gold, and stop at the starting point of the second phase of circulation; for that, reason any M —C dovetails in actual circulation with any C —M; the second chapter in the life-course of one commodity with the first chapter of that of another commodity. A, e. g., sells £2 worth of iron. He thus completes the transaction C —M or the first metamorphosis of commodity iron, but postpones his purchase until some other time. At the same time B, who sold 2 quarters of wheat for £6 a fortnight since, buys with the same £6 a coat and trousers of Moses & Son, thus completing M —C or the second metamorphosis of the commodity, wheat.

The two transactions M —C and C —M appear here merely as links of one chain, because a commodity expressed in gold looks like any other commodity, and one cannot tell by the looks of the gold whether it is transformed iron or transformed wheat. C —M —C appears, therefore, in the actual process of circulation as a jumble of countless accidentally coinciding or successively following members of different complete metamorphoses. The actual process of circulation thus appears not as a complete metamorphosis of a commodity, not as its movement through opposite phases, but as a mere agglomeration of many accidentally coinciding or successive purchases and sales. The process thus loses all clearness of outline which is so much more the case since every single act of circulation, e. g., sale, is at the same time its opposite, purchase, and vice versa. On the other hand, the process of circulation is nothing but the movement of metamorphoses in the world of commodities and, therefore, must reflect them also in its movement as a whole. How that reflection takes place we shall consider in the following chapter. It may be added here that in C —M —C the two extreme Cs constitute two forms of commodities which do not bear the same relation to M. The first C relates to money as a commodity of a special class to a universal commodity, while money relates to the second C as a universal commodity to an individual commodity. C —M —C can, therefore, be reduced by abstract logic to the final form

S —U —I in which S, standing for species, forms the first extreme; U, signifying universality, forms the connecting medium, and I, individuality, constitutes the last extreme.

The owners of commodities entered the sphere of circulation simply as guardians of commodities. Within that sphere they confront each other in the opposite roles of buyer and seller, one as a personified sugar-loaf, the other as personified gold. As soon as the sugar-loaf is turned into gold, the seller becomes a buyer. These definite social functions are no outgrowths of human nature, but are the products of relations of exchange between men who produce their goods in the form of commodities. They are so far from being purely individual relations between buyer and seller that both enter this relation only to the extent that their individual labor is disregarded and is turned into money as labor of *no* individual. Just as it is, therefore, childish to consider these economic bourgeois roles of buyer and seller as eternal social forms of human individuality, so it is on the other hand, preposterous to lament in them the extinction of individuality.[67] They are the necessary manifestations of individuality at a certain stage of the social system of production. Moreover, in the opposition of buyer and seller the antagonistic nature of capitalistic production is expressed as yet so superficially and as mere matter of form, that this opposition belongs also to precapitalistic forms of society, since it merely requires that the mutual relations of individuals should be those of owners of commodities.

Now, if we consider the result of C —M —C, it comes down to mere interchange of matter, C —C. A commodity has been exchanged for a commodity, a use-value for a use-value, and the transformation of the commodity into money, or the commodity in its form of money, serves merely as a means of effecting this interchange of matter. Money thus appears merely as a *medium of exchange* of commodities; not as a medium of exchange in general, but as a means of exchange in the sphere of circulation, i. e., a *medium of circulation*.[68]

We have seen that the process of circulation of commodities comes to a completion in C —C, appearing as mere barter carried on by means of money; further, that C —M —C represents in general not only two isolated processes, but their dynamic union as well; but to draw from that the conclusion that purchase and sale form an indivisible unit, is a mode of thinking the criticism of which belongs to the domain of logic, and not to that of economics. The separation of purchase and sale in the process of exchange destroys all local, primitive, patriarchal and naively genial barriers to interchange of matter in society. It is, moreover, the general form of the separation of the points of coincidence and opposition in this interchange, carrying within it the possibility of commercial crises, because the antagonism of commodity and money is the abstract and general form of all antagonisms with which the capitalistic system of labor is pregnant. Hence, circulation of money is possible without crises, but crises can not occur without money circulation. In other words, where labor based on the system of private exchange has not reached the stage marked by the existence of money, it is less capable of producing those phenomena which presuppose the full development of the capitalistic mode of production. Bearing this in mind we can appreciate the depth of the criticism which proposes to do away with the "shortcomings" of capitalistic production by abolishing the "privilege" enjoyed by the precious metals and introducing a so-called "rational monetary system." As a sample of economic defence of an opposite character may serve the following piece of reasoning which has been proclaimed exceedingly keen. JAMES MILL, the father of the well-known English economist, John Stuart Mill, says: "Whatever ...be the amount of the annual produce, it never can exceed the amount of the annual demand....Of two men who perform an exchange, the one does not come with only a supply, the other with only a demand; each of them comes with both a demand and a supply....The supply which he brings is the instrument of his demand; and his demand and supply are of course exactly equal to one another. It is therefore, impossible that there should ever be in any country a commodity or commodities in quantity greater than the demand, without there being, to an equal amount, some other commodity or commodities in quantity less than the demand."[69]

Mill restores the balance by turning the process of circulation into direct barter and then smuggling into direct barter the character of buyer and seller borrowed by him from the process of circulation. To put it in his own confused language, during certain periods when all commodities are unsaleable there are really more buyers than sellers of one commodity, *money*, and more sellers than buyers of *all other money*, commodities; such was, e. g., the case at certain moments during the commercial crisis of 1857-58 in London and Hamburg. The metaphysical balance of purchases and sales amounts to this, that every purchase is a sale and every sale is a purchase, which is a poor consolation to the guardian of the commodity who can not bring about its sale and therefore can not buy.[70]

The separation of sale and purchase makes possible a large number of fictitious transactions side by side with genuine trade before the final exchange between the producer and the consumer of commodities takes place. It enables a host of parasites to penetrate the process of production and exploit the separation. But this, again, means that with money as the universal form of labor under the capitalist system, there is *the possibility* of the development of its contradictions.

b. THE CIRCULATION OF MONEY.

Actual circulation appears at first sight as a mass of purchases and sales accidentally taking place side by side. In buying as in selling, commodities and money always stand in the same mutual relation: the seller, on the side of the commodity; the buyer, on that of money. Money as a medium of circulation always appears therefore as *a means of purchase*; and in that way the difference in its destinations in the opposite phases of the metamorphosis of the commodity becomes indistinguishable.

Money passes into the hands of the seller in the same transaction in which the commodity passes into the hands of the buyer. Commodities and money thus flow in opposite directions and this change of place in which the commodity passes over to one side and money to the other side, occurs simultaneously at an indefinitely large number of points on the entire surface of bourgeois society. But the first step which the commodity makes in the sphere of circulation is also its last step.[71] Whether it leaves its place on account of its attraction for gold (C —M), or on account of its attraction by gold (M —C), with one move, with one change of place it falls out of the sphere of circulation into that of consumption. Circulation is a continuous flow of commodities, but different commodities all the time, since each commodity makes but one move. Every commodity enters upon the second phase of its circulation not as the same commodity, but as another commodity, gold. Hence the movement of a metamorphosed commodity is the movement of gold. The same piece of gold or the identical gold coin which changed places with one commodity in the act C —M, reappears from the opposite end as the starting point for M —C and thus changes places for the second time with another commodity. Just as it passed from the hands of buyer B into those of seller A, it now leaves A's hands who has become a buyer and passes into C's hands. The path described by a commodity in its transformation into money and its retransformation from money, i. e., the movement of a complete metamorphosis of a commodity assumes the aspect of an apparent movement of the same coin that changes places twice with two different commodities. No matter in how scattered and haphazard fashion purchases and sales may take place near each other, there is always in actual circulation a seller for each buyer and the money which moves into the place of the commodity sold, before it came into the hands of the buyer, must have already changed places with another commodity. Sooner or later it again leaves the hands of the seller, who turns buyer, to pass into the hands of a new seller and this frequently repeated change of place forms the interlacing of the metamorphoses of commodities. The same coins are moving, some more, others less frequently, from one place in the sphere of circulation to another, always in the direction opposite to that of the commodities moved, thus describing a longer or shorter circulation-curve. The different movements of the same coin can follow each other in point of time only, and on the contrary, the many scattered purchases and sales which appear as so many separate changes of place between commodities and money, occur simultaneously separated only in point of space.

The circulation of commodities C —M —C in its elementary form is completely described in the transition of money from the hands of the buyer into those of the seller and from the hands of the latter, as soon as he has turned buyer, into those of a new seller. This completes the metamorphosis of the commodity and with it the movement of money in so far as that movement is the expression of the metamorphosis. But since new use-values are continually produced in the shape of new commodities and must thus be constantly thrown anew into circulation, the process C —M —C is repeatedly renewed by the same commodity owners. The money which they have spent as buyers gets back into their hands as soon as they appear again as vendors of commodities. The constant renewal of the circulation of commodities finds its reflection in the continual circulation over the entire surface of bourgeois society of a quantity of money which, passing from hand to hand, describes at the same time a number of different small cycles starting from numberless points and returning each to its own starting point, to repeat the same movement over again.

The change of form on the part of commodities appears as a mere change of place on the part of money and the continuity of the circulation movement is all on the side of money, since the commodity always makes but one step in the direction opposite to money, while the latter makes in each case the second step for the commodity; the entire movement seems, therefore, to proceed from money, although in the case of a sale the commodity draws money out of its place, i. e., it circulates money as much as it is circulated by the latter in the case of a purchase. Furthermore, owing to the fact that money always confronts commodities in its capacity of a means of purchase, and in that capacity moves commodities only by realizing their price, the entire movement of circulation appears as a change of place between money and commodities, the former realizing the prices of the latter either by separate acts of circulation taking place simultaneously and side by side, or by successive transactions when the same coin realizes the prices of different commodities one after another. If we consider, e. g., the series C —M —C' —M —C" —M —C"', etc., without regard to the qualitative aspects which become indistinguishable in the process of circulation, we witness the same monotonous operation. After realizing the price of C, M successively realizes those of C', C", etc., and commodities C', C", C"', etc., constantly take the place which money has left. Money thus appears to keep commodities in circulation by realizing their prices. In discharging this function of realization of prices, money is itself constantly circulating, now changing its place, now describing a curve of circulation, now completing a small circuit where the starting and returning points coincide. As a medium of circulation, money is subject to a circulation of its own. The change of form of the circulating commodities appears, therefore, as a movement of money which furthers the exchange of commodities, motionless in themselves. The movement of the circulation process of commodities thus takes on the form of the movement of gold as a medium of circulation, i. e. of the *circulation of money.*

Since owners of commodities give the products of their individual labor the appearance of products of social labor by turning one object, viz. gold, into the direct expression of universal labor-time and therefore into money, their own movement by which all of them effect the interchange of the material products of their labor now appears to them as the direct movement of that one object, as the circulation of gold. The social movement itself appears to the owners of commodities partly as an outward necessity and partly as a mere formal intermediary process which enables every individual who puts any use-value into circulation to get other use-values out of it of an equal value. The use-value of commodities comes into play with their disappearance from the sphere or circulation, while the use-value of money as a medium of circulation is in its very circulation. The movement of a commodity in the sphere of circulation is of a transitory kind, while ceaseless motion in that sphere constitutes the function of money. Through this special function which it performs within the sphere of circulation money acquires a new capacity, which we have to consider now more closely.

In the first place, we see that the circulation of money forms an endlessly split up movement, since it reflects the splitting up of the process of circulation into an infinitely large number of purchases and sales and the independent separation of the mutually supplementary phases of metamorphoses of commodities. In the small cycles described by money, where the starting and returning points coincide, we do find a return movement, i. e., an actual circular movement, but the fact that there are as many starting points as there are commodities and that the number of these cycles is infinitely large puts them beyond all control, measurement, or computation. The time between the start and the return of a commodity is just as indefinite. Moreover, it is immaterial whether or not such a circuit has been actually described in a given case. No economic fact is more generally known than that one can spend money with one hand without getting it back with the other. Money proceeds from an endless number of points and returns to as many different points, but the coincidence of the starting and returning points is a matter of chance, because in the movement C —M —C the turning of the buyer again into a seller is not a necessary condition. Still less does the circulation of money resemble a movement radiating from a common centre to all points of the periphery and back from the peripheral points to the centre. The so-called cycle described by money, as it is pictured, amounts simply to this, that at all points we observe its appearance and disappearance, its never ceasing transition from place to place. In a higher, more involved form of money circulation, e. g. bank-note circulation, we shall find that the conditions of emission of money include those for its return. But in the simple money circulation it is a matter of chance for the same buyer to become again a seller. Where we really see constant cycle motions taking place, they are only reflections of deeper forces in the sphere of production, e. g., the manufacturer draws money from his banker on Friday, pays it out to his working-men on Saturday, the men immediately pay out the greater part of it to the storekeepers, etc., and the latter turn it in on Monday back to the banker.

We have seen that money realizes simultaneously a certain number of prices in the variegated purchases and sales which take place side by side at the same time. On the other hand, in so far as its movement represents the movement of the combined metamorphoses of commodities and the interlacing of these metamorphoses, the same coin realizes the prices of different commodities and thus makes a larger or smaller number of moves. If we take the circulation of a country for a given length of time, say a day, the quantity of gold required for the realization of prices and, consequently, for the circulation of commodities, will be determined by two conditions: first, the sum total of the prices; second, the average number of moves made by one coin. This number of moves or the rapidity of circulation of money is in its turn determined by or expresses the average rapidity with which commodities go through the different phases of their metamorphoses, the rapidity with which these metamorphoses succeed one another, and with which those commodities that have gone through their metamorphoses are replaced by new commodities in the process of circulation. We have seen that in the process of the determination of prices the exchange value of all commodities is ideally converted into a certain quantity of gold of the same value and that the same amount of value is present in a double form in either of the isolated acts of circulation M —C and C —M, first embodied in the commodity, and second, in gold; yet gold enjoys the capacity of a medium of circulation not by virtue of its isolated relation to separate commodities in a state of rest, but owing to its active presence in the dynamic world of commodities, viz., its function of expressing the change of form of commodities by its change of place and expressing the rapidity of their change of form by the rapidity of its change of place. The extent to which it is present in the sphere of circulation, i. e., the actual quantity of gold in circulation, is thus determined by the extent to which it is discharging its function throughout the entire process.

The circulation of money implies the circulation of commodities; money circulates commodities which have prices, i. e., which are beforehand ideally equated to certain quantities of gold. In the determination of the prices of commodities, the value of the quantity of gold which serves as a unit of measure, or the value of gold, is assumed to be given. Under that assumption the quantity of gold necessary for circulation is determined first of all by the sum total of the prices of commodities that are to be realized. But this sum is itself determined: 1. By the level of prices, the relatively high or low exchange value of commodities estimated in gold; and 2. By the mass of commodities circulating at fixed prices, i. e. by the number of purchases and sales at given prices.[72] If one quarter of wheat is worth 60 shillings, then twice as much gold is required to circulate it or to realize its price as would be the case if it were worth only 30 shillings. To circulate 500 quarters of wheat at 60 shillings, twice as much gold is necessary as for the circulation of 250 quarters at the same price. Finally, to circulate 10 quarters at 100 shillings only half as much money is necessary as when circulating 40 quarters at 50 shillings. It follows that the quantity of gold required for circulation may fall in spite of a rise in price, if the mass of commodities in circulation declines in a greater ratio than the rise of the combined sum of prices; and, inversely, the quantity of the circulating medium may rise in spite of a decline of the mass of commodities in circulation, if the sum total of prices rises in a greater ratio. Thorough and minute English investigations have demonstrated e. g. that in the early stages of a dearth of grain in England the quantity of money in circulation increases, because the total price of the diminished supply of grain is greater than the former total price of a larger supply of grain, while the circulation of the other commodities continues undisturbed for some time at their old prices. At a later stage of the dearth of grain, there is a decline in the quantity of circulating money, either because less goods are sold at old prices besides grain, or the same quantity of those goods is sold at lower prices.

But, as we have seen, the quantity of money in circulation is determined not only by the sum total of prices of commodities that are to be realized, but also by the rapidity with which money circulates or with which it completes this work of realization. If the same sovereign makes ten purchases a day, each of a commodity having a price of one sovereign, and thus changes hands ten times, it does as much work as would be accomplished by ten sovereigns each performing but a single act of circulation a day.[73] Consequently, rapidity of gold circulation can make up for its quantity, or the presence of gold in the sphere of circulation is determined not only by its presence as an equivalent of a commodity side by side with it, but also by its participation in the movement of metamorphoses of commodities. The rapidity of the circulation of money, however, can serve as a substitute for its quantity only to a limited extent, since at any given moment an endless number of isolated purchases and sales takes places in different localities.

If the total price of the commodities in circulation rises, but in a smaller ratio than the increase in the rapidity of circulation of money, the volume of the circulating medium will diminish. If on the contrary the rapidity of circulation decreases in a greater ratio than the total price of the commodities in circulation, the volume of currency will increase. An increasing volume of currency combined with a general fall of prices or a diminishing volume of currency in connection with a general rise of prices is one of the best known phenomena in the history of prices. But the consideration of the causes which bring about a simultaneous rise in the level of prices and a still greater rise in the rate of velocity of circulation of money, or the opposite phenomenon, falls outside of the sphere of simple circulation. By way of illustration, it may be mentioned that in periods of prevailing credit, the rapidity of circulation of money grows faster than the prices of commodities, while in times of declining credit the prices of commodities fall slower than the rapidity of circulation. The shallow and artificial character of the simple circulation of money is manifested in the fact that all the elements which have a determining influence on the volume of currency, such as the volume of commodities in circulation, prices, the rise or fall of prices, the number of simultaneous purchases and sales, the rapidity of the circulation of money, —depend on the metamorphic process which takes place in the world of commodities, and that again depends on the general character of the methods of production, the size of population, the relation between city and country, the development of the means of transportation, the greater or less division of labor, credit, etc.; in short, on circumstances all of which lie *outside* of the sphere of simple circulation of money and are only reflected in it.

The rapidity of circulation being given, the volume of currency is simply determined by the prices of commodities. Hence, prices are not high or low, because there is more or less money in circulation, but on the contrary, there is more or less money in circulation, because prices are high or low. This is one of the most important laws, whose demonstration in detail by means of the history of prices constitutes perhaps the only merit of the post-Ricardian English Political Economy. If experience shows, that the level of metallic circulation or the mass of gold and silver in circulation in a given country is subject to temporary ebbs and tides and very violent ones at times,[74] but on the whole remains stationary for long periods, the deviations forming but small oscillations about the average level, this is explained by the antagonistic nature of the circumstances which determine the quantity of money in circulation. Their simultaneous modifications neutralize their effects and leave everything where it was before.

The law, that with a given rapidity of circulation of money and a given total sum of prices of commodities the quantity of the circulating medium is determined, may also be expressed as follows. If the exchange values of commodities and the average rapidity of their metamorphoses are given, the quantity of gold in circulation depends on its own value. If, therefore, the value of gold, i. e. the labor-time necessary for its production, should rise or fall, the prices of commodities will rise or fall in inverse ratio, and corresponding to that rise or fall of prices, the rapidity of circulation remaining the same, a larger or smaller quantity of gold would be required to keep the same volume of commodities in circulation. The same change would occur, if the old standard of value were superseded by a more or less valuable metal. Thus, Holland required from fourteen to fifteen times as much silver as it had previously required gold, in order to circulate the same volume of commodities, when out of tender regard for the government creditors and out of fear of the effects of the discoveries in California and Australia it substituted silver for gold money.

From the fact that the quantity of gold in circulation depends on the variable sum total of prices of commodities and the varying rapidity of circulation, it follows that the volume of the circulating medium must be capable of contraction and expansion; in short, that according to the requirements of circulation, gold must now enter, now leave the sphere of circulation in its capacity of a medium of circulation. How the circulation process itself realizes these conditions, we shall see later on.

c. COIN AND SYMBOLS OF VALUE.

In its capacity of a medium of circulation, gold acquires a shape of its own, it becomes *coin*. In order to prevent any technical difficulties in the way of its circulation, it is coined according to the standard of the money of account. Gold pieces whose imprints and legends show that they contain certain weights of gold corresponding to the reckoning names of money, £, s., etc., are coins. The establishment of a mint-price, as well as the technical work of coining, are the business of the state. Both as money of account and as coin, money acquires a *local and political character*; it speaks different languages and wears different national uniforms. The sphere in which money circulates as coin, is distinguished as an *internal* sphere of circulation which is separated from the *universal* sphere of circulation in the commodity world by national boundaries.

Yet, the only difference between gold bullion and gold coin is that between coin denomination and weight denomination. What seems to be a difference in name in the latter case appears as a difference in shape in the former. Gold coin can be thrown into the melting-pot and thus be converted again into gold *sans phrase*, just as, on the contrary, gold bars only have to be sent to the mint to receive the shape of coins. The conversion and reconversion from one form into another appears to be a purely technical matter.

For 100 pounds or 1200 ounces troy of 22 carat gold one can get £4,672-1/2 or gold sovereigns at the English mint; if these sovereigns be put on one side of the weighing scale and one hundred pounds of gold bullion on the other, the two will balance each other, which proves that the sovereign is nothing but a piece of gold of certain weight bearing this name in English coinage and having a shape and stamp of its own. The 4,672-1/2 sovereigns are put into circulation at different points, and once in its grasp they make a certain number of moves per day, some sovereigns more, others less. If the average number of moves per day of each ounce be ten, the 1200 ounces of gold would realize 12,000 ounces or 46,725 sovereigns as the total price of commodities. You may turn and toss an ounce of gold in any way you like, and it will never weigh ten ounces. But here in the process of circulation one ounce practically does weigh ten ounces. The work performed by a coin in the sphere of circulation is equivalent to the quantity of gold it contains multiplied by the number of its moves. Besides the actual importance which a coin possesses by virtue of its being an individual piece of gold of a definite weight, it acquires an ideal significance due to its function. But whether the sovereign circulates once or ten times, in each particular purchase or sale it acts only as one sovereign. It is like a general who by timely appearance at ten different points on the battle field does the work of ten generals, but still remains the same identical general at each point. The idealization of the means of circulation which is due to the supplanting of quantity by rapidity in money circulation, affects only the function of the coin within the sphere of circulation, but not the nature of the individual coin.

The circulation of money is a movement through the outside world, and the sovereign, though it *non olet*, keeps rather mixed company. In the course of its friction against all kinds of hands, pouches, pockets, purses, money-belts, bags, chests and strong-boxes, the coin rubs off, loses one gold atom here and another one there and thus, as it wears off in its wanderings over the world, it loses more and more of its intrinsic substance. By being used it gets used up. Let us take up a sovereign at the moment when its natural, inborn character has been slightly affected. A baker, says Dodd,[75] who receives from the bank to-day a brand new sovereign and pays it to-morrow to the miller, does not pay the same veritable sovereign; the latter has become lighter than it was at the time he received it. It is clear, says an anonymous writer,[76] that in the very nature of things, coins must depreciate one by one as a result of ordinary and unavoidable friction. It is a physical impossibility to entirely exclude light coins from circulation at any time, even for one day. Jacob estimates that of the 380 million pounds sterling which were in existence in Europe in 1809, nineteen million pounds sterling entirely disappeared by 1829, i. e., within a period of twenty years.[77] Thus, while a commodity at its first step into the sphere of circulation, falls out of it, a coin, after a couple of steps within that sphere represents more metal than it actually contains. The longer a coin remains in circulation, the rapidity of circulation remaining the same, or the greater its rapidity of circulation within the same period of time, the greater the discrepancy between its form as coin and its actual gold or silver substance. What remains is *magni nominis umbra*. The body of the coin becomes but a shadow. If at first it became heavier through the process of circulation, it now becomes lighter on account of it, but continues to represent the original quantity of gold in each single purchase or sale. The sovereign, as a fictitious sovereign, as fictitious gold, continues to perform the function of a legitimate coin. While other beings lose their idealism in contact with the outer world, the coin is idealized by practice, being gradually transformed into a mere phantom of its golden or silver body. This second idealization of metal money springing from the very process of circulation, or from the discrepancy between its nominal weight and its real weight is exploited in all kinds of coin counterfeiting practiced partly by governments, partly by private adventurers. The entire history of coinage from the beginning of the middle ages until late in the eighteenth century is nothing but a history of these two-fold and antagonistic adulterations, and Custodi's voluminous collection of writings of Italian economists turns mostly about this point.

But the fictitious importance of gold due to its function, comes in conflict with its real substance. One gold coin has lost more, another, less of its metal substance in the course of circulation, and one of them is, as a matter of fact, worth more now than the other. But since in the discharge of their function of coins they are taken at the same value, the sovereign weighing a quarter of an ounce passing for no more than the sovereign which only stands for a quarter of an ounce, the full-weight sovereigns are subjected in the hands of unscrupulous owners to surgical operations which produce artificially what the circulation process has caused in a natural way to their more light-weighted brothers. They are clipped and reduced and the superfluous gold fat lands in the melting pot. If 4,672-1/2 gold sovereigns when put on one side of the weighing scale weigh on an average only 800 ounces instead of 1200, they will buy when brought to the gold market only 800 ounces of gold; that is, the market price of gold would rise above its mint price. Every coin, even if of full weight would pass in its mint form for less than in bullion form. The full weight sovereigns would be reconverted into bullion, a form in which a greater quantity of gold is always worth more than a smaller quantity. As soon as this decline of metallic weight would affect a sufficiently large number of sovereigns to bring about a permanent rise of the market price of gold above its mint price, the reckoning names of the coins, though remaining the same, would begin to denote a smaller quantity of gold. That is to say, the standard of money would change and gold would be coined in the future according to this new standard. By virtue of its idealization as a medium of circulation, gold would react upon and change the legally determined ratios under which it acted as the standard of price. The same revolution would be repeated after a certain length of time and thus gold would be subject to constant change both as a standard of price and as a medium of circulation, a change under one of these forms leading to a change under the other and vice versa. This explains the phenomenon mentioned above, namely that in the history of all modern nations the same money-name stands for a constantly diminishing quantity of metal. The contradiction between gold as coin and gold as standard of price becomes also one between gold as coin and gold as the universal equivalent; in the latter capacity it circulates not only within the limits of national boundaries, but in the world market. As a measure of value gold was always of full weight, because it served only as ideal gold. In its capacity of equivalent in the isolated transaction C —M it passes at once from a state of motion to a state of rest; but in its capacity of coin its natural substance comes in constant conflict with its function. The transformation of the gold sovereign into fictitious gold can not be wholly avoided, but legislation seeks to prevent its unlimited circulation as coin by prescribing its withdrawal from circulation as soon as its shortage of metallic substance reaches a certain degree. According to the English law, e. g., a sovereign which lacks more than 0.747 grains of its weight ceases to be legal tender. The Bank of England which weighed forty-eight million gold sovereigns in the short period between 1844 and 1848, possesses in Mr. Cotton's gold weighing scale a machine which not only detects a difference of 1-100 part of a grain between two sovereigns, but like a sensible being, immediately throws out the light-weight coin on a board where it lands under another machine which cuts it up with oriental cruelty.

That being the case, gold coins could not circulate at all were not their circulation confined to definite spheres in which they do not wear off so rapidly. In so far as a gold coin weighing only one-fifth of an ounce passes in circulation for a quarter of an ounce of gold, it is practically merely a sign or a symbol for one-twentieth of an ounce of gold, and in that way all gold coins are transformed by the very process of circulation into more or less of a mere sign or symbol of their substance. But no thing can be its own symbol. Painted grapes are no symbol of real grapes, they are imaginary grapes. Still less can a light-weight sovereign be a symbol of a full-weighted one, just as a lean horse can not serve as a symbol of a fat one. Since gold thus becomes a symbol of its own self, but at the same time can not serve in that capacity, it receives a symbolical, silver or copper substitute in those spheres of circulation in which it is most subject to wear and tear, namely where purchases and sales are constantly taking place on the smallest scale. In these spheres, even if not the same identical coins, still a certain part of the entire supply of gold money would constantly circulate as coin. To that extent gold is substituted by silver or copper tokens. Thus, while only a specific commodity can perform in a given country the function of a measure of value and therefore of money, different commodities can serve as coin side by side with gold. These subsidiary mediums of circulation, such as silver or copper coins, represent definite fractions of a gold coin within the sphere of circulation. Their own silver or copper weight is, therefore, not determined by the proportions of the respective values of silver and copper to that of gold, but is arbitrarily fixed by law. They may be issued only in such quantities in which the diminutive fractions of gold coin which they represent would constantly circulate either for purposes of change for gold coins of higher denominations, or for realizing equally small prices of commodities. In retail trade silver and copper tokens belong to distinct spheres of circulation. In the nature of things, the rapidity of their circulation is in inverse ratio to the price which they realize in each separate purchase or sale, or to the size of the fraction of gold coin which they represent. If we consider how immense the volume of the daily retail trade in a country like England is, we will understand from the comparatively insignificant proportions of its combined volume how rapid and steady the circulation of the subsidiary coin must be. From a parliamentary report of recent date we see, e. g., that in 1857 the English mint coined £4,859,000 worth of gold, £733,000 of silver nominal value which contained metal actually worth £363,000. The total amount of gold coined in the ten years ending December 31, 1857, was £55,239,000, and of silver only £2,434,000. The supply of copper coin in 1857 amounted only to £6,720 nominal value containing £3,492 worth of copper; of this £3,136 was in pennies, £2,464 in half-pennies, and £1,120 in farthings. The total value of copper coined in the ten years was £141,477 nominal, the metallic value being £73,503. Just as gold coin is prevented from permanently retaining its function of coin by the legal provision of the loss of weight which demonetizes it, so are the silver and copper tokens prevented from passing from their spheres of circulation into that of gold coin and acquiring the character of money by the provision of the maximum amount for which they are legal tender. In England e. g. copper is legal tender only to the amount of six pence and silver up to forty shillings. If silver and copper tokens were to be issued in greater quantities than the requirements of their spheres of circulation call for, prices of commodities would not rise as a result, but the accumulation of these tokens in the hands of retail dealers would reach such an extent that they would be finally compelled to sell them as metal. Thus in 1798 English copper coins, issued by private individuals, accumulated in the hands of small traders to the amount of £20,350 which they tried in vain to put again in circulation, being finally compelled to throw them as metal on the copper market.[78]

The silver and copper tokens which represent gold coin in certain spheres of circulation in the interior of the country, contain a definite quantity of silver and copper prescribed by law, but after they get into circulation, they wear off like gold coins and become even more rapidly mere phantoms, according to the rapidity and steadiness of their circulation. To draw again a line of demonetization beyond which silver and copper tokens would lose their character of coins, they would have to be replaced in turn within certain spheres of their own circulation by some other symbolic money, say iron and lead, and such representation of one kind of symbolic money by another kind would form an endless process. In all countries with a well developed circulation the very requirements of money circulation make it necessary that the character of silver and copper tokens as money be made independent of any loss of weight in those coins. Thus, as it was in the nature of things, it appears that they serve as symbols of gold coin not because they are symbols made of silver or copper, not because they have certain value, but only in so far as they have no value.

Relatively worthless things, such as *paper*, can consequently perform the function of symbols of gold money. That subsidiary currency consists of metal tokens, such as silver, copper, etc., is mainly due to the fact that in most countries the less valuable metals such as silver in England, copper in ancient Rome, Sweden, Scotland, etc., had circulated as money before they were degraded by the process of circulation to the rank of small change and replaced by a more precious metal. Besides, it is natural that the money symbol which grows directly out of metallic circulation, should itself be a metal. Just as that portion of gold which would always have to circulate as small change, is replaced by metal tokens; so can the other portion of gold which is constantly absorbed as coin by circulation in the interior of the country and, therefore, must continually circulate, be replaced with worthless tokens. The level below which the mass of circulating coin never sinks is determined in each country by experience. Thus, the originally imperceptible difference between the nominal weight and the metallic weight of a metal coin can grow apace until it reaches the point of absolute separation. The mint name of money parts company with its substance and exists outside of it in worthless slips of paper. Just as the exchange value of commodities is crystallized by their process of exchange into gold money, so is gold money sublimated in its currency into its own symbol first in the form of worn coin, then in the form of subsidiary metal currency, and finally in the form of a worthless token, paper, mere *sign of value*.

Gold coin has produced its substitutes, first metallic and then paper, only because in spite of its loss of metallic weight it continued to perform the function of coin. It did not circulate because of its wear and tear; on the contrary, it wore out to a symbol because it continued to circulate. Only in so far as gold money becomes simply a token of its own value in the process of circulation, can mere tokens of value take its place.

In so far as the movement C —M —C represents a dynamic unity of two processes C —M and M —C which pass directly one into the other, or in so far as a commodity passes through the complete process of its metamorphosis, it express its exchange value in price and in money only to discard that form at once and to become again a commodity or, rather, a use-value. That is to say, it develops *only an apparent assertion of the independence* of its exchange value. On the other hand, we have seen that gold, in so far as it performs the function of coin or in so far as it continually circulates, actually forms only a connecting link between the metamorphoses of commodities and constitutes *but their transitory money form*; furthermore, that it realizes the price of one set of commodities only in order to realize that of another, but in no case does it constitute a stable form of exchange value or appear itself as a commodity in a state of rest. The reality which the exchange value of commodities acquires in the process and which is represented by gold in its circulation, is the reality of an electric spark. Although real gold, it plays the part of fictitious gold, and can, therefore, be replaced in this function by a token of itself.

The token of value, say paper, which plays the part of coin, is the token of a quantity of gold expressed in its currency name, i. e., it is a gold token. Just as a certain quantity of gold does not in itself express a value ratio, so is that true of the token which takes its place. In so far as a certain quantity of gold, as embodied labor-time, has a value of a certain magnitude, the gold token represents value. But the magnitude of the value which it represents depends all the time on the value of the quantity of gold for which it stands. As regards commodities the token of value expresses *the reality of their price*, it is *signum pretii* and sign of their value only because their value is expressed in their price. In the process C —M —C, in so far as it represents the dynamic unity or direct alternation of the two metamorphoses-and that is the aspect it assumes in the sphere of circulation in which the token of value discharges its function-the exchange value of commodities acquires in price only an ideal expression and in money only an imaginary symbolic existence. Exchange value thus acquires *only* an imaginary though material expression, but it has no real existence except in the commodities themselves, in so far as a certain quantity of labor-time is embodied in them. It *appears*, therefore, that the token of value represents *directly* the value of commodities, by figuring not as a token of gold but as a token of the value which exists in the commodity alone and is only expressed in price. But it is a false appearance. The token of value is directly only *a token of price*, i. e., a *token of gold*, and only indirectly a token of value of a commodity. Unlike Peter Shlemihl, gold has not sold its shadow, but buys with its shadow. The token of value operates only in so far as it represents the price of one commodity as against that of another within the sphere of circulation, or in so far as it *represents gold* to every owner of commodities. A certain comparatively worthless object such as a piece of leather, a slip of paper, etc., becomes by force of custom a token of money material, but maintains its existence in that capacity only so long as its character as a symbol of money is guaranteed by the general acquiescence of the owners of commodities, i. e., so long as it enjoys a legally established conventional existence and compulsory circulation. Paper money issued by the state and circulating as legal tender is the perfected form of the token of value, and the only form of paper money, which has its immediate origin in metallic circulation or even in the simple circulation of commodities. *Credit money* belongs to a higher sphere of the social process of production and is governed by entirely different laws. Symbolic paper money does not in fact, differ in the least from subsidiary metal coin, except that it reaches wider spheres of circulation. We have seen that the mere technical development of the standard of price or of the mint price and later the shaping of gold bullion into coin have called forth the interference of the state; this circumstance brought about a visible separation of national circulation from the world circulation of commodities: this separation is completed by the evolution of coin into a token of value. As a mere medium of circulation money can assume an independent existence only within the sphere of national circulation.[79]

Our presentation has shown that the coin form of gold as a token of value differentiated from the gold substance itself, has its direct origin in the process of circulation and not in any agreement or state interference. Russia offers a striking example of the natural origin of the token of value. At the time when hides and furs played there the part of money, the conflict between the perishable and bulky nature of the material and its function as a medium of circulation resulted in the custom of replacing it by small pieces of stamped leather which thus became a kind of draft payable in hides and furs. Later on they became under the name of copecs mere tokens for fractions of the silver rouble and remained in use in some parts until 1700, when Peter the Great ordered their withdrawal in exchange for small copper coins issued by the state. Ancient writers who could observe the phenomena of exclusively metallic circulation, already took the view of coin as a symbol or token of value. That is true both of *Plato*[80] and *Aristotle*.[81] In countries where credit is not developed, as e. g. in China, legal tender paper money is found at an early date[82]. Early advocates of paper money expressly point out the fact that metallic coin is transformed into a token of value in the very process of circulation. So Benjamin Franklin[83] and Bishop Berkeley.[84]

How many reams of paper cut up into bills can circulate as money? Put in that way, the question would be absurd. The worthless tokens are signs of value only in so far as they represent gold within the sphere of circulation and they represent it only to the extent to which it would itself be absorbed as coin by the process of circulation; this quantity is determined by its own value, the exchange values of the commodities and the rapidity of their metamorphoses being given. Bills of a denomination of £5 could circulate in a quantity five times less than those of £1 denomination, and if all payments were made in shilling bills, then twenty times as many shilling bills would have to be in circulation as are one pound bills. If the gold currency were represented by bills of different denominations, e. g. five pound, one pound and ten shilling bills, then the quantity of these different tokens of value would be determined not only by the quantity of gold necessary for circulation as a whole, but also by that required in the sphere of circulation of each kind of bills. If fourteen million pounds sterling (this is the provision of the English Bank Law, not for the entire currency but only for credit money) were the level below which the circulation of a country never sank, then fourteen million paper bills, each a token of value of one pound, could circulate. If the value of gold fell or rose because the labor-time necessary for its production had fallen or risen, then, the exchange value of the same volume of commodities remaining the same, the number of one pound bills in circulation would rise or fall in inverse ratio to the change in the value of gold. If gold were replaced by silver as a measure of value, the ratio of the respective values of silver and gold being 1:15, and if each bill were to represent now the same quantity of silver as it represented gold before, then there would be 210 million one pound bills in circulation instead of the previous fourteen million. The number of paper bills is thus determined by the quantity of gold money which they represent in circulation, and since they are tokens of value only in so far as they represent it, their value is simply determined by their *quantity*. Thus, while the quantity of gold in circulation is determined by the prices of commodities, the value of the paper bills in circulation, on the contrary, depends exclusively on their own quantity.

The interference of the state which issues paper money as legal tender-and we are treating of paper money of that kind only-seems to do away with the economic law. The state which in its mint price gave a certain name to a piece of gold of certain weight, and in the act of coinage only impressed its stamp on gold, seems now to turn paper into gold by the magic of its stamp. Since paper bills are legal tender, no one can prevent the state from forcing as large a quantity of them as it desires into circulation and from impressing upon it any coin denomination, such as £1, £5, £20. The bills which have once gotten into circulation can not be removed, since on the one hand their course is hemmed in by the frontier posts of the country and on the other they lose all value, use-value, as well as exchange-value, outside of circulation. Take away from them their function and they become worthless rags of paper. Yet this power of the state is a mere fiction. It may throw into circulation any desired quantity of paper bills of whatever denomination, but with this mechanical act its control ceases. Once in the grip of circulation and the token of value or paper money becomes subject to its intrinsic laws.

If fourteen million pounds sterling were the quantity of gold required for the circulation of commodities and if the state were to put into circulation two hundred and ten million bills each of the denomination of £1, then these two hundred and ten millions would become the representatives of gold to the amount of fourteen million pounds sterling. It would be the same as if the state were to make the one pound bills represent a fifteen times less valuable metal or a fifteen times smaller weight of gold. Nothing would be changed but the nomenclature of the standard of price, which by its very nature is conventional, no matter whether such change takes place as a direct result of a change of the mint standard or indirectly owing to an increase of paper bills to an extent required by a new lower standard. Since the name £ would stand now for a fifteen times smaller quantity of gold, the prices of all commodities would increase fifteen times and two hundred and ten million one pound bills would now be actually as necessary as fourteen million had been before. To the same extent to which the combined quantity of tokens of value would increase now, the quantity of gold which each of them represents would decrease. The rise of prices would constitute but a reaction on the part of the process of circulation which forcibly equates the tokens of value to the quantity of gold which they are supposed to replace.

In the history of the debasement of money in England and France by their governments, we find repeatedly that prices had not risen in the same proportion in which the silver coinage had been debased. That was simply due to the fact that the proportion in which the currency was increased did not correspond to the proportion in which it had been debased; that is to say, because an inadequate quantity of coins of the poorer metallic composition was issued, if the exchange values of commodities were to be estimated in the future in the new coin as a measure of value and be realized in coins corresponding to this smaller unit of measure. This solves the difficulty left unsettled in the controversy between Locke and Lowndes. The ratio which a token of value, whether made of paper or of debased gold or silver, bears to certain weights of gold or silver estimated according to the mint price, depends not on its own composition but on the quantity in which it is found in circulation. The difficulty in understanding this is due to the fact that money in its two functions of a measure of value and a medium of circulation is subject to two not only opposite but apparently contradictory laws corresponding to the difference in the two functions. In the discharge of its function of a measure of value where money serves merely as money of account and gold only as ideal gold, everything depends on the natural substance of money. Estimated in silver or expressed in silver prices exchange values are naturally estimated quite differently than when measured in gold or as gold prices. On the contrary, in its function of a medium of circulation, where gold is not only imagined but is actually present side by side with other commodities, its substance is immaterial and everything depends on its quantity. For the unit of measure the determining factor is whether it consists of a pound of gold, silver or copper; while in the case of coin, no matter what its own composition is, it will become the embodiment of each of these units of measure in accordance with its quantity. But it goes against common sense that in the case of mere imaginary money everything should depend on its material substance, while in that of the palpably present coin all should be determined by an ideal ratio of numbers.

The rise or fall of prices of commodities following a rise or fall of the quantity of paper notes-the latter only where paper currency constitutes the exclusive medium of circulation-is thus nothing but an assertion through the process of circulation of a law mechanically violated from without; namely, that the quantity of gold in circulation is determined by the prices of commodities, and the quantity of tokens of value in circulation is determined by the quantity of gold coin which it represents. For that reason any desired number of paper notes will be absorbed and equally digested by the process of circulation, because the token of value, no matter with what gold title it may enter circulation, will be compressed within the latter to a token of that quantity of gold which could actually circulate in its place.

In the case of the circulation of tokens of value all laws pertaining to the circulation of real money appear to be reversed and standing on their heads. While gold circulates because it has value, paper has value because it circulates. While with a given exchange value of commodities, the quantity of gold in circulation depends on its own value, the value of paper depends on its own quantity in circulation. While the quantity of gold in circulation rises or falls with the rise or fall of prices of commodities, the prices of commodities seem to rise or fall with the change in the quantity of paper in circulation. While the circulation of commodities can absorb only a definite quantity of gold coin and as a result of that the alternating contraction and expansion of the currency appears as a necessary law, paper money seems to enter circulation in any desired amount. While the state is guilty of debasing gold and silver coin and of disturbing their function of a medium of circulation, if it turns out a coin, only 1-100 of a grain below its nominal weight; it performs a perfectly proper operation by issuing absolutely worthless paper notes which contain nothing of the metal except its mint denomination. While gold coin apparently represents the value of commodities only in so far as that value is itself estimated in gold or is expressed in price, the token of value seems to represent directly the value of commodities. It is, therefore, clear why students who examined one-sidedly the phenomena of circulation of money by confining their observations to the circulation of legal tender paper money, should have failed to grasp the intrinsic laws governing the circulation of money. As a matter of fact, these laws appear not only reversed but extinct in the circulation of tokens of value, since paper currency, if issued in the right quantity, goes through certain movements which are not in its nature as a token of value, while its proper movement instead of growing directly out of the metamorphosis of commodities, springs from the violation of its proper proportion to gold.

3. MONEY.

Money as distinguished from coin, the result of the circulation process C —M —C, forms the starting point of the circulation process M —C —M, i. e. the exchange of money for commodity in order to exchange commodity for money. In the form C —M —C, commodity forms the starting and final points of the movement; in the form M —C —M, money plays that part. In the former case money is the medium of exchange of commodities, in the latter the commodity helps money to become money. Money which appears merely as a means of circulation in the first form becomes an end in the second form; while commodity which appeared first as the end, now becomes but a means. Since money is itself the result of circulation C —M —C, the result of circulation appears at the same time as its starting point in the form M —C —M. While in the case of C —M —C the interchange of matter constituted the real import of the process, the form of the commodity resulting from this first process constitutes the import of the second process M —C —M.

In the form C —M —C the two extreme members are commodities of the same value, but qualitatively different use-values. Their mutual exchange C —C constitutes actual interchange of matter. In the form M —C —M the two extremes are gold and at the same time gold of equal value. To exchange gold for a commodity in order to exchange the commodity for gold, or if we consider the final result M —M, to exchange gold for gold, seems absurd. But if we translate the formula M —C —M into the expression: *to buy* in order *to sell*, which means nothing but to exchange gold for gold through an intervening movement, we recognize at once the prevailing form of capitalist production. In actual practice, however, people do not buy in order to sell, but they buy cheap in order to sell dear. Money is exchanged for a commodity in order to exchange the same commodity for a larger amount of money, so that the extremes M, M are, if not qualitatively, then quantitatively different. Such a quantitative difference presupposes the *exchange of non-equivalents*, yet commodity and money as such are only opposite forms of the same commodity, i. e. they are different forms of the same magnitude of value. The circuit M —C —M thus conceals under the forms of money and commodity more highly developed relations of production, and is but a reflection within the sphere of simple circulation of a movement of a more advanced character. Money, as distinguished from the medium of circulation, must therefore be developed from the direct form of circulation of commodities, C —M —C.

Gold, i. e., the specific commodity which serves as a measure of value and a medium of circulation, becomes money without any further assistance on the part of society. In England, where silver is neither the measure of value nor the prevailing medium of circulation, it does not become money, just as gold in Holland, as soon as it had been dethroned as a measure of value, ceased to be money. A commodity thus becomes money only in its combined capacity of a measure of value and medium of circulation; or, the unity of the measure of value and medium of circulation is money. As such a unity, however, gold has a separate existence independent of its existence in the two functions. As a measure of value it is only ideal money and ideal gold; as a mere medium of circulation it is symbolic money and symbolic gold; but in its plain metallic bodily form gold is money or money is real gold.

Let us now consider for a moment the commodity gold when it is in a state of rest, and plays the part of money in its relation to other commodities. All commodities represent in their prices a certain quantity of gold, that is to say, they are merely imaginary gold or imaginary money, representatives of gold, just as, on the other hand, money in the form of a token of value appeared as a mere representative of prices of commodities.[85] Since all commodities are thus but imaginary money, money is the only real commodity. Contrary to commodities, which only represent the independently existing exchange value, i. e., universal social labor, or abstract wealth, gold is the *material form of abstract wealth*. Through its use-value, every commodity, by its relation to some particular want, expresses only one aspect of material wealth, but one side of wealth. Money, however, satisfies every want since it can be directly converted into the object of any want. Its own use-value is realized in the endless series of use-values which form its equivalents. In its virgin metallic state it holds locked up all the material wealth which lies unfolded in the world of commodities. Thus, while commodities represent in their prices the universal equivalent or abstract wealth, viz., gold, the latter represents in its use-value the use-values of all commodities. Gold is, therefore, *the bodily representative of material wealth*. It is the "precis de toutes les choses" (Boisguillebert), the compendium of the wealth of society. At one and the same time, it is the direct incarnation of universal labor in its form, and the aggregate of all concrete labor in its substance. It is universal wealth individualized.[86] As a medium of circulation it underwent all kinds of injury, was clipped, and even reduced to the condition of a mere symbolic paper rag. As money it is restored to its golden glory.[87] From a serve it becomes a lord. From a mere understrapper it rises to the position of Lord of commodities.[88]

a. HOARDING.

Gold separates itself as money from the process of circulation whenever a commodity interrupts the process of its metamorphosis and remains in its form of a gold chrysalis. This occurs every time a sale is not immediately followed by purchase. The independent isolation of gold as money is, thus, a material expression of the disintegration of the process of circulation, or of the metamorphosis of commodities, into two separate acts independent of each other. The coin itself becomes money as soon as its course is interrupted. In the hands of the seller who takes it in exchange for his commodity, it is money and not coin; as soon as it passes out of his hands it is again coin. Everybody is a seller of the one commodity which he produces, but a buyer of all other commodities which he needs for his existence in society. While his selling is determined by the labor-time required for the production of his commodity, his buying is determined by the continual renewal of the wants of life. In order to be able to buy without having sold anything, he must sell without buying. In fact, the circulation process C —M —C is a dynamic unity of sale and purchase only in so far as it constitutes at the same time the constant process of its separation. In order that money should flow continuously as coin, coin must constantly coagulate as money. The continuous flow of coin depends on its constant accumulations in the form of reserve-funds of coin which spring up throughout the sphere of circulation and form sources of supply; the formation, distribution, disappearance, and reformation of these reserve funds is constantly changing, their existence constantly disappears, their disappearance constantly exists. Adam Smith expressed this never-ceasing transformation of coin into money and of money into coin by saying that every owner of commodities must always keep in supply besides the particular commodity which he sells, a certain quantity of the universal commodity with which he buys. We saw, that in the process C —M —C the second member M —C splits up into a series of purchases which do not take place at once, but at intervals of time, so that one part of M circulates as money while the other rests as money. Money is in that case only *suspended coin* and the separate parts of the circulating mass of coins appear now in one form, now in another, constantly changing. This first transformation of the medium of circulation into money represents, therefore, but a technical aspect of money circulation.[89]

The primitive form of wealth is that of a surplus or superabundance, i. e., that part of the products which are not immediately required as use-values, or the possession of such products whose use-value falls outside the sphere of mere necessaries. When considering the transition of commodity into money we saw that this surplus or superabundance of products constitutes the proper sphere of exchange at a low stage of development of production. Superfluous products become exchangeable products or commodities. The adequate form of this surplus is gold and silver, the first form in which wealth as abstract social wealth is preserved. Commodities can not only be stored up in the form of gold and silver, i. e., in the substance of money, but gold and silver are wealth in preserved form. While every use-value performs its service as such by being consumed, i. e., destroyed, the use-value of gold as money consists in its being the bearer of exchange value, in embodying universal labor-time as a shapeless raw material. As shapeless metal, exchange value possesses an indestructible form. Gold or silver thus brought to rest as money, forms a *hoard*. Among nations with an exclusively metallic circulation, such as the ancients were, hoarding is practiced universally from the individual to the state which guards its state hoard. In more ancient times, in Asia and Egypt, these hoards under the protection of kings and priests appear rather as a mark of their power. In Greece and Rome it was part of public policy to accumulate state hoards as the safest and most available form of surplus. The quick transfer of such hoards by conquerors from one country to another and the sudden outpour of a part of these hoards into the general circulation constitute a peculiar feature of ancient economy.

As the incarnation of labor-time gold is a pledge for its own value, and since it is the embodiment of *universal* labor-time, the process of circulation pledges gold its constant rôle of exchange value. Owing to the mere fact that the owner of commodities can retain his commodity in the form of exchange value or retain the exchange-value as a commodity, the exchange of commodities for the purpose of retaining them in the transformed shape of gold becomes circulation's own motive. The metamorphosis C —M takes place for the sake of the metamorphosis, i. e., in order to transform it from particular natural wealth into universal social wealth. Instead of change of matter, change of form becomes its own purpose. From a mere form of the movement exchange value becomes its substance. Commodity is preserved as wealth, as commodity, only in so far as it keeps within the sphere of circulation, and it keeps in that fluent state only in so far as it solidifies in the form of silver and gold. It remains in the stream of circulation as its crystal. At the same time gold and silver themselves become money only in so far as they do not play the part of mediums of circulation. *As non-mediums of circulation they become money.* The withdrawal of a commodity from circulation in the form of gold is therefore the only means of keeping it constantly within the sphere of circulation.

The owner of commodities can receive money from circulation only in return for a commodity which he gives to it. Constant selling, continual throwing of commodities into circulation is, therefore, the first condition of hoarding from the standpoint of the circulation of commodities. On the other hand, money as a medium of circulation constantly disappears in the very process of circulation by being realized all the time in use-values and becoming dissolved in fleeting pleasures. It must, therefore, be taken out of the all-consuming stream of circulation or the commodity must be kept up in its first metamorphosis, so that money is prevented from performing its function of a means of purchase. The commodity owner who has now become a hoarder, must sell as much as possible and buy as little as possible, as old Cato had taught: "patrem familias vendacem, non emacem esse." While industry constitutes the positive condition of hoarding, saving forms the negative one. The less the equivalent of a commodity is withdrawn from circulation in the form of particular commodities or use-values, the more it is withdrawn in the shape of money or exchange value.[90] The acquisition of wealth in its universal form thus requires abstinence from wealth in its material reality. Thus the stimulating impulse for hoarding is *greed*, the objects of which are not commodities as use-values, but exchange value as commodity. In order to get possession of the surplus in its universal form, the particular wants must be treated as so much luxury and excess. Thus the Cortes presented a report to Philipp II., in 1593, in which, among other things, was said: "The Cortes of Valladolid in the year 1586 petitioned Your Majesty not to allow the further importation into the Kingdom of candles, glassware, jewelry, knives and similar articles; these things useless to human life come from abroad to be exchanged for gold, as though the Spaniards were Indians." The hoarder despises the worldly, temporary and transitory enjoyments in his hunt after the eternal treasure, which neither moth nor rust can eat, which is perfectly celestial and earthly at the same time. "The general remote cause of our want of money is the great excess of this Kingdom in consuming the Commodities of Forreine Countries, which prove to us discommodities, in hindering us of so much treasure, which otherwise would bee brought in, in lieu of those toyes....Wee ... consume amongst us, that great abundance of the Wines of Spaine, of France, of the Rhene, of the Levant ... the Raisins of Spaine, the Corints of the Levant, the Lawnes and Cambricks of Hannaults ... the Silkes of Italie, the Sugers and Tobaco of the West Indies, the Spices of the East Indies: All which are of no necessetie unto us and yet are bought with ready mony."[91]

In the form of gold and silver, wealth is indestructible, both because exchange value is preserved in the shape of indestructible metal, and, especially, because gold and silver are prevented from becoming, as mediums of circulation, mere vanishing money forms of the commodity. The destructible substance is thus sacrificed for the indestructible form. "If money be taken (by means of taxation) from him, who spendeth the same ... upon eating and drinking, or any other perishing Commodity; and the same transferred to one that bestoweth it on Cloaths; I say that even in this case the Commonwealth hath some little advantage; because Cloaths do not altogether perish so soon as Meats and Drinks. But if the same be spent in Furniture of Houses, the advantage is yet a little more; if in Building of Houses, yet more; if in improving of Lands, working of Mines, Fishing, etc., yet more; but most of all, in bringing Gold and Silver into the Country; because those things are not only not perishable, but are esteemed for Wealth at all times and everywhere; whereas other Commodities which are perishable, or whose value depends upon the Fashion; or which are contingently scarce and plentiful, are Wealth, but pro hic et nunc."[92] The withdrawal of money from the stream of circulation and the saving of it from the social interchange of matter reaches its extreme form in the *burying* of money, so that social wealth is brought as an underground indestructible treasure into a perfectly secret private relation with the owner of commodities. Dr. Bernier, who stayed for some time at the court of Aurenzeb at Delhi, tells us how the merchants, especially the Mohammedan heathens, who control nearly all the trade and all money, secretly bury their money deep in the ground, "being imbued with the faith that the gold and silver which they put away during their lives will serve them after death in the next world."[93] However, in so far as the asceticism of the hoarder is combined with active industry, he is rather a Protestant by religion and still more a Puritan. "It can not be denied that buying and selling are necessary, that one can not get along without them, and that one can buy like a Christian especially things that serve in need and in honor; for the patriarchs had also bought and sold cattle, wool, grain, butter, milk and other goods. They are gifts of God which He gives out of the earth and divides among men. But foreign trade which brings over from Calcutta, India and other such places commodities consisting of costly silks, and gold ware, and spices which only serve for luxury and are of no use, draining the land and the people of their money, should not be tolerated if we but had a government of princes. Yet I do not wish to write of that now, for I believe it will have to stop of itself, when we have no money any longer; and so will luxury and gluttony; for no writing or teaching will help until want and poverty will force us."[94]

In times of disturbance in the process of the social interchange of matter, the burying of money takes place even in bourgeois societies which are at a high stage of development. The social bond in its compact form is being saved from the social movement (with the owner of commodities this bond is the commodity and the adequate form of the commodity is money). The social *nervus rerum* is buried next to the body whose nerve it is.

The hoard would now become mere useless metal, its money soul would depart from it and it would remain as the burnt ashes of circulation, as its caput mortuum, if it did not constantly tend to get back into circulation. Money, or crystallized exchange value, is, according to its nature, the form of abstract wealth; but, on the other hand, any given sum of money is a quantitatively limited magnitude of value. The quantitative limitation of exchange value is in contradiction with its qualitative universality and the hoarder conceives in it a barrier which turns, in fact, into a qualitative barrier as well and makes of the hoard merely a limited representative of material wealth. Money, in its capacity of a universal equivalent, appears, as we have seen, as a member of an equation, the other member of which consists of an endless series of commodities. It depends on the magnitude of the exchange value to what extent money will be realized in such an endless series, i. e., to what degree it corresponds to the conception of it as an exchange value. The automatic movement of exchange value as exchange value can only tend to its passing beyond its quantitative limits. But by exceeding the quantitative limits of the hoard a new limit is created which must be removed in its turn. There is no definite limit which appears as a barrier to further hoarding, every limit plays that part. Hoard accumulation has, therefore, no inherent limits, no inherent measure; it is an endless process which finds in each successive result an impulse for a new beginning. While the hoard is increased only by being preserved, it is preserved only by being increased.

Money is not only *an* object of the passion for riches; it is *the* object of that passion. The latter is essentially *auri sacra fames*. The passion for riches, contrary to that for special kinds of natural wealth or use-values, such as clothing, ornaments, herds, etc., is possible only when universal wealth has been individualized as such in a particular object and can, therefore, be retained in the form of a single commodity. Money appears then no less as an object than as a source of the passion for riches.[95] The underlying fact of the matter is that exchange value as such and with it its increase become the final aim. Greed holds the hoard fast by not allowing the money to become a medium of circulation, but the thirst for gold saves the money soul of the hoard by keeping up the lasting affinity of gold for circulation.

To sum up, the activity by which hoards are built up resolves itself into withdrawal of money from circulation by continually repeated sales, and simple hoarding or *accumulation*. In fact, it is only in the sphere of simple circulation and, especially, in the form of hoarding, that accumulation of wealth as such takes place, while, as we shall see later, in the case of other so-called forms of accumulation it is only a misnomer to call them by that name in mere recollection of the simple accumulation of money. All other commodities are hoarded either as use-values, in which case the manner of storing them up is determined by the peculiarities of their use-value: the storing of grain, e. g., requires special equipment; the accumulation of sheep makes one a shepherd; the accumulation of slaves and land creates relations of master and servant, etc.; the accumulation of particular kinds of wealth requires special processes different from the simple act of hoarding, and develops special individual traits. Or, wealth in the form of commodities is hoarded as exchange-value and in that case hoarding appears as a commercial or a specific economic operation. The one who carries on such operations becomes a dealer in corn, in cattle, etc. Gold and silver are money not through some activity of the individual who accumulates it, but as crystals of the process of circulation which goes on without any aid on his part. He has nothing to do but to put them aside, adding new weights of metal to his hoard, a perfectly senseless operation which, if applied to all other commodities, would deprive them of all value.[96]

Our hoarder appears as a martyr of exchange value, a holy ascetic crowning the metal pillar. He cares for wealth only in its social form and therefore he buries it away from society. He wants to have the commodity in the form in which it is always capable of entering circulation and therefore he withdraws it from circulation. He dreams of exchange value and therefore does not exchange. The fluid form of wealth and its petrification, the elixir of life and the stone of wisdom madly haunt each other in alchemic fashion. In his imaginary unlimited passion for enjoyment he denies himself all enjoyment. Because he wishes to satisfy all social wants, he barely satisfies his elementary natural wants. While holding fast to his wealth in its metallic bodily form, the latter escapes him as a phantom. As a matter of fact, however, the hoarding of money for the sake of money is the barbaric form of production for production's sake, i. e., the development of the productive forces of social labor beyond the limits of ordinary wants. The less the production of commodities is developed, the more important is the first crystallization of exchange value into money, or hoarding, which plays, therefore, an important part among the ancient nations, in Asia until the present day, and among modern agricultural nations where exchange value has not as yet taken hold of all the relations of production. Before taking up the consideration of the specific economic function of hoarding within the sphere of metallic circulation, let us mention another form of hoarding.

Quite apart from their aesthetic properties, silver and gold commodities are convertible into money, since the material of which they are made is a money material; and, inversely, gold money and gold bullion can be converted into commodities. Because gold and silver constitute the material of abstract wealth, the greatest display of wealth consists of the utilization of these metals as concrete use-values, and if the owner of commodities hides his treasure at certain stages of production, he is very anxious to appear before other owners of commodities as *rico hombre* whenever he can do so with safety. He gilds himself and his house.[97] In Asia, especially in India, where, unlike under the capitalist system, the hoarding of wealth appears not as a subordinate function of the system of production, but as an end in itself, gold and silver commodities are practically but aesthetic forms of hoards. In mediaeval England gold and silver commodities were considered before the law as mere forms of treasure, since their value was but slightly increased by the crude labor spent upon them. They were destined to re-enter circulation and their fineness was therefore prescribed in the same manner as that of coin. The increasing use of gold and silver as objects of luxury with the growth of wealth is such a simple matter that it was perfectly clear to the ancients,[98] while modern economists have advanced the erroneous proposition that the use of silver and gold articles increases not in proportion to the growth of wealth, but in proportion to the fall in value of the precious metals. Their otherwise accurate references to the use of Californian and Australian gold are inconclusive, since the increased consumption of gold as a raw material does not find justification, according to their theory, in any corresponding decline in its value. From 1810 to 1830, in consequence of the struggle of the American colonies against Spain and the interruption of mining caused by revolutions, the annual average production of precious metals declined by more than one-half. The decline of coin in circulation in Europe amounted to nearly one-sixth, comparing the years 1829 and 1809. Although the quantity produced had thus declined and the cost of production, if it had changed at all, had increased, yet the consumption of precious metals as objects of luxury increased to an extraordinary extent in England during the very war and on the continent after the Peace of Paris. The consumption increased with the general growth of wealth.[99] It may be stated as a general law that the conversion of gold and silver money into articles of luxury prevails in times of peace, while their reconversion into bullion or even coin takes place in stormy periods.[100] How considerable the proportion is of the gold and silver treasure in the form of articles of luxury to the quantity of precious metals serving as money may be seen from the fact that in 1829 the proportion in England, according to Jacob, was two to one, and in entire Europe and America the precious metals in the form of articles of luxury exceeded those in the form of money by one-fourth.

We have seen that the circulation of money is but the manifestation of the metamorphoses of commodities, or of the form under which the social interchange of matter takes place. With the change in the total price of commodities in circulation or in the volume of their simultaneous metamorphoses, the rapidity of their change of form in each case being given, the total quantity of gold in circulation must always expand or contract. That is possible only under the condition that the total quantity of money in the country continually bear a varying ratio to the quantity of money in circulation. This condition is met by the process of hoarding. With a fall in prices or rise in the rapidity of circulation, the hoard-reservoirs absorb that part of money which is thrown out of circulation; with a rise in price or a decline in the rapidity of circulation, the hoards open up and return a part of their contents to the stream of circulation. The solidification of circulating money into hoards and the outpouring of hoards into circulation is a constantly oscillating movement in which the prevalence of the one or the other tendency is determined exclusively by fluctuations in the circulation of commodities. Hoards thus serve as conduits for the supply and withdrawal of money to or from circulation, so that every time only that quantity of money circulates as coin which is required by the immediate needs of circulation. If the volume of the entire circulation suddenly expands and the fluent unity of sale and purchase assumes such dimensions that the total sum of prices to be realized increases more rapidly than the rapidity of the circulation of money, the hoards decrease perceptibly; but when the combined movement slackens to an unusual extent, or the movement of buying and selling steadies itself, the medium of circulation solidifies into money in large measure, and the treasure reservoirs fill up far above their average level. In countries with an exclusively metallic circulation or where production is at a low stage of development, the hoards are endlessly split up and scattered all over the land, while in countries where the capitalist system is developed they are concentrated in bank reservoirs. Hoards are not to be confounded with coin reservoirs, which form a constituent part of the total supply of money in circulation, while the interaction between hoards and currency implies the decline or rise of its total supply. Gold and silver commodities form, as we have seen, both conduits for the withdrawal of precious metals, as well as sources of their supply. In ordinary times only their former function is of importance to the economy of metallic circulation.[101]

b. MEANS OF PAYMENT.

The two forms which have so far distinguished money from the circulating medium are those of *suspended coin* and of the *hoard*. The temporary transformation of coin into money in the case of the former means that the second phase of C —M —C, namely purchase M —C, must break up within a certain sphere of circulation into a series of successive purchases. As to hoarding, it is simply based on the isolation of the act C —M when it does not immediately pass into M —C, or is but an independent development of the first metamorphosis of a commodity; it represents money as the result of the alienation of all commodities in contra-distinction to the medium of circulation as the embodiment of commodities in their always alienable form. Coin reserves and hoards are money only as non-circulating mediums and are non-circulating mediums only because they do not circulate. In the capacity in which we consider money now, it circulates or enters circulation, but does not perform the function of a circulating medium. As a medium of circulation money is always a means of purchase, now it does not act in that capacity.

As soon as money develops through the process of hoarding into the embodiment of abstract social wealth and the tangible representative of material wealth, it assumes in that capacity special functions within the process of circulation. If money circulates merely as a medium of circulation and therefore as a means of purchase, it is understood that commodity and money confront each other at the same time, i. e., that the same value is present in a double form: at one pole, as a commodity in the hands of the seller; at the other pole as money in the hands of the buyer. This simultaneous existence of the two equivalents at opposite poles and their simultaneous change of places or mutual alienation presupposes in its turn that seller and buyer enter into relations as owners of equivalents that are on hand. But in the course of time, the process of the metamorphosis of commodities which produces the different forms of money, transforms also the owners of commodities or changes the character in which they appear before each other in the community. In the process of metamorphosis of the commodity the guardian of the latter changes his skin as often as the commodity changes place or as the money assumes new forms. Thus, the owners of commodities originally confronted each other only as commodity owners, but later on they became one a buyer, the other a seller; then each became alternately buyer and seller, then hoarders, and finally rich men. In that manner, the owners of commodities do not come out of the process of circulation the same men that they entered. In fact the different forms which money assumes in the process of circulation are but crystallized changes of form of the commodities themselves, which in their turn are but concrete expressions of the changing social relations in which commodity owners carry on the interchange of matter with one another. New trade relations spring up in the process of circulation, and, as representatives of these changed relations, commodity owners assume new economic roles. Just as gold becomes idealized within the process of circulation and plain paper, in its capacity of a representative of gold, performs the function of money, so does the same process of circulation lend the weight of actual seller and buyer to the buyer and seller who enter it merely as representatives of future money and future commodities.

All the forms in which gold develops into money, are but the unfolding of potentialities which the metamorphosis of commodities bears within itself. These forms did not become distinctly differentiated in the process of simple money circulation where money appears as coin and the movement C —M —C forms a dynamic unity; at most, they appeared as mere potentialities as, e. g., in the case of the break in the metamorphosis of a commodity. We have seen that in the process C —M the relations between the commodity and money were those of an actual use-value and ideal exchange-value to an actual exchange value and only ideal use-value. By alienating his commodity as a use-value the seller realized its own exchange value and the use-value of money. On the contrary, the buyer, by alienating his money as exchange value, realized its own use-value and the price of the commodity. Commodity and money changed places accordingly. When it comes to a realization in actual life of this bi-polar contrast, a new break occurs. The seller actually alienates his commodity, but realizes its price only in idea: he has sold his commodity at its price, which is to be realized, however, only subsequently, at a time agreed upon. The purchaser buys as the representative of future money, while the vender sells as the owner of present goods. On the part of the vender, the commodity as use-value is actually alienated, without the price being actually realized; on the part of the purchaser, money is actually realized in the use-value of the commodity, without being actually alienated as exchange value. Instead of a token of value representing money symbolically as was the case before, the purchaser himself performs that part now. And just as in the former case the symbolic nature of the token of value called forth the guarantee of the state which has made it legal tender, so does the personal symbolism of the buyer bring about legally enforcible private contracts among commodity owners.

The contrary may happen in the process M —C, where the money can be alienated as a real means of purchase, and in that way the price of the commodity can be realized before the use-value of the money is realized and the commodity actually delivered. This occurs constantly under the everyday form of pre-payments. And it is under this form that the English government purchases opium from the ryots of India, or, foreign merchants residing in Russia mostly buy agricultural products. In these cases, however, the money always acts in its well known role of a means of purchase and therefore, does not assume any new forms.[102] We need not dwell, therefore, on this case any longer; but with reference to the changed form which the two processes M —C and C —M assume now, we may note that the difference between purchase and sale which appeared but imaginary in the direct process of circulation, now becomes a real difference, since in the former case only the money is present and in the latter only the commodity, and in either case only that extreme is present from which the initiative comes. Besides, the two forms have this in common: that in either, one of the equivalents is present only in the common will of the buyer and seller, —a will that is binding on both and assumes definite legal forms.

Seller and buyer become creditor and debtor. While the commodity owner looked comical as the guardian of a treasure, he now becomes awe-inspiring, since he no longer identifies himself but his neighbor with a certain sum of money and makes him and not himself a martyr of exchange value. From a believer he becomes a creditor, for religion he substitutes law.

"I stay here on my bond!"

Thus, in the modified form C —M in which the commodity is present and money is only represented, money plays first of all the part of a measure of value. The exchange value of the commodity is estimated in money as its measure; but as exchange value, established by contract, price exists not only in the mind of the seller, but also as a measure of obligation on the part of the buyer. Besides serving as a measure of value, money plays here the part of a means of purchase, although in that capacity it only casts ahead the shadow of its future existence. It attracts the commodity from its position in the hand of the seller into that of the buyer. As soon as the term of the contract expires, money enters circulation, since it changes its position by passing from the hands of the former buyer into those of the former seller. But it does not enter circulation as a circulating medium or as a means of purchase. It performed those functions before it was present and it appears after it has ceased to perform them. It now enters circulation as the only adequate equivalent of the commodity, as the absolute form of existence of exchange value, as the last word of the process of exchange, in short as money, and money in its distinct role of a *universal means of payment*. In this capacity of a means of payment money appears as the absolute commodity, but within the sphere of circulation and not without it as was the case with hoards. The difference between the means of purchase and the means of payment makes itself unpleasantly felt in periods of commercial crises.[103]

Originally, the conversion of the product into money in the sphere of circulation appears only as an individual necessity for the commodity owner in so far as his own product has no use-value to him, but has to acquire it first by being alienated. But in order to pay at the expiration of the contract, he must have sold commodities before that. Thus, entirely apart from his individual wants, the movement of the circulation process makes selling a social necessity with every owner of commodities. As a former buyer of a commodity he is compelled to become a seller of another commodity in order to get money not as a means of purchase but as a means of payment, as the absolute form of exchange value. The conversion of commodity into money as a final act, or the first metamorphosis of a commodity as an end in itself which in the case of hoarding seemed to be a matter of caprice on the part of the commodity owner, becomes now an economic function. The motive and essence of sale for the sake of payment becomes from a mere form of the process of circulation its self emanating substance.

In this form of sale the commodity completes its change of position; it circulates while it postpones its first metamorphosis, viz. its transformation into money. On the contrary, on the part of the buyer the second metamorphosis is completed, i. e. money is reconverted into a commodity before the first metamorphosis has taken place, i. e., before the commodity has been turned into money. The first metamorphosis thus takes place after the second in point of time; and thereby, money i. e. the form of the commodity in its first metamorphosis, acquires a new destination. Money or the spontaneous development of exchange value, is no longer a mere intermediary form of the circulation of commodities, but its final result.

That such *time sales* in which the two poles of the sale are separated in point of time, have their natural origin in the simple circulation of commodities, requires no elaborate proof. In the first place, the development of circulation leads to a continual repetition of the mutual transactions between the same commodity owners who confront each other as seller and buyer. The repetition is not accidental; on the contrary, goods are ordered, let us say, for a certain date in the future when they are to be delivered and paid for. In that case the sale is ideal, i. e. it is legally accomplished without the actual presence of the goods and money. Both forms of money, those of a medium of circulation and of a means of payment still coincide here, since in the first place, commodity and money change places simultaneously, and secondly, the money does not buy the commodity, but realizes the price of the commodity purchased before. In the second place, the nature of a great many use-values makes the simultaneous alienation and delivery of the goods impossible, and delivery has to be postponed for a certain time; e. g., when the use of a house is sold for one month, the use-value of the house is delivered only at the expiration of the month, although it changes hands at the beginning of the month. Since the actual transfer of the use-value and its virtual alienation are separated here in point of time, the realization of its price occurs also after its change of place. Finally, the difference in the seasons and in the length of time required for the production of various commodities brings about a situation where one tries to sell his goods, while the other is not ready to buy; and with the repeated purchases and sales between the same commodity owners the two ends of sale fall apart according to the conditions of production of the respective commodities. Thus arises a relation of creditor and debtor between the owners of commodities which, though constituting the natural foundation of the credit system, may be fully developed before the latter comes into existence. It is clear that with the extension of the credit system, and, consequently, with the development of the capitalist system of production in general, the function of money as a means of payment will extend at the expense of its function as a means of purchase and, still more, as an element of hoarding. In England, e. g., money as coin has been almost completely banished into the sphere of retail and petty trade between producers and consumers, while it dominates the sphere of large commercial transactions as a means of payment.[104]

As the universal means of payment money becomes the *universal commodity* of all contracts, at first only in the sphere of circulation of commodities.[105] But with the development of this function of money, all other forms of payment are gradually converted into money payments. The extent to which money is developed as the exclusive means of payment indicates the degree to which exchange value has taken hold of production in its depth and breadth.[106]

The volume of money in circulation, as a means of payment, is determined in the first place, by the amount of payments, i. e. by the sum total of the prices of the commodities alienated, but not about to be alienated, as in the case of the simple circulation of money. The quantity thus determined is subject, however, to two modifications. The first modification is due to the rapidity with which the same piece of money repeats the same function, i. e. with which the several payments succeed one another. A pays B, whereupon B pays C, and so forth. The rapidity with which the same coin repeats its function as a means of payment, depends first, upon the continuity of the relation of creditor and debtor among the owners of commodities, the same commodity owner being the creditor of one person and the debtor of another, etc., and secondly, upon the interval which separates the times of various payments. This chain of payments or of supplementary first metamorphoses of commodities is qualitatively different from the chain of metamorphoses which is formed by the circulation of money as a circulating medium. The latter not only makes its appearance gradually, but is even formed in that manner.

A commodity is first converted into money, then again into a commodity, thereby enabling another commodity to become money, etc.; or, seller becomes buyer, whereby another commodity owner turns seller. This successive connection is accidentally formed in the very process of the exchange of commodities. But when the money which A has paid to B is passed on from B to C, from C to D, etc., and that, too, at intervals rapidly succeeding one another, then this external connection reveals but an already existing social connection. The same money passes through different hands not because it appears as a means of payment; it passes as a means of payment because the different hands have already clasped each other. The rapidity with which money circulates as a means of payment thus shows that individuals have been drawn into the process of circulation much deeper than would be indicated by the same rapidity of the circulation of money as coin or as a means of purchase.

The sum total of prices made up by all the purchases and sales taking place at the same time, and, therefore, side by side, constitutes the limit for the substitution of the volume of coin by the rapidity of its circulation. If the payments that are to be made simultaneously are concentrated at one place-which naturally arises at first at points where the circulation of commodities is largest-the payments balance each other as negative and positive quantities: A is under obligations to pay B, while he has to be paid by C. etc. The quantity of money required as a means of payment will, therefore, be determined not by the total amount of payments which have to be made simultaneously, but by the greater or less concentration of the same and by the magnitude of the balance remaining after their mutual neutralization as negative and positive quantities. Special arrangements are made for settlements of this kind even where the credit system is not developed at all, as was the case e. g. in ancient Rome. The consideration of these arrangements, however, as well as that of the general time limits of payment, which are everywhere established among certain elements in the community, does not belong here. We may add that the specific influence which these time settlements exert on the periodic fluctuations in the quantity of money in circulation, has been scientifically investigated but lately.

In so far as the payments mutually balance as positive and negative quantities, no money actually appears on the scene. It figures here only in its capacity of a measure of value: first, in the prices of commodities, and second, in the magnitude of mutual obligations. Aside from its ideal form, exchange value does not exist here independently, not even in the form of a token of value; that is to say, money plays here only the part of ideal money of account. The function of money as a means of payment thus implies a contradiction. On the one hand, in so far as payments balance, it serves only ideally as a measure of value. On the other hand, in so far as a payment has actually to be made, money enters circulation not as a transient circulating medium, but as the final resting form of the universal equivalent, as the absolute commodity, in a word, as money. Therefore, whenever such a thing as a chain of payments and an artificial system of settling them, is developed, money suddenly changes its visionary nebulous shape as a measure of value, turning into hard cash or means of payment, as soon as some shock causes a violent interruption of the flow of payments and disturbs the mechanism of their settlement. Thus, under conditions of fully developed capitalist production, where the commodity owner has long become a capitalist, knows his Adam Smith, and condescendingly laughs at the superstition that gold and silver alone constitute money or that money differs at all from other commodities as the absolute commodity, money suddenly reappears not as a medium of circulation, but as the only adequate form of exchange value, as the only form of wealth, exactly as it is looked upon by the hoarder. In its capacity of such an exclusive form of wealth, it reveals itself, unlike under the monetary system, not in mere imaginary, but in actual depreciation and worthlessness of all material wealth. That is what constitutes the particular phase of crises of the world market which is known as a money crisis. The *summum bonum* for which everybody is crying at such times as for the only form of wealth, is cash, hard cash; and by the side of it all other commodities just because they are use-values, appear useless like so many trifles and toys, or, as our Dr. Martin Luther says, as mere objects of ornament and gluttony. This sudden reversion from a system of credit to a system of hard cash heaps theoretical fright on top of the practical panic; and the dealers by whose agency circulation is affected shudder before the impenetrable mystery in which their own economical relations are involved.[107]

Payments, in their turn, require the formation of reserve funds, the accumulation of money as a means of payment. The building up of reserve funds appears no longer as a practice carried on outside of the sphere of circulation, as in the case of hoarding; nor as a mere technical accumulation of coin, as in the case of coin reserves; on the contrary, money must now be gradually accumulated to be available on certain future dates when payments become due. While hoarding, in its abstract form as a means of enrichment, declines with the development of the capitalist system of production, that species of hoarding which is directly called for by the process of production, increases; or, to put it differently, a part of the treasure which is generally formed in the sphere of circulation of commodities, is absorbed as a reserve fund of means of payment. The more developed the capitalist system of production, the more these reserve funds are limited to the necessary minimum. Locke, in his work "On the Lowering of Interest"[108] furnishes interesting data with reference to the size of these reserve funds in his time. They show what a considerable part of the total money in circulation the reservoirs for means of payment absorbed in England just at the time when banking began to develop.

The law as to quantity of money in circulation, as it has been formulated in the analysis of the simple circulation of money, receives an essential modification when the circulation of the means of payment is taken into account. The rapidity of the circulation of money whether as circulating medium or as means of payment-being given, the total amount of money in circulation at a given time will be determined by the sum total of the prices of commodities to be realized, *plus* the total amount of payments falling due at the same time, *minus* the amount of payments balancing each other. The general law that the volume of money in circulation depends on the prices of commodities is not affected by this in the least, since the extent of the payments is itself determined by the prices stipulated in contracts. What is, however, strikingly demonstrated, is that even if the rapidity of circulation and the economy of payments be assumed to remain the same, the sum total of the prices of the commodities circulating in a given period of time, say one day, and the volume of money in circulation on the same day are by no means equal, because there is a large number of commodities in circulation whose prices have yet to be realized in money at a future date, and there is a quantity of money in circulation which constitutes the payment for commodities which have long gone out of circulation. The latter amount will depend on the sum of payments falling due on the same day although contracted for at entirely different periods.

We have seen that a change in the values of gold and silver does not affect their function as measures of value or money of account. But this change is of decisive importance for money as a hoard, since with the rise or fall of value of gold and silver, the total value of a gold or silver hoard will also rise or fall. Of still greater importance is the effect of this change on money as a means of payment. The payment takes place after the sale of the commodity, or the money serves in two different capacities at two different periods; first, as a measure of value, then as a means of payment corresponding to the measurement. If, during this interval, the value of the precious metals or the labor-time necessary for their production undergoes a change, the same quantity of gold or silver will be worth more or less when it appears as a means of payment than what it was when it served as a measure of value, i. e., when the contract was concluded. The function of a particular commodity, like gold or silver, to serve as money or independent exchange value comes here in conflict with the nature of the particular commodity whose magnitude of value depends on changes in the cost of its production. The great social revolution which caused the fall in value of the precious metals in Europe, is as well known as the revolution of an opposite character which had been brought about at an early period in the history of the ancient Roman republic by the rise in value of copper in terms of which the debts of the plebeians had been contracted. Without attempting here to follow any further the fluctuations of value of the precious metals and their effect on the system of bourgeois political economy, it is at once apparent that a fall in the value of the precious metals favors the debtors at the expense of the creditors, while a rise in their value favors the creditors at the expense of the debtors.

c. WORLD MONEY.

Gold becomes money as distinguished from coin only after it is withdrawn from circulation in the shape of a hoard; it then enters circulation as a non-medium of circulation, and finally breaks through the barriers of home circulation to assume the part of a universal equivalent in the world of commodities. It becomes *world money*.

While the general measures of weight of the precious metals served as their original measures of value, the reverse process takes place now in the world market, and the reckoning names of money are turned back into corresponding weight names. In the same way, while shapeless crude metal (aes rude) was the original form of the medium of circulation and the coin form constituted but the official stamp certifying that a given piece of metal was of a certain weight, now the precious metal in its capacity of a world coin throws off its stamp and shape and reassumes the indistinguishable bullion form; and even if national coins, such as Russian imperials, Mexican dollars, and English sovereigns, do circulate abroad, their name is of no importance, and only their contents count. Finally, as international money, the precious metals come again to perform their original function of mediums of exchange, which, like the exchange of commodities, arose first not within the various primitive communities, but at their points of contact with one another. As world money, money thus reassumes its primitive form. On leaving the sphere of home circulation, it strips off the particular forms which it has acquired in the course of the development of the process of exchange within that particular national sphere, those local garbs of standard of price, of coin, of auxiliary coin, and of token of value.

We have seen that in the home circulation of a country, only one commodity serves as a measure of value. Since, however, that function is performed by gold in some countries and by silver in others, there is a double standard of value in the world market and money assumes two forms in all its other functions. The translation of the values of commodities from gold prices into silver prices and vice versa depends in each case upon the relative value of the two metals, which is constantly changing and, therefore, appears to be constantly in the process of determination. Commodity owners in every national sphere of circulation have to use gold and silver alternately for foreign circulation and thus to exchange the metal which is accepted as money at home for the metal which they happen to need as money abroad. Every nation is, therefore, utilizing both metals, gold and silver, as world money.

In the international circulation of commodities, gold and silver appear not as mediums of circulation, but as universal mediums of exchange. The universal medium of exchange performs its function only under its two developed forms of a means of purchase and of a means of payment, whose mutual relation in the world market is the very reverse of what it is at home. In the sphere of home circulation, money in the form of coin, played exclusively the part of a means of purchase, either as the intermediary in the dynamic unity C —M —C or as the representative of the transient form of exchange value in the unceasing change of positions by commodities. In the world market it is just the contrary. Gold and silver appear here as a means of purchase when the exchange of matter is but one-sided, and purchase and sale do not coincide. The frontier trade at Kiachta e. g. is both actually and according to treaty, one of barter, in which silver plays only the part of a measure of value. The war of 1857-58 compelled the Chinese to sell without buying. Silver suddenly appeared now as a means of purchase. Out of regard to the letter of the treaty, the Russians made up the French five frank coins into crude silver commodities, which were made to serve as a means of exchange. Silver has always served as a means of purchase between Europe and America on one side and Asia on the other, where it settles down in the form of hoards. Furthermore, the precious metals serve as international means of purchase whenever the ordinary balance of exchange of matter between two nations is suddenly upset, as e. g. when a failure of crops forces one of them to buy on an extraordinary scale. Finally, the precious metals are international means of purchase in the hands of gold and silver producing countries, in which case they directly constitute a product and commodity and not merely a converted form of a commodity. The more the exchange of commodities between different national spheres of circulation is developed, the more important becomes the function of world money to serve as a *means of payment* for the settlement of international balances.

Like home circulation, international circulation requires a constantly changing quantity of gold and silver. A part of the accumulated hoards serves therefore, in each country as a reserve fund of world money, which now declines, now rises, according to the fluctuations of the exchange of commodities.[109] Besides the special movements which take place between national spheres of circulation, world-money possesses a universal movement, whose starting points are at the sources of production from which gold and silver streams spread out in different directions all over the world market. Here gold and silver enter the world circulation as commodities and are exchanged for commodity equivalents in proportion to the labor-time contained in them, before they penetrate national spheres of circulation. In the latter, they appear now with a given magnitude of value. Every fall or rise in the cost of their production equally affects, therefore, their relative value throughout the world market; on the other hand, that value is entirely independent of the extent to which the different national spheres of circulation absorb gold or silver. The part of the metal stream which is caught up by every separate sphere in the world of commodities, partly enters directly the home circulation of money to make up for worn out coin; partly is dammed up in the different reservoirs containing hoards of coin, means of payment and world-money; partly is turned into articles of luxury, while the rest simply forms a treasure. At an advanced stage of development of the capitalist system of production the formation of hoards is reduced to the minimum required by the various processes of circulation for the free play of their mechanism. The hoard as such becomes idle wealth, unless it appears as a temporary form of a surplus resulting from a favorable balance of payments or as the result of an interrupted exchange of matter, i. e. as the solidification of a commodity in its first metamorphosis.

Gold and silver, in their capacity of money, being by conception universal commodities, assume in their capacity of world money the form adapted to a universal commodity. To the extent to which all commodities are exchanged for them, they become the transformed impersonation of all commodities and, therefore, universally alienable commodities. Their function of serving as the embodiment of universal labor-time is realized more and more as the interchange of matter produced by concrete labor embraces increasing parts of the world. They become universal equivalents to the extent to which the series of particular equivalents which constitute their spheres of exchange, increases. Since in the sphere of world circulation commodities unfold their own exchange value on a universal scale, they assume the form of world money when transformed into gold and silver. As commodity owning nations are thus turning gold into money by their diversified industry and universal trade, industry and trade appear to them only as a means of getting money out of the world market in the shape of gold and silver. Gold and silver, as world money, are, therefore, as much products of the universal circulation of commodities as they are means of widening its sphere. Like chemistry which grew up behind the backs of the alchemists who tried to find a way of making gold, so do the sources of world industry and world trade spring up behind the backs of the owners of commodities, while they are hunting for the commodity in its magic form. Gold and silver help to create the world market by anticipating its existence in their conception of money. That this magic effect of the precious metals is by no means confined to the period of infancy of capitalist society but is a necessary outgrowth of the perverse conception which the representatives of the commodity world have of their own work in society, is shown by the extraordinary influence exerted in the middle of the nineteenth century by the discovery of new gold fields.

Just as money develops into world-money, so the commodity owner develops into a cosmopolitan. The cosmopolitan relation of men is originally only a relation of commodity owners. The commodity as such rises above all religious, political, national, and language barriers. Price is its universal language and money, its common form. But with the development of world-money as distinguished from national coin, there develops the cosmopolitanism of the commodity owner as the faith of practical reason opposed to traditional, religious, national and other prejudices which hinder the interchange of matter among mankind. As the identical gold that lands in England in the form of American eagles, turns there into sovereigns and three days later circulates in Paris in the form of Napoleons, only to emerge in Venice in a few weeks as so many ducats, retaining all the while the same value, it becomes clear to the commodity owner that nationality "is but the guinea's stamp." The lofty idea which he conceives of the entire world is that of a market, the *world market*.[110]

4. THE PRECIOUS METALS.

The process of capitalist production first of all takes hold of the metallic circulation as of a ready, transmitted organ which, though undergoing a gradual transformation, always retains its fundamental structure. The question as to why gold and silver and not other commodities serve as money material falls outside the limits of the capitalist system. We shall, therefore, confine ourselves to summing up the most essential points.

Since universal labor-time admits of quantitative differences only, the object which is to serve as its specific incarnation must be capable of representing purely quantitative differences, i. e., it must be homogeneous and uniform in quality throughout. That is the first condition a commodity must satisfy to perform the function of a measure of value. If commodities were estimated in oxen, hides, grain, etc., they would really have to be estimated in an ideal average ox, or average hide, since there are qualitative differences between an ox and an ox, grain and grain, hide and hide. On the contrary, gold and silver, as elementary substances, are always the same, and equal quantities of them represent, therefore, values of equal magnitude.[111] The other condition which a commodity that is to serve as a universal equivalent must satisfy and which follows directly from its function of representing purely quantitative differences, is that it must be capable of being divided and re-united at will, so that money of account may be represented materially as well. Gold and silver possess these properties to a superior degree.

As mediums of circulation, gold and silver have this advantage over other commodities, that their high specific gravity which condenses much weight in little space, corresponds to their economic specific gravity which condenses relatively much labor-time, i. e. a great quantity of exchange value in a small volume. This insures facility of transport, of transition from hand to hand and from one country to another, the ability to appear as rapidly as to disappear, in short, that material mobility which constitutes the *sine qua non* of the commodity that is to serve as the *perpetuum mobile* of the process of circulation.

The high specific value of the precious metals, their durability, comparative indestructibility, insusceptibility of oxidation through the action of the air, in the case of gold insolubility in acids except in aqua regia, —all these natural properties make the precious metals the natural material for hoarding. Peter Martyr who seems to have been a great lover of chocolate, remarks, therefore, of the cacao-bags which formed a species of Mexican gold: "O felicem monetam, quae suavem utilemque praebet humano generi potum, et a tartarea peste avaritiae suos immunes servat possessores, quod suffodi aut diu servari nequeat."[112]

The great importance of metals in general in the direct process of production is due to the part they play as instruments of production. Apart from their scarcity, the great softness of gold and silver as compared with iron and even copper (in the hardened state in which it was used by the ancients), makes them unfit for that application and deprives them, therefore, to a great extent, of that property on which the use-value of metals is generally based. Useless as they are in the direct process of production, they are easily dispensed with as means of existence, as articles of consumption. For that reason any desired quantity of them may be absorbed by the social process of circulation without disturbing the processes of direct production and consumption. Their individual use-value does not come in conflict with their economic function. Furthermore, gold and silver are not only negatively superfluous, i. e. dispensable articles, but their aesthetic properties make them the natural material of luxury, ornamentation, splendor, festive occasions, in short, the positive form of abundance and wealth. They appear, in a way, as spontaneous light brought out from the underground world, since silver reflects all rays of light in their original combination, and gold only the color of highest intensity, viz. red light. The sensation of color is, generally speaking, the most popular form of aesthetic sense. The etymological connection between the names of the precious metals, and the relations of colors, in the different Indo-Germanic languages has been established by Jacob Grimm (see his History of the German Language).

Finally, the susceptibility of gold and silver of being turned from coin into bullion, from bullion into articles of luxury and vice versa, i. e. the advantage they possess as against other commodities in not being tied down to a definite, exclusive form in which they can be used, makes them the natural material of money, which must constantly change from one form to another.

Nature no more produces money than it does bankers or discount rates. But since the capitalist system of production requires the crystallization of wealth as a fetich in the form of a single article, gold and silver appear as its appropriate incarnation. Gold and silver are not money by nature, but money is by nature gold and silver. In the first place, the silver or gold money crystal is not only the product of the process of circulation, but in fact its only final product. In the second place, gold and silver are ready and direct products of nature, not distinguished by any difference of form. The universal product of the social process or the social process itself as a product is a peculiar natural product, a metal hidden in the bowels of the earth and extracted therefrom.[113]

We have seen that gold and silver are unable to fulfill the requirements which they are expected to meet in their capacity of money, viz. to remain values of unvarying magnitude. Still, as Aristotle had already observed, they possess a more constant value than the average of other commodities. Apart from the universal effect of an appreciation or depreciation of the precious metals, the fluctuations in the ratio between the values of gold and silver has a special importance, since both serve side by side in the world market as money material. The purely economic causes of this change of value must be traced to the change in the labor-time required for the production of these metals; conquests and other political upheavals which exercised a great influence on the value of metals in the ancient world, have nowadays only a local and transitory effect. The labor-time required for the production of the metals will depend on the degree of their natural scarcity, as well as on the greater or less difficulty with which they can be obtained in a purely metallic state. As a matter of fact, gold is the first metal discovered by man. This is due to the fact that nature itself furnishes it partly in pure crystalline form, individualized, free from chemical combination with other substances, or, as the alchemists used to say, in a virgin state; and so far as it does not appear in that state, nature does the technical work in the great gold washeries of rivers. Only the crudest kind of labor is thus required of man in the extraction of gold, either from rivers or from alluvial deposits; while the extraction of silver presupposes the development of mining and a comparatively high degree of technical skill generally. For that reason the value of silver is originally greater than that of gold in spite of the lesser absolute scarcity of the former. Strabo's assertion that a certain Arabian tribe gave ten pounds of gold for one pound of iron and two pounds of gold for one pound of silver, seems by no means incredible. But as the productive powers of labor in society are developed and the product of unskilled labor rises in value as compared with the product of skilled labor; as the earth's crust is more thoroughly broken up and the original superficial sources of gold supply give out, the value of silver begins to fall in proportion to that of gold. At a given stage of development of engineering and of the means of communication, the discovery of new gold or silver fields become the decisive factor. In ancient Asia the ratio of gold to silver was 6 to 1 or

8 to 1; the latter ratio prevailed in China and Japan as late as the beginning of the nineteenth century; 10 to 1, the ratio in Xenophon's time, may be considered as the average ratio of the middle period of antiquity. The exploitation of the Spanish silver mines by Carthage and later by Rome had about the same effect in antiquity, as the discovery of the American mines in modern Europe. For the period of the Roman empire 15 or 16 to 1 may be assumed as a rough average, although we frequently find cases of still greater depreciation of silver in Rome. The same movement beginning with the relative depreciation of gold and concluding with the fall in the value of silver, is repeated in the following epoch which has lasted from the Middle Ages to the present time. As in Xenophon's times the average ratio in the Middle Ages was 10 to 1, changing to 16 or 15 to 1 in consequence of the discovery of the American mines. The discovery of the Australian, Californian and Columbian gold sources makes a new fall in the value of gold probable.[114]

C. Theories of the Medium of Circulation and of Money

As the universal thirst for gold prompted nations and princes in the sixteenth and seventeenth centuries, the period of infancy of modern bourgeois society, to crusades beyond the sea in search of the golden grail,[115] the first interpreters of the modern world, the founders of the monetary system, of which the mercantile system is but a variation, proclaimed gold and silver, i. e. money, as the only thing that constitutes wealth. They were quite right when, from the point of view of the simple circulation of commodities, they declared that the mission of bourgeois society was to make money, i. e. to build up everlasting treasures which neither moth nor rust could eat. It is no argument with the monetary system to say that a ton of iron whose price is £3 constitutes a value of the same magnitude as £3 worth of gold. The point here is not the magnitude of the exchange value, but as to what constitutes its adequate form. If the monetary and mercantile systems single out international trade and the particular branches of national industry directly connected with that trade as the only true sources of wealth or money, it must be borne in mind, that in that period the greater part of national production was still carried on under forms of feudalism and was the source from which producers drew directly their means of subsistence. Products, as a rule, were not turned into commodities nor, therefore, into money; they did not enter into the general social interchange of matter; did not, therefore, appear as embodiments of universal abstract labor; and did not, in fact, constitute bourgeois wealth. Money as the end and object of circulation is exchange value or abstract wealth, but it is no material element of wealth and does not form the directing goal and impelling motive of production. True to the conditions as they prevailed in that primitive stage of bourgeois production, those unrecognized prophets held fast to the pure, tangible, and resplendent form of exchange value, to its form of a universal commodity as against all special commodities. The proper bourgeois economic sphere of that period was the sphere of the circulation of commodities. Hence, they judged the entire complex process of bourgeois production from the point of view of that elementary sphere and confounded money with capital. The unceasing war of modern economists against the monetary and mercantile system is mostly due to the fact that this system blabs out in brutally naive fashion, the secret of bourgeois production, viz. its subjection to the domination of exchange value. Ricardo, though wrong in the application he makes of it, remarks somewhere that even in times of famine, grain is imported not because the nation is starving, but because the grain dealer is making money. In its criticism of the monetary and mercantile system, political economy, by attacking that system as a mere illusion and as a false theory, fails to recognize in it the barbaric form of its own fundamental principles. Furthermore, this system has not only an historic justification, but within certain spheres of modern economy retains until now the full rights of citizenship. At all stages of the bourgeois system of production in which wealth assumes the elementary form of a commodity, exchange value assumes the elementary form of money and in all phases of the process of production wealth

74

reassumes for a moment the universal elementary commodity form. Even at the most advanced stage of bourgeois economy, the specific functions of gold and silver to serve as money, in contradistinction to their function of mediums of circulation —a function which distinguishes them from all other commodities-is not done away with, but only limited, hence the monetary and mercantile system retains its right of citizenship. The Catholic fact that gold and silver are contrasted with other profane commodities as the direct incarnation of social labor, that is as the expression of abstract wealth, naturally offends the Protestant point d'honneur of bourgeois economy, and out of fear of the prejudices of the monetary system it had lost for a long time its grasp of the phenomena of money circulation, as will be shown presently.

It was quite natural that, contrary to the monetary and mercantile system which knew money only in its form of a crystallized product of circulation, classical political economy should have conceived money first of all in its fluent form of exchange value arising and disappearing within the process of the metamorphosis of commodities. And since the circulation of commodities is regarded exclusively in the form of C —M —C and the latter in its turn, exclusively in its aspect of a dynamic unity of sale and purchase, money comes to be regarded in its capacity of a medium of circulation as opposed to its capacity of money. And when that medium of circulation is isolated in its function of coin, it turns, as we have seen, into a token of value. But since classical political economy had to deal with metallic circulation as the prevailing form of circulation, it defined metallic money as coin, and metallic coin as a mere token of value. In accordance with the law governing the circulation of tokens of value, the proposition was advanced that the prices of commodities depend on the quantity of money in circulation instead of the opposite principle that the quantity of money in circulation depends on the prices of commodities. We find this view more or less clearly expressed by the Italian economists of the seventeenth century; LOCKE now asserts, now denies that principle; it is clearly elaborated in the "Spectator" (of October 19, 1711) by MONTESQUIEU AND HUME. Since Hume was by far the most important representative of this theory in the eighteenth century, we shall commence our review with him.

Under certain assumptions, an increase or decrease in the quantity either of the metallic money in circulation, or of the tokens of value in circulation seems to affect *uniformly* the prices of commodities. With each fall or rise of the *value* of gold or silver in which the exchange values of commodities are estimated as prices, there is a rise or fall of prices, because of the change in their measure of value; as a result of the rise or fall of prices, a greater or smaller quantity of gold and silver is circulating as coin. But the apparent phenomenon is the fall in prices-the exchange value of commodities remaining the same-accompanied by an increased or diminished quantity of the medium of circulation. On the other hand, if the quantity of tokens of value rises above or falls below its required level, it is forcibly reduced to the latter by a fall or rise of prices. In either case the same effect seems to be brought about by the same cause, and Hume holds fast to this semblance.

Every scientific inquiry into the relation between the volume of the circulating medium and the movement of prices must assume the value of the money material as given. Hume, on the contrary, considers exclusively periods of revolution in the value of the precious metals, i. e. revolutions in the measure of value. The rise of prices which occurred simultaneously with the increase of metallic money after the discovery of the American mines forms the historical background of his theory, while his polemic against the monetary and mercantile system furnishes its practical motive. The importation of precious metals can naturally increase while their cost of production remains the same. On the other hand, a decrease in their value, i. e. in the labor-time required for their production will reveal itself first of all in their increased imports. Hence, said the later followers of Hume, a decrease in the value of the precious metals, reveals itself in an increased volume of the circulating medium, and the increased volume of the latter is shown in the rise of prices. As a matter of fact, however, the rise in price affects only exported commodities, which are exchanged for gold and silver as commodities and not as mediums of circulation. Thus, the prices of these commodities, which are now estimated in gold and silver of lower value, rise as compared with the prices of all other commodities whose exchange value continues to be estimated in gold or silver according to the standard of their old cost of production. This two-fold appraisement of the exchange values of commodities in the same country can naturally be only temporary, and the gold and silver prices must become equalized in the proportions determined by the exchange values themselves, so that finally the exchange values of all commodities come to be estimated according to the new value of the money material. The development of this process, as well as the ways and means in which the exchange value of commodities asserts itself within the limits of the fluctuations of market prices, do not fall within the scope of this work. But that this equalization takes place but gradually in the early periods of development of bourgeois production and extends over long periods of time, never keeping pace with the increase of cash in circulation, has been strikingly demonstrated by new critical investigations of the movement of prices of commodities in the sixteenth century.[116] The favorite references of Hume's followers to the rise of prices in ancient Rome in consequence of the conquests of Macedonia, Egypt and Asia Minor, are quite irrelevant. The characteristic method of antiquity of suddenly transferring hoarded treasures from one country to another, which was accomplished by violence and thus brought about a temporary reduction of the cost of production of precious metals in a certain country by the simple process of plunder, affects just as little the intrinsic laws of money circulation, as the gratuitous distribution of Egyptian and Sicilian grain in Rome affected the universal law governing the price of grain. Hume, as well as all other writers of the eighteenth century, was not in possession of the material necessary for the detailed observation of the circulation of money. This material, which first becomes available with the full development of banking, includes in the first place a critical history of prices of commodities, and in the second, official and current statistics relating to the expansion and contraction of the circulating medium, the imports and exports of the precious metals, etc. Hume's theory of circulation may be summed up in the following propositions: 1. The prices of commodities in a country are determined by the quantity of money existing there (real or symbolic money); 2. The money current in a country represents all the commodities to be found there. In proportion "as there is more or less of this representation," i. e. of money, "there goes a greater or less quantity of the thing represented to the same quantity of it"; 3. If commodities increase in quantity, their price falls or the value of money rises. If money increases in quantity, then, on the contrary, the price of commodities rises and the value of money declines.[117]

"The dearness of everything," says Hume, "from plenty of money, is a disadvantage, which attends an established commerce, and sets bounds to it in every country, by enabling the poorer states to undersell the richer in all foreign markets."[118] "Where coin is in greater plenty; as a greater quantity of it is required to represent the same quantity of goods; it can have no effect, either good or bad, taking a nation within itself; any more than it would make an alteration on a merchant's books, if, instead of the Arabian method of notation, which requires few characters, he should make use of the Roman, which requires a great many. Nay, the greater quantity of money, like the Roman characters, is rather inconvenient, and requires greater trouble both to keep and transport it."[119] In order to prove anything, Hume should have shown that under a *given* system of notation the quantity of characters used does not depend on the magnitude of the numbers, but that on the contrary, the magnitude of the numbers depends on the quantity of the characters used. It is perfectly true that there is no advantage in estimating or "counting" values of commodities in depreciated gold and silver, and that is the reason why nations have always found it more convenient with the growth of the value of the commodities in circulation to count in silver in preference to copper, and in gold rather than in silver. In proportion as the nations became richer, they converted the less valuable metals into subsidiary coin and the more valuable ones into money. Furthermore, Hume forgets that in order to count values in gold and silver, it is not necessary that either gold or silver should be "on hand." Money of account and the medium of circulation are identical with him and both are "coin." Hume concludes that a rise or fall of prices depends on the quantity of money in circulation, because a change in the value of the measure of value, i. e. of the precious metals which serve as money of account, causes a rise or fall of prices and, consequently, also a change in the amount of money in circulation, the rapidity of the latter remaining the same. That not only the quantity of gold and silver increased in the sixteenth and seventeenth centuries, but that the cost of their production had declined at the same time, Hume could know from the closing up of the European mines. In the sixteenth and seventeenth centuries the prices of commodities increased in Europe with the influx of the mass of American gold and silver; hence the prices of commodities in every land are determined by the mass of gold and silver to be found there. This was Hume's first "necessary consequence."[120] In the sixteenth and seventeenth centuries prices had not risen uniformly with the increase of the quantity of precious metals; more than half a century passed before *any* change in prices became perceptible, and even then it took a long time before the exchange values of commodities came to be generally estimated according to the depreciated value of gold and silver, i. e. before the revolution affected the general price level. Hence, concludes Hume, who, quite contrary to the principles of his philosophy, generalizes indiscriminately from imperfectly observed facts, prices of commodities or the value of money depend not on the total amount of money to be found in the country, but rather on the quantity of gold and silver which is actually in circulation; but in the long run all the gold and silver in the country must be absorbed by circulation in the form of coin.[121] It is clear that if gold and silver have a value of their own, then, apart from all other laws of circulation, only a definite quantity of gold and silver can circulate as the equivalent of commodities of a given value. If, therefore, every quantity of gold and silver which happens to be in a country must enter the sphere of exchange of commodities as a medium of circulation without regard to the total value of the commodities, then gold and silver have no intrinsic value and are in fact no real commodities. That is Hume's third "necessary consequence." He makes commodities enter the process of circulation without price and gold and silver without value. That is the reason why he never speaks of the value of commodities and of gold, but only of their relative quantities. Locke had already said that gold and silver had merely an imaginary or conventional value; the first brutal expression of opposition to the assertion of the monetary "system" that gold and silver alone have true value. That gold and silver owe their character of money to the function they perform in the social process of exchange is interpreted to the effect that they owe their own value and therefore the magnitude of their value to a social function.[122] Gold and silver are thus worthless things, which, however, acquire a fictitious value within the sphere of circulation *as representatives of commodities.* They are converted by the process of circulation not into money, but into value. This value of theirs is determined by the proportion between their own volume and that of the commodities, since the two must balance each other. Thus, Hume makes gold and silver enter the world of commodities as non-commodities; but as soon as they appear in the form of coin, he turns them, on the contrary, into mere commodities, which must be exchanged for other commodities by simple barter. In that manner, if the world of commodities consisted of but one commodity, say one million quarters of grain, the idea would work itself out very simply; viz., one quarter of grain would be exchanged for two ounces of gold if there were altogether two million ounces of gold, and for twenty ounces of gold, if there were a total of twenty million ounces, the price of the commodity and the value of money rising or falling in inverse ratio to the quantity of gold in existence.[123] But the world of commodities consists of an endless variety of use-values, whose relative values are by no means determined by their relative quantities. How, then, does Hume conceive this exchange of the volume of commodities for the volume of gold? He contents himself with the meaningless, hollow idea that every commodity is exchanged as an aliquot part of the entire volume of commodities for a corresponding aliquot part of the volume of gold. The process of the movement of commodities due to the antagonism between exchange value and use-value which commodities bear within themselves, and which manifests itself in the circulation of money, becoming crystallized in different forms of the latter, is thus done away with, giving place to the imaginary mechanical equalization process between the quantity of precious metals to be found in a country and the volume of commodities existing there at the same time.

SIR JAMES STEUART opens his inquiry into the nature of coin and money with an elaborate criticism of Hume and Montesquieu.[124] He is really the first to ask this question: is the quantity of current money determined by the prices of commodities, or are the prices of commodities determined by the quantity of current money? Although his analysis is obscured by his fantastic conception of the measure of value, his vacillating view of exchange value and by reminiscences of the mercantile system, he discovers the essential forms of money and the general laws of the circulation of money, because he makes no attempt at a mechanical separation of commodities from money, but proceeds to develop its different functions from the different aspects of the exchange of commodities. Money is used, he says, for two principal purposes: for the payment of debts and for the purchase of what one needs; the two together form "ready money demands." The state of trade and industry, the mode of living, the customary expenditures of the people, taken all together regulate and determine the volume of "ready money demands," i. e. the number of "alienations." In order to effect this multitude of payments, a certain proportion of money is required. This proportion may increase or decrease according to circumstances, even while the number of alienations remains the same. At any rate, the circulation of a country can absorb only a definite quantity of money.[125] "It is the complicated operations of demand and competition which determines the standard price of everything"; the latter "does not in the least depend on the quantity of gold and silver in the country."[126] What then will become of the gold and silver that is not required as coin? They are hoarded or used in the manufacture of articles of luxury. If the quantity of gold and silver fall below the level required for circulation, symbolic money or other substitutes take its place. If a favorable rate of exchange brings about a surplus of money in the country and cuts off at the same time the demand for its shipment abroad, it will accumulate in strong-boxes, where the "riches will remain without producing more effect than if they had remained in the mine."

The second law discovered by Steuart is that of the reflux of credit circulation to its starting point. Finally, he works out the effects which the disparity of the rates of interest in different countries produces upon the international export and import of precious metals. The last two points we mention here only for the sake of completeness, since they have but a remote bearing on the subject of our discussion.[127] Symbolic money or credit money-Steuart does not as yet distinguish between the two forms of money-may take the place of precious metals as a means of purchase or means of payment in the sphere of home circulation, but never in the world market. Paper notes are therefore "money of the society," while gold and silver are "money of the world."[128]

It is characteristic of nations with an "historical" development, in the sense in which the term is used by the historical school of law, to keep forgetting their own history. Although the controversy as to the relation of prices of commodities to the volume of the circulating medium has been continually agitating Parliament for the last half a century, and has precipitated in England thousands of pamphlets, large and small, Steuart has remained even more of a "dead dog" than Spinoza seemed to be to Moses Mendelson in Lessing's time. Even the latest writer on the history of "currency," Maclaren, makes Adam Smith the original author of Steuart's theory, and Ricardo of Hume's theory.[129]

While Ricardo elaborated Hume's theory, Adam Smith registered the results of Steuart's investigations as dead facts. Adam Smith applied the Scotch saying that "mony mickles mak a muckle" even to his spiritual wealth, and therefore concealed with petty care the sources to which he owed the little out of which he tried to make so much. More than once he prefers to break off the point of the discussion, whenever he feels that an attempt on his part clearly to formulate the question would compel him to settle his accounts with his predecessors. So in the case of the money theory. He tacitly adopts Steuart's theory when he says that the gold and silver existing in a country is partly utilized as coin; partly accumulated in the form of reserve funds for merchants in countries without banks, or of bank reserves in countries with a credit currency; partly serves as a hoard for the settling of international payments; partly is turned into articles of luxury. He passes over without remark the question as to the quantity of coin in circulation, treating money quite wrongly as a mere commodity.[130] His vulgarizer, the dull J. B. Say, whom the French have proclaimed *prince de la science* —like Johann Christoph Gottsched, who proclaimed his Schönaich a Homer and himself a Pietro Aretino to the *terror principum and lux mundi* —has with great pomp raised this not altogether innocent oversight of Adam Smith to a dogma.[131] It must be said, however, that his hostile attitude to the illusions of the mercantile system prevented Adam Smith from taking an objective view of the phenomena of metallic circulation, while his views on credit money are original and deep. As in the eighteenth century petrification theories there is always felt the presence of an undercurrent which springs from either a critical or apologetic attitude toward the biblical tradition of the flood, so there is concealed behind all the money theories of the eighteenth century a secret struggle with the monetary system, the ghost which had stood guard over the cradle of bourgeois economy and continued to throw its shadow over legislation.

In the nineteenth century, inquiries into the nature of money were not prompted directly by phenomena of metallic circulation, but rather by those of banknote circulation. The former was touched upon only in order to discover the laws governing the latter. The suspension of specie payments by the Bank of England in 1797, the rise of prices of many commodities which followed it, the fall of the mint price of gold below its market price, the depreciation of bank-notes, especially since 1809, furnished the direct practical occasion for a party struggle in parliament and a theoretical tournament outside of it, both conducted with like passion. The historical background for the controversy was furnished by the history of paper money during the eighteenth century: the fiasco of Law's bank; the depreciation of the provincial bank-notes of the English Colonies in North America from the beginning to the middle of the eighteenth century which went hand in hand with the increase in the number of tokens of value; further, the Continental bills issued as legal tender by the American government during the War of Independence; and finally, the experiment with the French *assignats* carried out on a still larger scale. Most of the English writers of that period confound the circulation of bank-notes, which is governed by quite different laws, with the circulation of tokens of value or government legal tender paper money; and while they claim to explain the phenomena of this legal tender circulation by the laws of metallic circulation, they proceed, as a matter of fact, just the opposite way, viz., deducting laws for the latter from phenomena observed in connection with the former. We omit all the numerous writers of the period of 1800-1809 and turn directly to RICARDO, both because he embodies the views of his predecessors, which he formulates with greater precision, and because the shape he gave to the theory of money governs English bank legislation until this moment. Ricardo, like his predecessors, confounds the circulation of bank-notes, or credit money, with the circulation of mere tokens of value. The fact which impresses him most is the depreciation of paper currency accompanied by the rise of prices of commodities. What the American mines had been to Hume, the paper-bill presses in Threadneedle street were to Ricardo, and he himself expressly identifies the two factors at some place in his works. His first writings, which dealt exclusively with the money question belong to the time of the most violent controversy between the Bank of England, which had on its side the ministers and the war party, and its opponents about whom were centered the parliamentary opposition, the Whigs and the Peace party. They appeared as immediate forerunners of the famous Report of the Bullion Committee of 1810, in which Ricardo's views were adopted.[132] The singular circumstance, that Ricardo and his adherents, who held money to be merely a token of value, are called bullionists, is due not only to the name of that committee, but also to the nature of their theory. In his work on political economy, Ricardo repeated and developed further the same views, but nowhere has he investigated the nature of money as such, as he had done in the case of exchange value, profit, rent, etc.

To begin with, Ricardo determines the value of gold and silver, like that of all other commodities, by the quantity of labor-time embodied in them.[133] By means of them, as commodities of a given value, the values of all other commodities are measured.[134] The volume of the circulating medium in a country is determined by the value of the unit of measure of money on the one hand, and by the sum total of the exchange values of commodities, on the other. This quantity is modified by economy in the method of payment.[135] Since the quantity of money, of a given value, which can be absorbed by circulation, is thus determined and since the value of money within the sphere of circulation manifests itself only in its quantity, it follows that mere tokens of value, if issued in proportions determined by the value of money, may replace it in circulation, and in fact, "a currency is in its most perfect state when it consists wholly of paper money, but of paper money of an equal value with the gold which it professes to represent."[136] So far Ricardo determines the volume of the circulating medium by the prices of commodities, assuming the value of money to be given; money as a token of value means with him a token of a definite quantity of gold and not a mere worthless representative of commodities as was the case with Hume.

When Ricardo suddenly gets off the straight path of his presentation and takes the very opposite view, he does so to turn his attention to the international circulation of precious metals and thus brings confusion into the problem by introducing considerations that are foreign to the subject. Let us follow his own course of reasoning, and, in order to remove everything that is artificial and incidental, let us assume that the gold and silver mines are located in the interior of the countries in which the precious metals circulate as money. The only inference which follows from Ricardo's reasoning as so far developed, is that, the value of gold being given, the quantity of money in circulation will be determined by the prices of commodities. Thus, at a given moment, the quantity of gold in circulation in a country is simply determined by the exchange value of the commodities in circulation. Let us suppose now that the sum total of these exchange values has declined either because there are less commodities produced at the old exchange values, or because, in consequence of an increased productivity of labor, the same quantity of commodities has a smaller value. Or, we may assume on the contrary that the sum total of exchange values has increased, either because the quantity of commodities has increased while the cost of their production has remained the same, or because the value of the same or of a smaller quantity of commodities has risen in consequence of a diminished productivity of labor. What becomes in either case of the *given* quantity of metal in circulation? If gold is money merely because it is current as a medium of circulation; if it is compelled to remain in circulation like government legal tender paper money (and that is what Ricardo has in mind), then the quantity of money in circulation will rise above the normal level, as determined by the exchange value of the metal, in the former case, and fall below that level in the latter. Although possessing a value of its own, gold will become in the former case a token of a metal of lower exchange value than its own, and in the latter, a token of a metal of higher value. In the former case it will remain as a token of value less than its own, in the latter greater than its own (again an abstract deduction from legal tender paper money). In the former case it is the same as though commodities were estimated in a metal of lower value than gold, in the latter, as though they were estimated in a metal of higher value. In the former case, prices of commodities would rise therefore, in the latter they would fall. In either case the movement of prices, their rise or fall, would appear as the effect of a relative expansion or contraction of the volume of gold in circulation above or below the level corresponding to its own value, i. e. above or below the normal quantity which is determined by the proportion between its own value and that of the commodities in circulation.

The same process would take place if the sum total of the prices of the commodities in circulation remained unchanged, while the volume of gold in circulation came to be below or above the right level: the former in case the gold coin worn out in the course of circulation were not replaced by the production of a corresponding quantity of gold in the mines; the latter, if the output of the mines exceeded the requirements of circulation. In either case it is assumed that the cost of production of gold or its value remain the same.

To sum up: the money in circulation is at its normal level, when its volume is determined by its own bullion value, the exchange value of commodities being given. It rises above that level, bringing about a fall in the value of gold below its own bullion value and a rise of prices of commodities, whenever the sum total of the exchange values of commodities declines, or the output of gold from the mines increases. It sinks below its right level, leading to a rise of gold above its own bullion value and to a fall of prices of commodities, whenever the sum total of the exchange values of the commodities or the gold output of the mines is not sufficient to replace the quantity of outworn gold. In either case the gold in circulation becomes a token of value greater or smaller than that it really possesses. It may become an appreciated or depreciated token of itself. As soon as all commodities would come to be estimated in gold of this new value and the general price level would accordingly rise or fall, the quantity of current gold would again answer the requirements of circulation (a consequence which Ricardo emphasizes with great pleasure), but would be at variance with the cost of production of the precious metals and, therefore, with their relation as commodities to all other commodities. According to the general Ricardian theory of exchange value, the rise of gold above its exchange value, i. e., above the value as determined by the labor-time contained in it, would cause an increase in the production of gold until the increased output of it would reduce its value to the proper magnitude. And in the same manner, a fall of gold below its value would cause a decline in its production until its value rose again to its proper magnitude. By these opposite movements the discrepancy between the bullion value of gold and its value as a medium of circulation would disappear, the normal level of the volume of gold in circulation would be restored, and the price level would again correspond to the measure of value. These fluctuations in the value of gold in circulation would to the same extent affect gold in the form of bullion, because by assumption, all gold that is not utilized as an article of luxury, is supposed to be in circulation. Since gold itself may become, both as coin and bullion, a token of value of greater or smaller magnitude than its bullion value, it is self understood that convertible bank-notes in circulation have to share the same fate. Although bank-notes are convertible, i. e. their real value and nominal value agree, "the aggregate currency consisting of metal and of convertible notes" may appreciate or depreciate according as to whether it rises or falls, for reasons already stated, above or below the level determined by the exchange value of the commodities in circulation and the bullion value of gold. Inconvertible paper money, has, from this point of view, only that advantage as against convertible paper money, that it may depreciate in a two-fold manner. It may fall below the value of the metal which it is supposed to represent, because it has been issued in too great quantity, or it may depreciate because the metal it represents has itself fallen in value. This depreciation, not of paper as compared with gold, but of gold and paper together, or of the aggregate currency of a country, is one of the principal discoveries of Ricardo, which Lord Overstone and Co. pressed into their service and made a fundamental principle of Sir Robert Peele's Bank legislation of 1844 and 1845.

What should have been proven was that the price of commodities or the value of gold depends on the quantity of gold in circulation. The proof consists in the assumption of what is to be proven, viz. that any quantity of the precious metal employed as money must become a medium of circulation or coin, and thereby a token of value for the commodities in circulation, no matter in what proportion to its own intrinsic value and no matter what the total value of those commodities may be. To put it differently, the proof consists in overlooking all the other functions which money performs besides its function of a medium of circulation. When hard pressed, as in his controversy with Bosanquet, Ricardo, completely under the influence of the phenomenon of depreciated tokens of value caused by their quality, takes recourse to dogmatic assurances.[137]

If Ricardo had built up this theory by abstract reasoning, as we have done it here, without introducing concrete facts and incidental matters which only distract his attention from the main question, its hollowness would be striking. But he takes up the entire subject in its *international* aspect. It will be easy to prove, however, that the apparent magnitude of scale does not make his fundamental ideas less diminutive.

His first proposition was as follows: the volume of metallic currency is normal when it is determined by the total value of the commodities in circulation estimated in its bullion value.

Expressed so as to apply to international conditions, it reads thus: in a normal state of circulation every country possesses a quantity of money "according to the state of its commerce and wealth." Money circulates at a value corresponding to its real value or to its cost of production, i. e. it has the same value *in all countries.*[138] That being the case, "there could be no temptation offered to either for their importation or exportation."[139] There would thus be established a balance of currencies between the different countries. The normal level of a national currency is now expressed in terms of an international balance of currencies, which practically amounts to the statement that nationality does not change anything in a universal economic law. We have reached again the same fatal point as before. How is the normal level disturbed? Or, speaking in terms of the new terminology, how is the international balance of currencies disturbed? Or, how does money cease to have the same value in all countries? Or, finally, how does it cease to pass at its own value in every country? We have seen that the normal level was disturbed by an increase or decrease of the volume of money in circulation while the total value of commodities remained the same; or, because the quantity of money in circulation remained the same while the exchange values of commodities rose or fell. In the same manner, the international level, determined by the value of the metal itself, is disturbed by an increase in the quantity of gold in a country brought about by the discovery of new gold mines,[140] or by an increase or decrease of the total exchange-value of the circulating commodities in any particular country. Just as in the former case the output of the precious metals decreased or increased according as to whether it was necessary to contract or expand the currency and thereby to lower or raise prices, so are the same effects produced now by export and import from one country to another. In the country in which prices would rise or the value of gold would fall below the bullion value in consequence of a redundant currency, gold would be depreciated, and the prices of commodities would rise as compared with other countries. Gold would, therefore, be exported, while commodities would be imported, and vice versa. Just as in the former case the output of gold, so now the import or export of gold and, with it, the rise or fall of prices of commodities would continue until, as we would have said before, the right value relation would be restored between the metal and commodities, or as we shall say now, the international balance of currencies would be restored. Just as in the former case the production of gold increased or decreased because gold stood above or below its value, so now the international migration of gold would take place for the same reason. Just as in the former case, every change in the production of the circulating metal affected its quantity and, thereby, prices, so would the same effect be produced now by international import and export. As soon as the relative values of gold and commodities or the normal quantity of currency would be restored, no further production would take place in the former case, and no further export or import in the latter, except in so far as would be necessary to replace outworn coin and to meet the demand of manufacturers of articles of luxury. It follows "that the temptation to export money in exchange for goods, or what is termed an unfavorable balance of trade, never arises but from a redundant currency."[141] "The exportation of the coin is caused by its cheapness, and is not the effect, but the cause of an unfavourable balance."[142] Since the increase or decrease in the production of gold in the former case and the importation or exportation of gold in the latter, take place only whenever its volume rises above or sinks below its normal level, i. e. whenever gold appreciates or depreciates in comparison with its bullion value, or whenever prices of commodities are too high or too low; it follows that every such movement works as a corrective,[143] since, through the resultant expansion or contraction of the currency, prices are restored to their true level: in the former case this level represents the balance between the respective values of gold and of commodities; in the latter, the international balance of currencies. To put it in other words: money circulates in different countries only in so far as it circulates as coin in every country. Money is but coin and all the gold existing in a country must therefore enter circulation, i. e. it can rise above or fall below its value as a token of value. Thus we safely land again, by the round-about way of this international complication, at the simple dogma which constituted our starting point.

With what violence to actual facts Ricardo has to explain them in the sense of his abstract theory, a few illustrations will suffice to show. He maintains, e. g. that in years of poor crops, which happened frequently in England during 1800-1820, gold is exported not because corn is needed and gold as money is at all times an effectual means of purchase in the world market, but because gold is in such cases depreciated in its value as compared with other commodities and, therefore, the currency of the country in which there has been a failure of crops is depreciated with respect to other national currencies. "In consequence of a bad harvest, a country having been deprived of a part of its commodities ... the currency which was before at its just level ... become(s) redundant," and prices of all commodities rise in consequence.[144] Contrary to this paradoxical interpretation it has been proven statistically that from 1793 to the present time, whenever England had a bad harvest the available supply of currency not only did not become superabundant, but became inadequate and that, therefore, more money circulated and had to circulate on such occasions.[145]

In the same manner, Ricardo maintained, with reference to Napoleon's Continental System and the English Blockade Decree, that the English exported gold instead of commodities to the Continent, because their money was depreciated with respect to the money on the Continent, that their commodities were, therefore, more high priced, which made it a more profitable commercial speculation to export gold than goods. According to him England was a market in which commodities were dear and money was cheap, while on the Continent commodities were cheap and money was dear. The trouble, according to an English writer, was "the ruinously low prices of our manufactures and of our colonial productions under the operation ... of the 'Continental System 'during the last six years of the war.... The prices of sugar and coffee, for instance, on the Continent, computed in gold, were four or five times higher than their prices in England, computed in bank-notes. I am speaking ... of the times in which the French chemists discovered sugar in beet-root, and a substitute for coffee in chicory; and when the English grazier tried experiments upon fattening oxen with treacle and molasses-of the times when we took possession of the island of Heligoland, in order to form there a depot of goods to facilitate, if possible, the smuggling of them into the north of Europe; and when the lighter descriptions of British manufactures found their way into Germany through Turkey.... Almost all the merchandise of the world accumulated in our warehouses, where they became impounded, except when some small quantity was released by a French License, for which the merchants at Hamburgh and Amsterdam had, perhaps, given Napoleon such a sum as forty or fifty thousand pounds. They must have been strange merchants ... to have paid so large a sum for liberty to carry a cargo of goods from a dear market to a cheap one. What was the ostensible alternative the merchant had?... Either to buy coffee at 6d. a pound in bank-notes, and send it to a place where it would instantly sell at 3s. or 4s. a pound in gold, or to buy gold with bank-notes at £5 an ounce, and send it to a place where it would be received at £3 17s. 10-1/2d. an ounce....It is too absurd, of course, to say ... that the gold was remitted instead of the coffee, as a preferable mercantile operation.... There was not a country in the world in which so large a quantity of desirable goods could be obtained, in return for an ounce of gold, as in England....Bonaparte ... was constantly examining the English Price Current....So long as he saw that gold was dear and coffee was cheap in England, he was satisfied that his 'Continental System 'worked well."[146]

At the very time when Ricardo first formulated his theory of money, and the Bullion Committee embodied it in its parliamentary report, namely in 1810, a ruinous fall of prices of all English commodities as compared with those of 1808 and 1809 took place, while gold rose in value accordingly. Only agricultural products formed an exception, because their importation from abroad met with obstacles and their domestic supply was decimated by unfavorable crop conditions.[147] Ricardo so utterly failed to comprehend the rôle of precious metals as an international means of payment, that in his testimony before the Committee of the House of Lords in 1819 he could say "that drains for exportation would cease altogether so soon as cash payments should be resumed, and the currency be restored to its metallic level." He died just in time, on the very eve of the crisis of 1825, which belied his prophesies.

The time when Ricardo wrote was generally little adapted for the observation of the function of precious metals as world money. Before the introduction of the Continental System, the balance of trade had almost always been in favor of England, and while that system lasted, the commercial intercourse with the European continent was too insignificant to affect the English rate of exchange. The money transmissions were mostly of a political nature and Ricardo seems to have utterly failed to grasp the part which subsidy payments played at that time in English gold exports.[148]

Among the contemporaries of Ricardo who formed the school which adopted his economic principles, JAMES MILL was the most important one. He attempted to work out Ricardo's theory of money on the basis of simple metallic circulation, without the irrelevant international complications which served Ricardo to hide the inadequacy of his theory, and without any controversial regard for the operations of the Bank of England. His main arguments are as follows:

"By value of money, is here to be understood the proportion in which it exchanges for other commodities, or the quantity of it which exchanges for a certain quantity of other things.... It is the total quantity of the money in any country, which determines what portion of that quantity shall exchange for a certain portion of the goods or commodities of that country. If we suppose that all the goods of the country are on one side, all the money on the other, and that they are exchanged at once against one another, it is evident ... that the value of money would depend wholly upon the quantity of it. It will appear that the case is precisely the same in the actual state of the facts. The whole of the goods of a country are not exchanged at once against the whole of the money; the goods are exchanged in portions, often in very small portions, and at different times, during the course of the whole year. The same piece of money which is paid in one exchange to-day, may be paid in another exchange tomorrow. Some of the pieces will be employed in a great many exchanges, some in very few, and some, which happen to be hoarded, in none at all. There will, amid all these varieties, be a certain average number of exchanges, the same which, if all the pieces had performed an equal number, would have been performed by each; that average we may suppose to be any number we please; say, for example, ten. If each of the pieces of the money in the country perform ten purchases, that is exactly the same thing as if all the pieces were multiplied by ten, and performed only one purchase each. The value of all the goods in the country is equal to ten times the value of all the money.... If the quantity of money instead of performing ten exchanges in the year, were ten times as great, and performed only one exchange in the year, it is evident that whatever addition were made to the whole quantity, would produce a proportional diminution of value, in each of the minor quantities taken separately. As the quantity of goods, against which the money is all exchanged at once, is supposed to be the same, the value of all the money is no more, after the quantity is augmented, than before it was augmented. If it is supposed to be augmented one-tenth, the value of every part, that of an ounce for example, must be diminished one-tenth.... In whatever degree, therefore, the quantity of money is increased or diminished, other things remaining the same, in that same proportion, the value of the whole, and of every part, is reciprocally diminished or increased. This, it is evident, is a proposition universally true. Whenever the value of money has either risen or fallen (the quantity of goods against which it is exchanged and the rapidity of circulation remaining the same), the change must be owing to a corresponding diminution or increase of the quantity; and can be owing to nothing else. If the quantity of goods diminish, while the quantity of money remains the same, it is the same thing as if the quantity of money had been increased;" and vice versa.... "Similar changes are produced by any alteration in the rapidity of circulation.... An increase in the number of these purchases has the same effect as an increase in the quantity of money; a diminution the reverse.... If there is any portion of the annual produce which is not exchanged at all, as what is consumed by the producer; or which is not exchanged for money; that is not taken into the account, because what is not exchanged for money is in the same state with respect to the money, as if it did not exist.... Whenever the coining of money ... is free, its quantity is regulated by the value of the metal....

Gold and silver are in reality commodities.... It is cost of production ... which determines the value of these, as of other ordinary productions."[149]

The whole wisdom of Mill resolves itself into a series of arbitrary and absurd assumptions. He wishes to prove that the price of commodities or the value of money is determined by "the total quantity of the money in any country." *Assuming* that the quantity and the exchange value of the commodities in circulation remain unchanged and that the same be true of the rapidity of circulation and of the value of precious metals as determined by the cost of production, and *assuming* at the same time that the quantity of the metallic currency increases or decreases in proportion to the quantity of money *existing* in a country, it becomes really "evident" that what was to have been proven has been assumed. Mill falls, moreover, into the same error as Hume by assuming that use-values and not commodities with a given exchange value are in circulation, and that vitiates his statement, even if we grant all of his "assumptions." The rapidity of circulation may remain the same; this may also be true of the value of the precious metals and of the *quantity* of commodities in circulation; and yet a change in the exchange value of the latter may require now a larger and now a smaller quantity of money for their circulation. Mill sees that a part of the money in a country is in circulation, while another is idle. With the aid of a most absurd average calculation he *assumes* that, although it really appears to be different, yet all the gold in a country does circulate. Assuming that ten million silver thalers circulate in a country twice a year, there could be twenty million such coins in circulation, if each circulated but once. And if the entire quantity of silver to be found in a country in any form amounts to one hundred million thalers, it may be supposed that the entire one hundred million can enter circulation, if each piece of money should circulate once in five years. One could as well assume that all the money of the world circulate in Hempstead, but that each piece of money instead of being employed three times a year, is employed once in 3,000,000 years. The one assumption is as relevant as the other for the purpose of determining the relation between the sum total of prices of commodities and the volume of currency. Mill feels that it is a matter of decisive importance to him to bring the commodities in direct contact not with the money in circulation, but with the entire supply of money existing in a country. He admits that "the whole of the goods of a country are not exchanged at once against the whole of the money," but that the goods are exchanged in different portions and at different times of the year for different portions of money. To do away with this difficulty he *assumes* that it does not exist. Moreover, this entire idea of direct contact of commodities and money and direct exchange is a mere abstraction from the movement of simple purchase and sale or the function of money as a means of purchase. Already in the movement of money as a means of payment, commodity and money cease to appear simultaneously.

The commercial crises of the nineteenth century, namely, the great crises of 1825 and 1836, did not result in any new developments in the Ricardian theory of money, but they did furnish new applications for it. They were no longer isolated economic phenomena, such as the depreciation of the precious metals in the sixteenth and seventeenth centuries which interested Hume, or the depreciation of paper money in the eighteenth and early nineteenth centuries which confronted Ricardo; they were the great storms of the world market in which the conflict of all the elements of the capitalist process of production discharge themselves, and whose origin and remedy were sought in the most superficial and abstract sphere of this process, the sphere of money circulation. The theoretical assumption from which the school of economic weather prophets proceeds, comes down in the end to the illusion that Ricardo discovered the laws governing the circulation of purely metallic currency. The only thing that remained for them to do was to subject to the same laws the circulation of credit and bank-note currency.

The most general and most palpable phenomenon in commercial crises is the sudden, general decline of prices following a prolonged general rise. The general decline of prices of commodities may be expressed as a rise in the relative value of money with respect to all commodities, and the general rise of prices as a decline of the relative value of money. In either expression the phenomenon is described but not explained. Whether I put the question thus: explain the general periodic rise of prices followed by a general decline of the same, or formulate the same problem by saying: explain the periodic decline and rise of the relative value of money with respect to commodities; the different wording leaves the problem as little changed as would its translation from German into English. Ricardo's theory of money was exceedingly convenient, because it lends a tautology the semblance of a statement of causal connection. Whence comes the periodic general fall of prices? From the periodic rise of the relative value of money. Whence the general periodic rise of prices? From the periodic decline of the relative value of money. It might have been stated with equal truth that the periodic rise and fall of prices is due to their periodic rise and fall. The problem itself is stated under the assumption that the intrinsic value of money, i. e., its value as determined by the cost of production of precious metals remains *unchanged*. If it is more than a tautology then it is based on a misconception of the most elementary principles. If the exchange value of A measured in terms of B, declines, we know that this may be caused by a decline of the value of A as much as by a rise of the value of B; the same being true of the case of a rise of the exchange value of A measured in terms of B. The tautology once admitted as a statement of cause, the rest follows easily. A rise of prices of commodities is caused by a decline of the value of money and a decline of the value of money is caused, as we know from Ricardo, by a redundant currency, i. e., by a rise of the volume of currency over the level determined by its own intrinsic value and the intrinsic value of the commodities. In the same manner, the general decline of prices of commodities is explained by the rise of the value of money above its intrinsic value in consequence of an inadequate currency. Thus, prices rise and fall periodically, because there is periodically too much or too little money in circulation. Should a rise of prices happen to coincide with a contracted currency, and a fall of prices with an expanded one, it may be asserted in spite of those facts that in consequence of a contraction or expansion of the volume of commodities in the market, which can not be proven statistically, the quantity of money in circulation has, although not absolutely, yet relatively increased or declined. We have seen that according to Ricardo these universal fluctuations must take place even with a purely metallic currency, but that they balance each other through their alternations; thus, e. g., an inadequate currency causes a fall of prices, the fall of prices leads to the export of commodities abroad, this export causes again an import of gold from abroad, which, in its turn, brings about a rise of prices; the opposite movement taking place in case of a redundant currency, when commodities are imported and money is exported. But, since in spite of these universal fluctuations of prices which are in perfect accord with Ricardo's theory of metallic currency, their acute and violent form, their crisis-form, belongs to the period of advanced credit, it is perfectly clear that the issue of bank-notes is not exactly regulated by the laws of metallic currency. Metallic currency has its remedy in the import and export of precious metals which immediately enter circulation and thus, by their influx or efflux, cause the prices of commodities to fall or rise. The same effect on prices must now be exerted by banks by the artificial imitation of the laws of metallic currency. If gold is coming in from abroad it proves that the currency is inadequate, that the value of money is too high and the prices of commodities too low, and, consequently, that bank notes must be put in circulation in proportion to the newly imported gold. On the contrary, notes have to be withdrawn from circulation in proportion to the export of gold from the country. That is to say, the issue of bank notes must be regulated by the import and export of the precious metals or by the rate of exchange. Ricardo's false assumption that gold is only coin, and that therefore all imported gold swells the currency, causing prices to rise, while all exported gold reduces the currency leading to a fall of prices, this theoretical assumption is turned into a practical experiment of putting in every case an amount of currency in circulation equal to the amount of gold in existence. Lord Overstone (the banker Jones Loyd), Colonel Torrens, Norman, Clay, Arbuthnot and a host of other writers, known in England as the adherents of the "currency principle," not only preached this doctrine, but with the aid of Sir Robert Peel succeeded in 1844 and 1845 in making it the basis of the present English and Scotch bank legislation. Its ignominious failure, theoretical as well as practical, following upon experiments on the largest national scale, can be treated only after we take up the theory of credit.[150] So much can be seen, however, that the theory of Ricardo which isolates money in its fluent form of currency, ends by ascribing to the ebbs and tides in the supply of precious metals an influence on bourgeois economy such as the believers in the superstitions of the monetary system had never dreamt of. Thus did Ricardo, who proclaimed paper currency as the most perfect form of money, become the prophet of the bullionists.

After Hume's theory or the abstract opposition to the monetary system was thus developed to its ultimate conclusions, Steuart's concrete conception of money was finally restored to its rights by THOMAS TOOKE.[151] Tooke arrives at his principles not from any theory, but by a conscientious analysis of the history of prices of commodities from 1793 to 1856. In the first edition of his History of Prices which appeared in 1823, Tooke is still under the complete influence of the Ricardian theory, and vainly tries to reconcile it with actual facts. His pamphlet "On the Currency," which appeared after the crisis of 1825 might even be considered as the first consistent presentation of the views which were later given the force of law by Overstone. Continued studies in the history of prices forced him, however, to the conclusion that the direct connection between prices and the volume of currency, as it is pictured by the theory, is a mere illusion; that the expansion and contraction of currency which takes place while the value of the precious metals remains unchanged, is always the effect but never the cause of price fluctuations; that the circulation of money is in any event but a secondary movement; and that money assumes quite different forms in the actual process of production in addition to that of a circulating medium. His detailed investigations belong to a sphere outside of that of simple metallic circulation and can be discussed here as little as the investigations of WILSON and FULLARTON which belong to the same class.[152] None of these writers takes a one-sided view of money, but treat it in its various aspects; the treatment, however, is mechanical, without an attempt to establish an organic connection either between these various aspects themselves, or between them and the combined system of economic categories. They fall, therefore, into the error of confusing *money* as distinguished from *medium of circulation* with *capital* or even with commodity, although they are forced elsewhere to differentiate it from both.[153] When gold, e. g., is shipped abroad, it practically means that capital is sent abroad, but the same thing takes place when iron, cotton, grain, or any other commodity is exported. Both are capital and are distinguished not as capital, but as money and commodity. The function of gold as the international medium of exchange springs, therefore, not from its being capital, but from its specific character of money. Similarly, when gold, or bank notes in its place, circulate in the home trade as means of payment, they constitute capital at the same time. But they could not be replaced by capital in the form of commodities, as has been demonstrated very palpably by crises, for instance. That is to say, it is the fact that gold is distinguished from commodities in its capacity of money and not in that of capital, that makes it the means of payment. Even when capital is exported directly as capital, as, e. g., when it is done for the purpose of lending abroad a certain amount on interest, it depends on circumstances, whether it will be exported in the form of commodities or in that of gold, and if in the latter form, it is due to the specific destination of the precious metals as distinguished from commodities to serve as money. In general, these writers do not consider money in its abstract form, as it is developed within the sphere of simple circulation of commodities, and as it spontaneously grows out of the relation of the circulating commodities. As a result, they constantly vacillate between the abstract forms of money which distinguish it from commodity and those forms of it beneath which are concealed concrete relations, such as capital, revenue, etc.[154]

**Introduction
to the
Critique of Political Economy**[155]

1. Production in General

The subject of our discussion is first of all *material* production by individuals as determined by society, naturally constitutes the starting point. The individual and isolated hunter or fisher who forms the starting point with Smith and Ricardo, belongs to the insipid illusions of the eighteenth century. They are Robinsonades which do not by any means represent, as students of the history of civilization imagine, a reaction against over-refinement and a return to a mis-understood natural life. They are no more based on such a naturalism than is Rosseau's "contrat social," which makes naturally independent individuals come in contact and have mutual inter-course by contract. They are the fiction and only the aesthetic fiction of the small and great Robinsonades. They are, moreover, the anticipation of "bourgeois society," which had been in course of development since the sixteenth century and made gigantic strides towards maturity in the eighteenth. In this society of free competition the individual appears free from the bonds of nature, etc., which in former epochs of history made him a part of a definite, limited human conglomeration. To the prophets of the eighteenth century, on whose shoulders Smith and Ricardo are still standing, this eighteenth century individual, constituting the joint product of the dissolution of the feudal form of society and of the new forces of production which had developed since the sixteenth century, appears as an ideal whose existence belongs to the past; not as a result of history, but as its starting point.

Since that individual appeared to be in conformity with nature and [corresponded] to their conception of human nature, [he was regarded] not as a product of history, but of nature. This illusion has been characteristic of every new epoch in the past. Steuart, who, as an aristocrat, stood more firmly on historical ground, contrary to the spirit of the eighteenth century, es-caped this simplicity of view. The further back we go into history, the more the individual and, therefore, the producing individual seems to depend on and constitute a part of a larger whole: at first it is, quite naturally, the family and the clan, which is but an enlarged family; later on, it is the community growing up in its different forms out of the clash and the amalgamation of clans. It is but in the eighteenth century, in "bourgeois society," that the different forms of social union confront the individual as a mere means to his private ends, as an outward necessity. But the period in which this view of the isolated individual becomes prevalent, is the very one in which the interrelations of society (general from this point of view) have reached the highest state of development. Man is in the most literal sense of the word a *zoon politikon*, not only a social animal, but an animal which can develop into an individual only in society. Production by isolated individuals outside of society-something which might happen as an exception to a civilized man who by accident got into the wilderness and already dynamically possessed within himself the forces of society-is as great an absurdity as the idea of the development of language without individuals living together and talking to one another. We need not dwell on this any longer. It would not be necessary to touch upon this point at all, were not the vagary which had its justification and sense with the people of the eighteenth century transplanted in all earnest into the field of political economy by Bastiat, Carey, Proudhon and others. Proudhon and others naturally find it very pleasant, when they do not know the historical origin of a certain economic phenomenon, to give it a quasi historico-philosopohical explanation by going into mythology. Adam or Prometheus hit upon the scheme cut and dried, whereupon it was adopted, etc. Nothing is more tediously dry than the dreaming *locus communis*.

Whenever we speak, therefore, of production, we always have in mind production at a certain stage of social development, or production by social individuals. Hence, it might seem that in order to speak of production at all, we must either trace the historical process of development through its various phases, or declare at the outset that we are dealing with a certain historical period, as, e. g., with modern capitalistic production which, as a matter of fact, constitutes the subject proper of this work. But all stages of production have certain landmarks in common, common purposes. *Production in general* is an abstraction, but it is a rational abstraction, in so far as it singles out and fixes the common features, thereby saving us repetition. Yet these general or common features discovered by comparison constitute something very complex, whose constituent elements have different destinations. Some of these elements belong to all epochs, others are common to a few. Some of them are common to the most modern as well as to the most ancient epochs. No production is conceivable without them; but while even the most completely developed languages have laws and conditions in common with the least developed ones, what is characteristic of their development are the points of departure from the general and common. The conditions which generally govern production must be differentiated in order that the essential points of difference be not lost sight of in view of the general uniformity which is due to the fact that the subject, mankind, and the object, nature, remain the same. The failure to remember this one fact is the source of all the wisdom of modern economists who are trying to prove the eternal nature and harmony of existing social conditions. Thus they say, e. g., that no production is possible without some instrument of production, let that instrument be only the hand; that none is possible without past accumulated labor, even if that labor consist of mere skill which has been accumulated and concentrated in the hand of the savage by repeated exercise. Capital is, among other things, also an instrument of production, also past impersonal labor. Hence capital is a universal, eternal natural phenomenon; which is true if we disregard the specific properties which turn an "instrument of production" and "stored up labor" into capital. The entire history of production appears to a man like Carey, e. g., as a malicious perversion on the part of governments.

If there is no production in general, there is also no general production. Production is always some special branch of production or an aggregate, as, e. g., agriculture, stock raising, manufactures, etc. But political economy is not technology. The connection between the general destinations of production at a given stage of social development and the particular forms of production, is to be developed elsewhere (later on).

Finally, production is not only of a special kind. It is always a certain body politic, a social personality that is engaged on a larger or smaller aggregate of branches of production. The connection between the real process and its scientific presentation also falls outside of the scope of this treatise. [We must thus distinguish between] production in general, special branches of production and production as a whole.

It is the fashion with economists to open their works with a general introduction, which is entitled "production" (see, e. g., John Stuart Mill) and deals with the general "requisites of production."

This general introductory part treats or is supposed to treat:

1. Of the conditions without which production is impossible, i. e., of the most essential conditions of production. As a matter of fact, however, it dwindles down, as we shall see, to a few very simple definitions, which flatten out into shallow tautologies;
2. Of conditions which further production more or less, as, e. g., Adam Smith's [discussion of] a progressive and stagnant state of society.

In order to give scientific value to what serves with him as a mere summary, it would be necessary to study the *degree of productivity* by periods in the development of individual nations; such a study falls outside of the scope of the present subject, and in so far as it does belong here is to be brought out in connection with the discussion of competition, accumulation, etc. The commonly accepted view of the matter gives a general answer to the effect that an industrial nation is at the height of its production at the moment when it reaches its historical climax in all respects. Or, that certain races, climates, natural conditions, such as distance from the sea, fertility of the soil, etc., are more favorable to production than others. That again comes down to the tautology that the facility of creating wealth depends on the extent to which its elements are present both subjectively and objectively. As a matter of fact a nation is at its industrial height so long as its main object is not gain, but the process of gaining. In that respect the Yankees stand above the English.

But all that is not what the economists are really after in the general introductory part. Their object is rather to represent production in contradistinction to distribution-see Mill, e. g. — as subject to eternal laws independent of history, and then to substitute bourgeois relations, in an underhand way, as immutable natural laws of society *in abstracto*. This is the more or less conscious aim of the entire proceeding. On the contrary, when it comes to distribution, mankind is supposed to have indulged in all sorts of arbitrary action. Quite apart from the fact that they violently break the ties which bind production and distribution together, so much must be clear from the outset: that, no matter how greatly the systems of distribution may vary at different stages of society, it should be possible here, as in the case of production, to discover the common features and to confound and eliminate all historical differences in formulating *general human* laws. E. g., the slave, the serf, the wage-worker —all receive a quantity of food, which enables them to exist as slave, serf, and wage-worker. The conqueror, the official, the landlord, the monk, or the levite, who respectively live on tribute, taxes, rent, alms, and the tithe, —all receive [a part] of the social product which is determined by laws different from those which determine the part received by the slave, etc. The two main points which all economists place under this head, are: first, property; second, the protection of the latter by the administration of justice, police, etc. The objections to these two points can be stated very briefly.

1. All production is appropriation of nature by the individual within and through a definite form of society. In that sense it is a tautology to say that property (appropriation) is a condition of production. But it becomes ridiculous, when from that one jumps at once to a definite form of property, e. g. private property (which implies, besides, as a prerequisite the existence of an opposite form, viz. absence of property). History points rather to common property (e. g. among the Hindoos, Slavs, ancient Celts, etc.) as the primitive form, which still plays an important part at a much later period as communal property. The question as to whether wealth grows more rapidly under this or that form of property, is not even raised here as yet. But that there can be no such a thing as production, nor, consequently, society, where property does not exist in any form, is a tautology. Appropriation which does not appropriate is a *contradictio in subjecto*.

2. Protection of property, etc. Reduced to their real meaning, these commonplaces express more than what their preachers know, namely, that every form of production creates its own legal relations, forms of government, etc. The crudity and the shortcomings of the conception lie in the tendency to see but an accidental reflective connection in what constitutes an organic union. The bourgeois economists have a vague notion that it is better to carry on production under the modern police, than it was, e. g. under club-law. They forget that club law is also law, and that the right of the stronger continues to exist in other forms even under their "government of law."

When the social conditions corresponding to a certain stage of production are in a state of formation or disappearance, disturbances of production naturally arise, although differing in extent and effect.

To sum up: all the stages of production have certain destinations in common, which we generalize in thought; but the so-called general conditions of all production are nothing but abstract conceptions which do not go to make up any real stage in the history of production.

2. The General Relation of Production to Distribution, Exchange, and Consumption

Before going into a further analysis of production, it is necessary to look at the various divisions which economists put side by side with it. The most shallow conception is as follows:

By production, the members of society appropriate (produce and shape) the products of nature to human wants; distribution determines the proportion in which the individual participates in this production; exchange brings him the particular products into which he wishes to turn the quantity secured by him through distribution; finally, through consumption the products become objects of use and enjoyment, of individual appropriation. Production yields goods adopted to our needs; distribution distributes them according to social laws; exchange distributes further what has already been distributed, according to individual wants; finally, in consumption the product drops out of the social movement, becoming the direct object of the individual want which it serves and satisfies in use. Production thus appears as the starting point; consumption as the final end; and distribution and exchange as the middle; the latter has a double aspect, distribution being defined as a process carried on by society, while exchange, as one proceeding from the individual. In production the person is embodied in things, in [consumption[156]] things are embodied in persons; in distribution, society assumes the part of go-between of production and consumption in the form of generally prevailing rules; in exchange this is accomplished by the accidental make-up of the individual.

Distribution determines what proportion (quantity) of the products the individual is to receive; exchange determines the products in which the individual desires to receive his share allotted to him by distribution.

Production, distribution, exchange, and consumption thus form a perfect connection, production standing for the general, distribution and exchange for the special, and consumption for the individual, in which all are joined together. To be sure this is a connection, but it does not go very deep. Production is determined [according to the economists] by universal natural laws, while distribution depends on social chance: distribution can, therefore, have a more or less stimulating effect on production: exchange lies between the two as a formal (?) social movement, and the final act of consumption which is considered not only as a final purpose, but also as a final aim, falls, properly, outside of the scope of economics, except in so far as it reacts on the starting point and causes the entire process to begin all over again.

The opponents of the economists-whether economists themselves or not-who reproach them with tearing apart, like barbarians, what is an organic whole, either stand on common ground with them or are *below* them. Nothing is more common than the charge that the economists have been considering production as an end in itself, too much to the exclusion of everything else. The same has been said with regard to distribution. This accusation is itself based on the economic conception that distribution exists side by side with production as a self-contained, independent sphere. Or [they are accused] that the various factors are not treated by them in their connection as a whole. As though it were the text books that impress this separation upon life and not life upon the text books; and the subject at issue were a dialectic balancing of conceptions and not an analysis of real conditions.

a. Production is at the same time also consumption. Twofold consumption, subjective and objective. The individual who develops his faculties in production, is also expending them, consuming them in the act of production, just as procreation is in its way a consumption of vital powers. In the second place, production is consumption of means of production which are used and used up and partly (as e. g. in burning) reduced to their natural elements. The same is true of the consumption of raw materials which do not remain in their natural form and state, being greatly absorbed in the process. The act of production is, therefore, in all its aspects an act of consumption as well. But this is admitted by economists. Production as directly identical with consumption, consumption as directly coincident with production, they call productive consumption. This identity of production and consumption finds its expression in Spinoza's proposition, *Determinatio est negatio.* But this definition of productive consumption is resorted to just for the purpose of distinguishing between consumption as identical with production and consumption proper, which is defined as its destructive counterpart. Let us then consider consumption proper.

Consumption is directly also production, just as in nature the consumption of the elements and of chemical matter constitutes production of plants. It is clear, that in nutrition, e. g., which is but one form of consumption, man produces his own body; but it is equally true of every kind of consumption, which goes to produce the human being in one way or another. [It is] consumptive production. But, say the economists, this production which is identical with consumption, is a second production resulting from the destruction of the product of the first. In the first, the producer transforms himself into things; in the second, things are transformed into human beings. Consequently, this consumptive production-although constituting a direct unity of production and consumption-differs essentially from production proper. The direct unity in which production coincides with consumption and consumption with production, does not interfere with their direct duality.

Production is thus at the same time consumption, and consumption is at the same time production. Each is directly its own counterpart. But at the same time an intermediary movement goes on between the two. Production furthers consumption by creating material for the latter which otherwise would lack its object. But consumption in its turn furthers production, by providing for the products the individual for whom they are products. The product receives its last finishing touches in consumption. A railroad on which no one rides, which is, consequently not used up, not consumed, is but a potential railroad, and not a real one. Without production, no consumption; but, on the other hand, without consumption, no production; since production would then be without a purpose. Consumption produces production in two ways.

In the first place, in that the product first becomes a real product in consumption; e. g., a garment becomes a real garment only through the act of being worn; a dwelling which is not inhabited, is really no dwelling; consequently, a product as distinguished from a mere natural object, proves to be such, first *becomes* a product in consumption. Consumption gives the product the finishing touch by annihilating it, since a product is the [result] of production not only as the material embodiment of activity, but also as a mere object for the active subject.

In the second place, consumption produces production by creating the necessity for new production, i. e. by providing the ideal, inward, impelling cause which constitutes the prerequisite of production. Consumption furnishes the impulse for production as well as its object, which plays in production the part of its guiding aim. It is clear that while production furnishes the material object of consumption, consumption provides the ideal object of production, as its image, its want, its impulse and its purpose. It furnishes the object of production in its subjective form. No wants, no production. But consumption reproduces the want.

In its turn, production:

First, furnishes consumption[157] with its material, its object. Consumption without an object is no consumption, hence production works in this direction by producing consumption.

Second. But it is not only the object that production provides for consumption. It gives consumption its definite outline, its character, its finish. Just as consumption gives the product its finishing touch as a product, production puts the finishing touch on consumption. For the object is not simply an object in general, but a definite object, which is consumed in a certain definite manner prescribed in its turn by production. Hunger is hunger; but the hunger that is satisfied with cooked meat eaten with fork and knife is a different kind of hunger from the one that devours raw meat with the aid of hands, nails, and teeth. Not only the object of consumption, but also the manner of consumption is produced by production; that is to say, consumption is created by production not only objectively, but also subjectively. Production thus creates the consumers.

Third. Production not only supplies the want with material, but supplies the material with a want. When consumption emerges from its first stage of natural crudeness and directness-and its continuation in that state would in itself be the result of a production still remaining in a state of natural crudeness-it is itself furthered by its object as a moving spring. The want of it which consumption experiences is created by its appreciation of the product. The object of art, as well as any other product, creates an artistic and beauty-enjoying public. Production thus produces not only an object for the individual, but also an individual for the object.

Production thus produces consumption: first, by furnishing the latter with material; second, by determining the manner of consumption; third, by creating in consumers a want for its products as objects of consumption. It thus produces the object, the manner, and the moving spring of consumption. In the same manner, consumption [creates] the *disposition* of the producer by setting (?) him up as an aim and by stimulating wants. The identity of consumption and production thus appears to be a three fold one.

First, direct identity: production is consumption; consumption is production. Consumptive production. Productive consumption. Economists call both productive consumption, but make one distinction by calling the former reproduction, and the latter productive consumption. All inquiries into the former deal with productive and unproductive labor; those into the latter treat of productive and unproductive consumption.

Second. Each appears as the means of the other and as being brought about by the other, which is expressed as their mutual interdependence; a relation, by virtue of which they appear as mutually connected and indispensable, yet remaining outside of each other.

Production creates the material as the outward object of consumption; consumption creates the want as the inward object, the purpose of production. Without production, no consumption; without consumption, no production; this maxim figures (?) in political economy in many forms.

Third. Production is not only directly consumption and consumption directly production; nor is production merely a means of consumption and consumption the purpose of production. In other words, not only does each furnish the other with its object; production, the material object of consumption; consumption, the ideal object of production. On the contrary, either one is not only directly the other, not (?) only a means of furthering the other, but while it is taking place, creates the other as such for itself (?). Consumption completes the act of production by giving the finishing touch to the product as such, by destroying the latter, by breaking up its independent material form; by bringing to a state of readiness, through the necessity of repetition, the disposition to produce developed in the first act of production; that is to say, it is not only the concluding act through which the product becomes a product, but also [the one] through which the producer becomes a producer. On the other hand, production produces consumption, by determining the manner of consumption, and further, by creating the incentive for consumption, the very ability to consume, in the form of want. This latter identity mentioned under point 3, is much discussed in political economy in connection with the treatment of the relations of demand and supply, of objects and wants, of natural wants and those created by society.

Hence, it is the simplest matter with a Hegelian to treat production and consumption as identical. And this has been done not only by socialist writers of fiction but even by economists, e. g. Say; the latter maintained that if we consider a nation as a whole, or mankind *in abstracto* —her production is at the same time her consumption. Storch pointed out Say's error by calling attention to the fact that a nation does not entirely consume her product, but also creates means of production, fixed capital, etc. To consider society as a single individual is moreover a false mode of speculative reasoning. With an individual, production and consumption appear as different aspects of one act. The important point to be emphasized here is that if production and consumption be considered as activities of one individual or of separate individuals, they appear at any rate as aspects of one process in which production forms the actual starting point and is, therefore, the predominating factor. Consumption, as a natural necessity, as a want, constitutes an internal factor of productive activity, but the latter is the starting point of realization and, therefore, its predominating factor, the act into which the entire process resolves itself in the end. The individual produces a certain article and turns again into himself by consuming it; but he returns as a productive and a self-reproducing individual. Consumption thus appears as a factor of production.

In society, however, the relation of the producer to his product, as soon as it is completed, is an outward one, and the return of the product to the individual depends on his relations to other individuals. He does not take immediate possession of it. Nor does the direct appropriation of the product constitute his purpose, when he produces in society. Between the producer and the product distribution steps in, which determines by social laws his share in the world of products; that is to say, distribution steps in between production and consumption.

Does distribution form an independent sphere standing side by side with and outside of production?

b. Production and Distribution. In perusing the common treatises on economics one can not help being struck with the fact that everything is treated there twice; e. g., under distribution, there figure rent, wages, interest, and profit; while under production we find land, labor, and capital as agents of production. As regards capital, it is at once clear that it is counted twice: first, as an agent of production; second, as a source of income; as determining factors and definite forms of distribution, interest and profit figure as such also in production, since they are forms, in which capital increases and grows, and are consequently factors of its own production. Interest and profit, as forms of distribution, imply the existence of capital as an agent of production. They are forms of distribution which have for their prerequisite capital as an agent of production. They are also forms of reproduction of capital.

In the same manner, wages is wage-labor when considered under another head; the definite character which labor has in one case as an agent of production, appears in the other as a form of distribution. If labor were not fixed as wage-labor, its manner of participation in distribution[158] would not appear as wages, as is the case e. g. under slavery. Finally, rent-to take at once the most developed form of distribution-by means of which landed property receives its share of the products, implies the existence of large landed property (properly speaking, agriculture on a large scale) as an agent of production, and not simply land, no more than wages represents simply labor. The relations and methods of distribution appear, therefore, merely as the reverse sides of the agents of production. An individual who participates in production as a wage laborer, receives his share of the products, i. e. of the results of production, in the form of wages. The subdivisions and organization of distribution are determined by the subdivisions and organization of production. Distribution is itself a product of production, not only in so far as the material goods are concerned, since only the results of production can be distributed; but also as regards its form, since the definite manner of participation in production determines the particular form of distribution, the form under which participation in distribution takes place. It is quite an illusion to place land under production, rent under distribution, etc.

Economists, like Ricardo, who are accused above all of having paid exclusive attention to production, define distribution, therefore, as the exclusive subject of political economy, because they instinctively[159] regard the forms of distribution as the clearest forms in which the agents of production find expression in a given society.

To the single individual distribution naturally appears as a law established by society determining his position in the sphere of production, within which he produces, and thus antedating production. At the outset the individual has no capital, no landed property. From his birth he is assigned to wage-labor by the social process of distribution. But this very condition of being assigned to wage-labor is the result of the existence of capital and landed property as independent agents of production.

From the point of view of society as a whole, distribution seems to antedate and to determine production in another way as well, as a pre-economic fact, so to say. A conquering people divides the land among the conquerors establishing thereby a certain division and form of landed property and determining the character of production; or, it turns the conquered people into slaves and thus makes slave labor the basis of production. Or, a nation, by revolution, breaks up large estates into small parcels of land and by this new distribution imparts to production a new character. Or, legislation perpetuates land ownership in large families or distributes labor as an hereditary privilege and thus fixes it in castes.

In all of these cases, and they are all historic, it is not distribution that seems to be organized and determined by production, but on the contrary, production by distribution.

In the most shallow conception of distribution, the latter appears as a distribution of products and to that extent as further removed from and quasi-independent of production. But before distribution means distribution of products, it is first, a distribution of the means of production, and second, what is practically another wording of the same fact, it is a distribution of the members of society among the various kinds of production (the subjection of individuals to certain conditions of production). The distribution of products is manifestly a result of this distribution, which is bound up with the process of production and determines the very organization of the latter. To treat of production apart from the distribution which is comprised in it, is plainly an idle abstraction. Conversely, we know the character of the distribution of products the moment we are given the nature of that other distribution which forms originally a factor of production. Ricardo, who was concerned with the analysis of production as it is organized in modern society and who was the economist of production *par excellence*, for that very reason declares *not* production but distribution as the subject proper of modern economics. We have here another evidence of the insipidity of the economists who treat production as an eternal truth, and banish history to the domain of distribution.

What relation to production this distribution, which has a determining influence on production itself, assumes, is plainly a question which falls within the province of production. Should it be maintained that at least to the extent that production depends on a certain distribution of the instruments of production, distribution in that sense precedes production and constitutes its prerequisite; it may be replied that production has in fact its prerequisite conditions, which form factors of it. These may appear at first to have a natural origin. By the very process of production they are changed from natural to historical, and if they appear during one period as a natural prerequisite of production, they formed at other periods its historical result. Within the sphere of production itself they are undergoing a constant change. E. g., the application of machinery produces a change in the distribution of the instruments of production as well as in that of products, and modern land ownership on a large scale is as much the result of modern trade and modern industry, as that of the application of the latter to agriculture.

All of these questions resolve themselves in the last instance to this: How do general historical conditions affect production and what part does it play at all in the course of history? It is evident that this question can be taken up only in connection with the discussion and analysis of production.

Yet in the trivial form in which these questions are raised above, they can be answered just as briefly. In the case of all conquests three ways lie open. The conquering people may impose its own methods of production upon the conquered (e. g. the English in Ireland in the nineteenth century, partly also in India); or, it may allow everything to remain as it was contenting itself with tribute (e. g. the Turks and the Romans); or, the two systems by mutually modifying each other may result in something new, a synthesis (which partly resulted from the Germanic conquests). In all of these conquests the method of production, be it of the conquerors, the conquered, or the one resulting from a combination of both, determines the nature of the new distribution which comes into play. Although the latter appears now as the prerequisite condition of the new period of production, it is in itself but a product of production, not of production belonging to history in general, but of production relating to a definite historical period. The Mongols with their devastations in Russia e. g. acted in accordance with their system of production, for which sufficient pastures on large uninhabited stretches of country are the main prerequisite. The Germanic barbarians, with whom agriculture carried on with the aid of serfs was the traditional system of production and who were accustomed to lonely life in the country, could introduce the same conditions in the Roman provinces so much easier since the concentration of landed property which had taken place there, died away completely with the older systems of agriculture. There is a prevalent tradition that in certain periods robbery constituted the only source of living. But in order to be able to plunder, there must be something to plunder, i. e. there must be production.[160] And even the method of plunder is determined by the method of production. A stockjobbing nation[161] e. g. can not be robbed in the same manner as a nation of shepherds.

In the case of the slave the instrument of production is robbed directly. But then the production of the country in whose interest he is robbed, must be so organized as to admit of slave labor, or (as in South America, etc.) a system of production must be introduced adapted to slavery.

Laws may perpetuate an instrument of production, e. g. land, in certain families. These laws assume an economic importance if large landed property is in harmony with the system of production prevailing in society, as is the case e. g. in England. In France agriculture had been carried on on a small scale in spite of the large estates, and the latter were, therefore, broken up by the Revolution. But how about the legislative attempt to perpetuate the minute subdivision of the land? In spite of these laws land ownership is concentrating again. The effect of legislation on the maintenance of a system of distribution and its resultant influence on production are to be determined elsewhere.

c. Exchange and Circulation. Circulation is but a certain aspect of exchange, or it may be defined as exchange considered as a whole. Since *exchange* is an intermediary factor between production and its dependent, distribution, on the one hand, and consumption, on the other; and since the latter appears but as a constituent of production, exchange is manifestly also a constituent part of production.

In the first place, it is clear that the exchange of activities and abilities which takes place in the sphere of production falls directly within the latter and constitutes one of its essential elements. In the second place, the same is true of the exchange of products, in so far as it is a means of completing a certain product, designed for immediate consumption. To that extent exchange constitutes an act included in production. Thirdly, the so-called exchange between dealers and dealers[162] is by virtue of its organization determined by production, and is itself a species of productive activity. Exchange appears to be independent of and indifferent to production only in the last stage when products are exchanged directly for consumption. But in the first place, there is no exchange without a division of labor, whether natural or as a result of historical development; secondly, private exchange implies the existence of private production; thirdly, the intensity of exchange, as well as its extent and character are determined by the degree of development and organization of production, as e. g. exchange between city and country, exchange in the country, in the city, etc. Exchange thus appears in all its aspects to be directly included in or determined by production.

The result we arrive at is not that production, distribution, exchange, and consumption are identical, but that they are all members of one entity, different sides of one unit. Production predominates not only over production itself in the opposite sense of that term, but over the other elements as well. With it the process constantly starts over again. That exchange and consumption can not be the predominating elements is self evident. The same is true of distribution in the narrow sense of distribution of products; as for distribution in the sense of distribution of the agents of production, it is itself but a factor of production. A definite [form of] production thus determines the [forms of] consumption, distribution, exchange, and *also the mutual relations between these various elements.* Of course, production *in its one-sided form* is in its turn influenced by other elements; e. g. with the expansion of the market, i. e. of the sphere of exchange, production grows in volume and is subdivided to a greater extent.

With a change in distribution, production undergoes a change; as e. g. in the case of concentration of capital, of a change in the distribution of population in city and country, etc.

Finally, the demands of consumption also influence production. A mutual interaction takes place between the various elements. Such is the case with every organic body.

3. The Method of Political Economy

When we consider a given country from a politico-economic standpoint, we begin with its population, then analyze the latter according to its subdivision into classes, location in city, country, or by the sea, occupation in different branches of production; then we study its exports and imports, annual production and consumption, prices of commodities, etc. It seems to be the correct procedure to commence with the real and concrete aspect of conditions as they are; in the case of political economy, to commence with population which is the basis and the author of the entire productive activity of society. Yet, on closer consideration it proves to be wrong. Population is an abstraction, if we leave out e. g. the classes of which it consists. These classes, again, are but an empty word, unless we know what are the elements on which they are based, such as wage-labor, capital, etc. Those imply, in their turn, exchange, division of labor, prices, etc. Capital, e. g. does not mean anything without wage-labor, value, money, price, etc. If we start out, therefore, with population, we do so with a chaotic conception of the whole, and by closer analysis we will gradually arrive at simpler ideas; thus we shall proceed from the imaginary concrete to loss and less complex abstractions, until we get at the simplest conception. This once attained, we might start on our return journey until we would finally come back to population, but this time not as a chaotic notion of an integral whole, but as a rich aggregate of many conceptions and relations. The former method is the one which political economy had adopted in the past at its inception. The economists of the seventeenth century, e. g., always started out with the living aggregate: population, nation, state, several states, etc., but in the end they invariably arrived, by means of analysis, at certain leading, abstract general principles, such as division of labor, money, value, etc. As soon as these separate elements had been more or less established by abstract reasoning, there arose the systems of political economy which start from simple conceptions, such as labor, division of labor, demand, exchange value, and conclude with state, international exchange and world market. The latter is manifestly the scientifically correct method. The concrete is concrete, because it is a combination of many objects with different destinations, i. e. a unity of diverse elements. In our thought, it therefore appears as a process of synthesis, as a result, and not as a starting point, although it is the real starting point and, therefore, also the starting point of observation and conception. By the former method the complete conception passes into an abstract definition; by the latter, the abstract definitions lead to the reproduction of the concrete subject in the course of reasoning. Hegel fell into the error, therefore, of considering the real as the result of self-coordinating, self-absorbed, and spontaneously operating thought, while the method of advancing from the abstract to the concrete is but a way of thinking by which the concrete is grasped and is reproduced in our mind as a concrete. It is by no means, however, the process which itself generates the concrete. The simplest economic category, say, exchange value, implies the existence of population, population that is engaged in production under certain conditions; it also implies the existence of certain types of family, clan, or state, etc. It can have no other existence except as an abstract one-sided relation of an already given concrete and living aggregate.

As a category, however, exchange value leads an antediluvian existence. And since our philosophic consciousness is so arranged that only the image of the man that it conceives appears to it as the real man and the world as it conceives it, as the real world; it mistakes the movement of categories for the real act of production (which unfortunately (?) receives only its impetus from outside) whose result is the world; that is true-here we have, however, again a tautology-in so far as the concrete aggregate is a thought aggregate, in so far as the concrete subject of our thought is in fact a product of thought, of comprehension; not, however, in the sense of a product of a self-emanating conception which works outside of and stands above observation and imagination, but of a mental consummation of observation and imagination. The whole, as it appears in our heads as a thought-aggregate, is the product of a thinking mind which grasps the world in the only way open to it, a way which differs from the one employed by the artistic, religious, or practical mind. The concrete subject continues to lead an independent existence after it has been grasped, as it did before, outside of the head, so long as the head contemplates it only speculatively, theoretically. So that in the employment of the theoretical method [in political economy], the subject, society, must constantly be kept in mind as the premise from which we start.

But have these simple categories no independent historical or natural existence antedating the more concrete ones? *Ça depend.* For instance, in his Philosophy of Law Hegel rightly starts out with possession, as the simplest legal relation of individuals. But there is no such thing as possession before the family or the relations of lord and serf, which are a great deal more concrete relations, have come into existence. On the other hand, one would be right in saying that there are families and clans which only *possess*, but do not *own* things. The simpler category thus appears as a relation of simple family and clan communities with respect to property. In earlier society the category appears as a simple relation of a developed organism, but the concrete substratum from which springs the relation of possession, is always implied. One can imagine an isolated savage in possession of things. But in that case possession is no legal relation. It is not true that the family came as the result of the historical evolution of possession. On the contrary, the latter always implies the existence of this "more concrete category of law." Yet so much may be said, that the simple categories are the expression of relations in which the less developed concrete entity may have been realized without entering into the manifold relations and bearings which are mentally expressed in the concrete category; but when the concrete entity attains fuller development it will retain the same category as a subordinate relation.

Money may exist and actually had existed in history before capital, or banks, or wage-labor came into existence. With that in mind, it may be said that the more simple category can serve as an expression of the predominant relations of an undeveloped whole or of the subordinate relations of a more developed whole, [relations] which had historically existed before the whole developed in the direction expressed in the more concrete category. In so far, the laws of abstract reasoning which ascends from the most simple to the complex, correspond to the actual process of history.

On the other hand, it may be said that there are highly developed but historically unripe forms of society in which the highest economic forms are to be found, such as co-operation, advanced division of labor, etc., and yet there is no money in existence, e. g. Peru.

In Slavic communities also, money, as well as exchange to which it owes its existence, does not appear at all or very little within the separate communities, but it appears on their boundaries in their inter-communal traffic; in general, it is erroneous to consider exchange as a constituent element originating within the community. It appears at first more in the mutual relations between different communities, than in those between the members of the same community. Furthermore, although money begins to play its part everywhere at an early stage, it plays in antiquity the part of a predominant element only in one-sidedly developed nations, viz. trading nations, and even in most cultured antiquity, in Greece and Rome, it attains its full development, which constitutes the prerequisite of modern bourgeois society, only in the period of their decay. Thus, this quite simple category attained its culmination in the past only at the most advanced stages of society. Even then it did not pervade (?) all economic relations; in Rome e. g. at the time of its highest development taxes and payments in kind remained the basis. As a matter of fact, the money system was fully developed there only so far as the army was concerned; it never came to dominate the entire system of labor.

Thus, although the simple category may have existed historically before the more concrete one, it can attain its complete internal and external development only in complex (?) forms of society, while the more concrete category has reached its full development in a less advanced form of society.

Labor is quite a simple category. The idea of labor in that sense, as labor in general, is also very old. Yet, "labor" thus simply defined by political economy is as much a modern category, as the conditions which have given rise to this simple abstraction. The monetary system, e. g. defines wealth quite objectively, as a thing (?)[163] in money. Compared with this point of view, it was a great step forward, when the industrial or commercial system came to see the source of wealth not in the object but in the activity of persons, viz. in commercial and industrial labor. But even the latter was thus considered only in the limited sense of a money producing activity. The physiocratic system [marks still further progress] in that it considers a certain form of labor, viz. agriculture, as the source of wealth, and wealth itself not in the disguise of money, but as a product in general, as the general result of labor. But corresponding to the limitations of the activity, this product is still only a natural product. Agriculture is productive, land is the source of production *par excellence*. It was a tremendous advance on the part of Adam Smith to throw aside all limitations which mark wealth-producing activity and [to define it] as labor in general, neither industrial, nor commercial, nor agricultural, or one as much as the other. Along with the universal character of wealth-creating activity we have now the universal character of the object defined as wealth, viz. product in general, or labor in general, but as past incorporated labor. How difficult and great was the transition, is evident from the way Adam Smith himself falls back from time to time into the physiocratic system. Now, it might seem as though this amounted simply to finding an abstract expression for the simplest relation into which men have been mutually entering as producers from times of yore, no matter under what form of society. In one sense this is true. In another it is not.

The indifference as to the particular kind of labor implies the existence of a highly developed aggregate of different species of concrete labor, none of which is any longer the predominant one. So do the most general abstractions commonly arise only where there is the highest concrete development, where one feature appears to be jointly possessed by many, and to be common to all. Then it can not be thought of any longer in one particular form. On the other hand, this abstraction of labor is but the result of a concrete aggregate of different kinds of labor. The indifference to the particular kind of labor corresponds to a form of society in which individuals pass with ease from one kind of work to another, which makes it immaterial to them what particular kind of work may fall to their share. Labor has become here, not only categorically but really, a means of creating wealth in general and is no longer grown together with the individual into one particular destination. This state of affairs has found its highest development in the most modern of bourgeois societies, the United States. It is only here that the abstraction of the category "labor," "labor in general," labor *sans phrase*, the starting point of modern political economy, becomes realized in practice. Thus, the simplest abstraction which modern political economy sets up as its starting point, and which expresses a relation dating back to antiquity and prevalent under all forms of society, appears in this abstraction truly realized only as a category of the most modern society. It might be said that what appears in the United States as an historical product, —viz. the indifference as to the particular kind of labor-appears among the Russians e. g. as a natural disposition. But it makes all the difference in the world whether barbarians have a natural predisposition which makes them applicable alike to everything, or whether civilized people apply themselves to everything. And, besides, this indifference of the Russians as to the kind of work they do, corresponds to their traditional practice of remaining in the rut of a quite definite occupation until they are thrown out of it by external influences.

This example of labor strikingly shows how even the most abstract categories, in spite of their applicability to all epochs-just because of their abstract character-are by the very definiteness of the abstraction a product of historical conditions as well, and are fully applicable only to and under those conditions.

The bourgeois society is the most highly developed and most highly differentiated historical organization of production. The categories which serve as the expression of its conditions and the comprehension of its own organization enable it at the same time to gain an insight into the organization and the conditions of production which had prevailed under all the past forms of society, on the ruins and constituent elements of which it has arisen, and of which it still drags along some unsurmounted remnants, while what had formerly been mere intimation has now developed to complete significance. The anatomy of the human being is the key to the anatomy of the ape. But the intimations of a higher animal in lower ones can be understood only if the animal of the higher order is already known. The bourgeois economy furnishes a key to ancient economy, etc. This is, however, by no means true of the method of those economists who blot out all historical differences and see the bourgeois form in all forms of society. One can understand the nature of tribute, tithes, etc., after one has learned the nature of rent. But they must not be considered identical.

Since, furthermore, bourgeois society is but a form resulting from the development of antagonistic elements, some relations belonging to earlier forms of society are frequently to be found in it but in a crippled state or as a travesty of their former self, as e. g. communal property. While it may be said, therefore, that the categories of bourgeois economy contain what is true of all other forms of society, the statement is to be taken *cum grano salis*. They may contain these in a developed, or crippled, or caricatured form, but always essentially different. The so-called historical development amounts in the last analysis to this, that the last form considers its predecessors as stages leading up to itself and perceives them always one-sidedly, since it is very seldom and only under certain conditions that it is capable of self-criticism; of course, we do not speak here of such historical periods which appear to their own contemporaries as periods of decay. The Christian religion became capable to assist us to an objective view of past mythologies as soon as it was ready for self-criticism to a certain extent, *dynamei* so-to-say. In the same way bourgeois political economy first came to understand the feudal, the ancient, and the oriental societies as soon as the self-criticism of the bourgeois society had commenced. So far as bourgeois political economy has not gone into the mythology of purely (?) identifying the bourgeois system with the past, its criticism of the feudal system against which it still had to wage war resembled Christian criticism of the heathen religions or Protestant criticism of Catholicism.

In the study of economic categories, as in the case of every historical and social science, it must be borne in mind that as in reality so in our mind the subject, in this case modern bourgeois society, is given and that the categories are therefore but forms of expression, manifestations of existence, and frequently but one-sided aspects of this subject, this definite society; and that, therefore, the origin of [political economy] *as a science* does not by any means date from the time to which it is referred *as such*. This is to be firmly held in mind because it has an immediate and important bearing on the matter of the subdivisions of the science.

For instance, nothing seems more natural than to start with rent, with landed property, since it is bound up with land, the source of all production and all existence, and with the first form of production in all more or less settled communities, viz. agriculture. But nothing would be more erroneous. Under all forms of society there is a certain industry which predominates over all the rest and whose condition therefore determines the rank and influence of all the rest.

It is the universal light with which all the other colors are tinged and are modified through its peculiarity. It is a special ether which determines the specific gravity of everything that appears in it.

Let us take for example pastoral nations (mere hunting and fishing tribes are not as yet at the point from which real development commences). They engage in a certain form of agriculture, sporadically. The nature of land-ownership is determined thereby. It is held in common and retains this form more or less according to the extent to which these nations hold on to traditions; such e. g. is land-ownership among the Slavs. Among nations whose agriculture is carried on by a settled population-the settled state constituting a great advance-where agriculture is the predominant industry, such as in ancient and feudal societies, even the manufacturing industry and its organization, as well as the forms of property which pertain to it, have more or less the characteristic features of the prevailing system of land ownership; [society] is then either entirely dependent upon agriculture, as in the case of ancient Rome, or, as in the middle ages, it imitates in its city relations the forms of organization prevailing in the country. Even capital, with the exception of pure money capital, has, in the form of the traditional working tool, the characteristics of land ownership in the Middle Ages.

The reverse is true of bourgeois society. Agriculture comes to be more and more merely a branch of industry and is completely dominated by capital. The same is true of rent. In all the forms of society in which land ownership is the prevalent form, the influence of the natural element is the predominant one. In those where capital predominates the prevailing element is the one historically created by society. Rent can not be understood without capital, nor can capital, without rent. Capital is the all dominating economic power of bourgeois society. It must form the starting point as well as the end and be developed before land-ownership is. After each has been considered separately, their mutual relation must be analyzed.

It would thus be impractical and wrong to arrange the economic categories in the order in which they were the determining factors in the course of history. Their order of sequence is rather determined by the relation which they bear to one another in modern bourgeois society, and which is the exact opposite of what seems to be their natural order or the order of their historical development. What we are interested in is not the place which economic relations occupy in the historical succession of different forms of society. Still less are we interested in the order of their succession "in idea" (*Proudhon*), which is but a hazy (?) conception of the course of history. We are interested in their organic connection within modern bourgeois society.

The sharp line of demarcation (abstract precision) which so clearly distinguished the trading nations of antiquity, such as the Phenicians and the Carthagenians, was due to that very predominance of agriculture. Capital as trading or money capital appears in that abstraction, where capital does not constitute as yet the predominating element of society. The Lombardians and the Jews occupied the same position among the agricultural nations of the middle ages.

As a further illustration of the fact that the same category plays different parts at different stages of society, we may mention the following: one of the latest forms of bourgeois society, viz. stock companies, appear also at its beginning in the form of the great chartered monopolistic trading companies. The conception of national wealth which is imperceptibly formed in the minds of the economists of the seventeenth century, and which partly continues to be entertained by those of the eighteenth century, is that wealth is produced solely for the state, but that the power of the latter is proportional to that wealth. It was as yet an unconsciously hypocritical way in which wealth announced itself and its own production as the aim of modern states considering the latter merely as a means to the production of wealth.

The order of treatment must manifestly be as follows: first, the general abstract definitions which are more or less applicable to all forms of society, but in the sense indicated above. Second, the categories which go to make up the inner organization of bourgeois society and constitute the foundations of the principal classes; capital, wage-labor, landed property; their mutual relations; city and country; the three great social classes, the exchange between them; circulation, credit (private). Third, the organization of bourgeois society in the form of a state, considered in relation to itself; the "unproductive" classes; taxes; public debts; public credit; population; colonies; emigration. Fourth, the international organization of production; international division of labor; international exchange; import and export; rate of exchange. Fifth, the world market and crises.

4. Production, Means of Production, and Conditions of Production, the Relations of Production and Distribution.[164] The Connection Between Form of State and Property on the One Hand and Relations of Production and Distribution(1) on the Other. Legal Relations. Family Relations.

Notes on the points to be mentioned here and not to be omitted:[165]

1. *War* attains complete development before peace; how certain economic phenomena, such as wage-labor, machinery, etc., are developed at an earlier date through war and in armies than within bourgeois society. The connection between productive force and the means of communication is made especially plain in the case of the army.

2. The relation between the idealistic and realistic methods of writing history; namely, the so-called history of civilization which is all a history of religion and states.

In this connection something may be said of the different methods hitherto employed in writing history. The so-called objective [method]. The subjective. (The moral and others). The philosophic.

3. *Secondary and tertiary.* Conditions of production which have been taken over or transplanted; in general, those that are not original. Here [is to be treated] the effect of international relations.

4. Objections to the materialistic character of this view. Its relation to naturalistic materialism.

5. The dialectics of the conceptions productive force (means of production) and relation of production, dialectics whose limits are to be determined and which does not do away with the concrete difference.

6. The unequal relation between the development of material production and art, for instance. In general, the conception of progress is not to be taken in the sense of the usual abstraction. In the case of art, etc., it is not so important and difficult to understand this disproportion as in that of practical social relations, e. g. the relation between education in the United States and Europe. The really difficult point, however, that is to be discussed here is that of the unequal (?) development of relations of production as legal relations. As, e. g., the connection between Roman civil law (this is less true of criminal and public law) and modern production.

7. This conception of development appears to imply necessity. On the other hand, justification of accident. Varia. (Freedom and other points). (The effect of means of communication). World history does not always appear in history as the result of world history.

8. The starting point [is to be found] in certain facts of nature embodied subjectively and objectively in clans, races, etc.

4. Produktion, Produktionsmittel und Produktionsverhältnisse. Produktionsverhältnis und Verkehrsverhältnisse. Staats- und Eigenthumsformen im Verhältnis zu den Produktions- und Verkehrsverhältnissen. Rechtsverhältnisse. Familienverhältnisse.

Notabene in bezug auf Punkte, die hier zu erwähnen und nicht vergessen werden dürfen:

1. Der *Krieg* ist früher ausgebildet, wie der Frieden: [Auszuführen wäre] die Art, wie durch den Krieg und in den Armeen etc. gewisse ökonomische Verhältnisse wie Lohnarbeit, Maschinerie etc. früher entwickelt [werden] als im Inneren der bürgerlichen Gesellschaft. Auch das Verhältnis von Produktivkraft und Verkehrsverhältnissen wird besonders anschaulich in der Armee.

2. Verhältnis der bisherigen idealen Geschichtsschreibung zur realen. Namentlich die sogenannte Kulturgeschichte, die alle Religions-und Staatengeschichte.

Bei der Gelegenheit kann auch etwas gesagt werden über die verschiedenen Arten der bisherigen Geschichtsschreibung. Sogenannte objektive. Subjektive. (Moralische und andere.) Philosophische.

3. *Sekundäres und Tertiäres.* Ueberhaupt *abgeleitete, übertragene* , nicht ursprüngliche Produktionsverhältnisse. Hier [ist das] Einspielen der internationalen Verhältnisse [zu behandeln].

4. Vorwürfe über Materialismus dieser Auffassung. Verhältnis zum naturalistischen Materialismus.

5. Dialektik der Begriffe Produktivkraft (Produktionsmittel) und Produktionsverhältnis, eine Dialektik, deren Grenzen zu bestimmen sind und den realen Unterschied nicht aufhebt.

6. Das unegale Verhältnis der Entwicklung der materiellen Produktion zum Beispiel zur künstlerischen. Ueberhaupt ist der Begriff des Fortschritts nicht in der gewöhnlichen Abstraktion zu fassen. Bei der Kunst etc. ist diese Disproportion noch nicht so wichtig und schwierig zu

fassen als innerhalb praktisch-sozialer Verhältnisse selbst, zum Beispiel das Bildungsverhältnis der Vereinigten Staaten zu Europa. Der eigentlich schwierige Punkt, der hier zu erörtern, ist aber der, wie die Produktionsverhältnisse als Rechtsverhältnisse in ungleiche (?) Entwicklung treten. Also zum Beispiel das Verhältnis des römischen Privatrechts (im Kriminalrecht und öffentlichen ist das wenige der Fall) zur modernen Produktion.

7. Diese Auffassung erscheint als nothwendige Entwicklung. Aber Berechtigung des Zufalls. Varia.[166] (Die Freiheit und anderes noch.) (Einwirkung der Kommunikationsmittel.) Weltgeschichte eigentlich[167] nicht immer in der Geschichte als weltgeschicht[liches] Resultat.

8. Der Ausgangspunkt [ist] natürlich von der Naturbestimmtheit [zu nehmen]; subjektiv und objektiv, Stämme, Rassen etc.

It is well known that certain periods of highest development of art stand in no direct connection with the general development of society, nor with the material basis and the skeleton structure of its organization. Witness the example of the Greeks as compared with the modern nations or even Shakespeare. As regards certain forms of art, as e. g. the epos, it is admitted that they can never be produced in the world-epoch making form as soon as art as such comes into existence; in other words, that in the domain of art certain important forms of it are possible only at a low stage of its development. If that be true of the mutual relations of different forms of art within the domain of art itself, it is far less surprising that the same is true of the relation of art as a whole to the general development of society. The difficulty lies only in the general formulation of these contradictions. No sooner are they specified than they are explained. Let us take for instance the relation of Greek art and of that of Shakespeare's time to our own. It is a well known fact that Greek mythology was not only the arsenal of Greek art, but also the very ground from which it had sprung. Is the view of nature and of social relations which shaped Greek imagination and Greek [art] possible in the age of automatic machinery, and railways, and locomotives, and electric telegraphs? Where does Vulcan come in as against Roberts & Co.; Jupiter, as against the lightning rod; and Hermes, as against the Credit Mobilier? All mythology masters and dominates and shapes the forces of nature in and through the imagination; hence it disappears as soon as man gains mastery over the forces of nature. What becomes of the Goddess Fame side by side with Printing House Square?[168] Greek art presupposes the existence of Greek mythology, i. e. that nature and even the form of society are wrought up in popular fancy in an unconsciously artistic fashion. That is its material. Not, however, any mythology taken at random, nor any accidental unconsciously artistic elaboration of nature (including under the latter all objects, hence [also] society). Egyptian mythology could never be the soil or womb which would give birth to Greek art. But in any event [there had to be] a mythology. In no event [could Greek art originate] in a society which excludes any mythological explanation of nature, any mythological attitude towards it and which requires from the artist an imagination free from mythology.

Looking at it from another side: is Achilles possible side by side with powder and lead? Or is the Iliad at all compatible with the printing press and steam press? Does not singing and reciting and the muses necessarily go out of existence with the appearance of the printer's bar, and do not, therefore, disappear the prerequisites of epic poetry?

But the difficulty is not in grasping the idea that Greek art and epos are bound up with certain forms of social development. It rather lies in understanding why they still constitute with us a source of aesthetic enjoyment and in certain respects prevail as the standard and model beyond attainment.

A man can not become a child again unless he becomes childish. But does he not enjoy the artless ways of the child and must he not strive to reproduce its truth on a higher plane? Is not the character of every epoch revived perfectly true to nature in child nature? Why should the social childhood of mankind, where it had obtained its most beautiful development, not exert an eternal charm as an age that will never return? There are ill-bred children and precocious children. Many of the ancient nations belong to the latter class. The Greeks were normal children. The charm their art has for us does not conflict with the primitive character of the social order from which it had sprung. It is rather the product of the latter, and is rather due to the fact that the unripe social conditions under which the art arose and under which alone it could appear can never return.

(End of Manuscript.)

Footnotes

1. Aristotle, d. Rep. L. l, c. 9 (edit. I Bekkeri Oxonii, 1837)

    "ἑκάστου γὰρ κτήματος διττὴ ἡ χρῆσις ἐστιν ... ἡ μὲν οἰκεία, ἡ δ᾽ οὐκ οἰκεια τοῦ ᾽πράγματος, οἷον ὑποδηματος ἥ τε ὑπόδησις καὶ ἡ μεταβλητική. Ἀμφότεραι γὰρ ὑποδηματος χρήσεις· καὶ γὰρ ἡ ἀλλαττομενος τῷ δεομένῳ ὑποδηματος ἀντὶ νομίσματος ἡ τροφῆς χρῆται τῷ ὑποδηματι ἥ ὑπόδημα, ἀλλ ᾽οὐ τὴν οἰκείαν χρῆσιν· οὐ γὰρ ἀλλαγης ἕνεκεν γέγονεν. Τὸν αὐτον δὲ τρόπον ἔχει καὶ περὶ τῶν ἄλλων κτημάτων."

    ("Of everything which we possess there are two uses: —one is the proper, and the other the improper or secondary use of it. For example, a shoe is used for wear, and is used for exchange; both are uses of the shoe. He who gives a shoe in exchange for money or food to him who wants one, does indeed use the shoe as a shoe, but this is not its proper or primary purpose, for a shoe is not made to be an object of barter. The same may be said of all possessions." The Politics of Aristotle, translated into English by B. Jowett, Oxford, 1885, v. I., p. 15.)

2. That is the reason why German compilers are so fond of dwelling on use-value, calling it a "good." See e. g. L. Stein, "System der Staatswissenschaften," v. I., chapter on "goods" (Gütter). For intelligent information on "goods" one must turn to treatises on commodities.

3. A ridiculous presumption has gained currency of late to the effect that common property in its primitive form is specifically a Slavonian, or even exclusively Russian form. It is the primitive form which we can prove to have existed among Romans, Teutons, and Celts; and of which numerous examples are still to be found in India, though in a partly ruined state. A closer study of the Asiatic, especially of Indian forms of communal ownership would show how from the different forms of primitive communism different forms of its dissolution have been developed. Thus e. g. the various original types of Roman and Teutonic private property can be traced back to various forms of Indian communism.

4. "La Ricchezza è una ragione tra due persone." ("Value is a relation between two persons") Galiani, "Della Moneta," p. 220 in vol. II. of Custodi's collection of "Scrittori classici Italiani di Economia Politica. Parte Moderna," Milano, 1803.

5. "In its natural state, matter ... is always destitute of value." McCulloch, "A Discourse on the Rise, Progress, Peculiar Objects, and Importance of Political Economy," 2nd edition, Edinburgh, 1825, pg. 48. It is evident how even a McCulloch stands above the fetishism of German "thinkers", who declare "matter" and half a dozen other foreign things to be elements of value. Cf. e. g. L. Stein, l. c. v. I., p. 110.

6. Berkeley, *The Querist*, London, 1750.

7. Thomas Cooper, Lectures on the Elements of Political Economy, London, 1831, p. 99.

8. F. List could never grasp the difference between labor as a source of use-value and labor as the creator of certain social form of wealth or exchange value, because comprehension was altogether foreign to his practical mind; he therefore saw in the modern English economists mere plagiarists of Moses, the Egyptian.

9. It can be readily understood what kind of "service" is rendered by the category "service" to economists of the type of J. B. Say and F. Bastiat, whose pondering sagacity, as Malthus has justly remarked, always abstracts from the specially definite forms of economic relations.

10. "Egli è proprio ancora delle misure d'aver si fatta relazione colle cose misurate, che in certo modo la misurata divien misura della misurante." Montanari, Della Moneta, p. 48 in v. III of Custodi's "Scrittori classici Italiani di Economia Politica. Parte Antica." ("It is the property of measure to be in such a relation to the things measured, that in a certain way the thing measured becomes the measure of the measuring thing.")

11. It is in that sense that Aristotle (see the passage quoted at the beginning of this chapter) conceives exchange value.

12. This expression is used by Genovesi.

13. Aristotle makes the same remark with reference to the private family as the primitive community. But the primitive form of family is the tribal family, from the historical dissolution of which the private family develops. ἐν μὲν οὖν τῇ πρώτῃ κοινωνίᾳ (τοῦτο δ̓ 'ἐστὶν οἰκία) φανερὸν ὅτι οὐδέν ἐστιν ἔργον αὐτῆς (namely τῆς ἀλλαγῆς) "And in the first community, which is the family, this art is obviously of no use." Jowett's transl. l. c.)

14. "Money is, in fact, only the instrument for carrying on buying and selling (but, if you please, what do you understand by buying and selling?) and the consideration of it no more forms a part of the science of political economy, than the consideration of ships, or steam engines, or of any other instrument employed to facilitate the production and distribution of wealth." Th. Hodgskin, Popular Political Economy, etc. London, 1827, p. 178, 179.

15. A comparative study of the writings and characters of Petty and Boisguillebert, outside of the light which it would throw upon the difference of French and English society at the end of the seventeenth and the beginning of the eighteenth centuries, would disclose the origin of the national contrast between English and French Political Economy. The same contrast reasserts itself in Ricardo and Sismondi.

16. Petty had illustrated the productive power inherent in the division of labor on a much grander scale than that was done later by Adam Smith. See his "Essay concerning the multiplication of mankind, etc.," 3rd edition, 1686, p. 35-36. He not only brings out the advantages of the division of labor on the example of the manufacture of a watch, as Adam Smith did later on that of a needle, but considers also a city and an entire country from the point of view of a large manufacturing establishment. The Spectator, of November 26, 1711, refers to this "illustration of the admirable Sir William Petty." McCulloch is, therefore, mistaken when he supposes that the Spectator confounded Petty with a writer forty years his junior. See McCulloch, "The Literature of Political Economy, a classified catalogue," London, 1845, p. 105. Petty is conscious of being the founder of a new science. His method, he says, "is not yet very usual, for instead of using only comparative and superlative Words, and intellectual Arguments," he has undertaken to speak "in Terms of Number, Weight or Measure; to use only Arguments of Sense, and to consider only such Causes, as have visible Foundations in Nature; leaving those that depend upon the mutable Minds, Opinions, Appetites, and Passions of particular Men, to the Consideration of others." (Political Arithmetick, etc., London, 1699. Preface.) (A new edition of "The Economic Writings of Sir William Petty," edited by Chas. Henry Hull, has been published by the University Press at Cambridge, 1899. The above passage will be found in vol. I., p. 244. The further references are given to this new, more accessible edition. Translator.) His wonderful keenness shows itself e. g. in the proposal to transport "all the moveables and people of Ireland, and of the Highlands of Scotland ... into the rest of Great Britain." Thereby much labor-time would be saved, the productivity of labor increased, and "the King and his Subjects would thereby become more Rich and Strong." (Political Arithmetick, ch. 4, p. 285.) Or in the chapter of his Political Arithmetic in which he

proves that England's mission is the conquest of the world's market at a time when Holland still played the leading part as a trading nation and France seemed to be on the way of becoming the ruling trading Power: "That the King of England's Subjects, have Stock competent and convenient, to drive the Trade of the whole Commercial World" (l. c., ch. 10, p. 311). "That the Impediments of England's greatness are but contingent and removable" (l. c., ch. 5, p. 298). A singular humor pervades all his writings. Thus, he shows that it was by material means that Holland-at that time the model country with English economists, just as England is with continental economists to-day —conquered the world market "without such Angelical Wits and Judgments, as some attribute to the Hollanders" (l. c., p. 258). He advocates "Liberty of Conscience" as a condition of trade, because "Dissenters ... are ... patient Men, and such as believe that Labour and Industry is their Duty towards God," and "They believe that ... for those who have less Wealth, to think they have the more Wit and Understanding, especially of the things of God which they think chiefly belong to the Poor." "From whence it follows that Trade is not fixt to any species of Religion as such; but rather ... to the Heterodox part of the whole" (l. c., p. 262-264). He advocates an "allowance by Publick Tax" for those "who live by begging, cheating, stealing, gaming, borrowing without intention of restoring," because "it were more for the publick profit" to tax the country for such persons "than to suffer them to spend extravagantly, at the only charge of careless, credulous, and good natured People" (p. 269-270). But he is opposed to taxes which transfer the wealth from industrious people "to such as do nothing at all, but eat and drink, sing, play, and dance; nay such as study the Metaphysicks" (ibid.). Petty's writings are rarities of the bookseller's trade and are to be found only in scattered poor old editions, which is the more surprising since William Petty was not only the father of English Political Economy, but also the ancestor of Henry Petty, alias Marquis of Lansdowne, the nestor of the English Whigs. However, the Lansdowne family could hardly bring out a complete edition of Petty's works without prefacing it with his biography, and what can be said of most origins of the great Whig families holds good also in this case, viz., "the less said of them the better." The keen-witted but cynical army surgeon who was as ready to plunder in Ireland under the shield of Cromwell as to crawl before Charles II. to get the title of baron which he needed for his plunderings, is a model hardly fit for public exhibition. Besides that, Petty seeks to prove in most of his writings which he published in his lifetime, that England's prosperity reached its climax under Charles II., a heterodox view for the hereditary exploiters of the "glorious revolution."

17. In contrast with the "black art of finance" of his time, Boisguillebert says: "La science financière n'est que la connaissance approfondie des intérêts de l'agriculture et du commerce." Le Détail de la France, 1697. Eugène Daire's edition of Economistes financiers du XVIII. siècle, Paris, 1843, vol. I., p. 241.

18. But not *Romance* Political Economy, since the Italians reproduce the contrast between the English and French economists in the two respective schools of Naples and Milan, while the Spaniards of the earlier period are either pure Mercantilists; modified mercantilists like Ustariz; or, like Jovellanos (see his Obras, Barcelona, 1839-40), hold to the "golden mean" with Adam Smith.

19. "La véritable richesse ... jouissance entière, non seulement des besoins de la vie, mais même de tous les superflus et de tout, ce qui peut fair plaisir à la sensualité," Boisguillebert, "Dissertation sur la nature de la richesse," etc., l. c., p. 403. But while Petty was a frivolous, rapacious and unprincipled adventurer, Boisguillebert, though an intendant under Louis XIV, championed the interests of the oppressed classes with a daring that was equal to his keenness of mind.

20. The French Socialism of the Proudhon type suffers from the same national hereditary disease.

21. "Benjamin Franklin, The Works of, etc.," ed. by I. Sparks, vol. II., Boston, 1836. "A Modest Inquiry into the Nature and Necessity of a Paper Currency."

22. L. c., p. 265.

23. L. c., p. 267.

24. L. c., "Remarks and Facts relative to the American Paper Money," 1764.

25. See "Papers on American Politics; Remarks and Facts relative to the American Paper Money," 1764, l. c.

26. See e. g. Galiani, "Della Moneta," in vol. 3 of Scrittori Classici italiani di Economia politica (Published by Custodi). Parte Moderna, Milano, 1803. "La fatica, he says, è l'unica che dà valore alla cosa" ("only effort can give value to any thing"). The designation of labor as "fatica," strain, effort, is characteristic of the southerner.

27. Steuart's work, "An Inquiry into the Principles of Political Economy, being an Essay on the Science of Domestic Policy in Free Nations," appeared first in London in two quarto volumes in the year 1767, ten years before Adam Smith's "Wealth of Nations." I quote from the Dublin edition of 1770. (The references to pages are the same for the standard London edition of 1767, except where otherwise stated. Translator.)

28. Steuart, l. c., vol. I., p. 181-183.

29. Steuart, l. c., vol. I., p. 361-362.

30. See chapter I., book II., vol. I. "of the reciprocal connections between Trade and Industry" (Translator).

31. He declares, therefore, the patriarchal form of agriculture which is devoted to the direct production of use-values for the owner of the land, to be an "abuse," not in Sparta, or Rome, or even in Athens, but in the industrial countries of the eighteenth century. This "abusive agriculture" is not "trade," but a "direct means of subsisting." Just as capitalistic agriculture clears the country of superfluous mouths, so does the capitalistic mode of manufacture clear the factory of superfluous hands.

32. Thus e. g., Adam Smith says: "Equal quantities of labour, at all times and places, may be said to be of equal value to the labourer. In his ordinary state of health, strength and spirits, in the ordinary degree of his skill and dexterity, he must always lay down the same portion of his ease, his liberty, and his happiness. The price which he pays must always be the same, whatever may be the quantity of goods which he receives in return for it. Of these, indeed, it may sometimes purchase a greater and sometimes a smaller quantity; but it is their value which varies, not that of the labour which purchases them....Labour alone, therefore, never varying in its own value ... is their [commodities'] real price, etc. Adam Smith (Book I., ch. V., p. 34, Oxford, 1869. Translator.)

33. David Ricardo, "On the Principles of Political Economy and Taxation," 3rd edition, London, 1821, p. 3.

34. Sismondi, "Etudes sur l'Economie Politique," t. II., Bruxelles, 1837. "C'est l'opposition entre la valeur usuelle ... et la valeur échangeable à laquelle le commerce a reduit toute chose," p. 161. [Paris edition, p. 229, Transl.]

35. Sismondi l. c., p. 163-166 seq. [Paris edition, 230 etf. Transl.]

36.   Perhaps the silliest to be found are the annotations of J. B. Say to the French translation of Ricardo, made by Constancio, and the most pedantically arrogant are the remarks of Mr. MacLeod in his newly published "Theory of Exchange," London, 1858.

37.   This objection raised against Ricardo by bourgeois economists was taken up later by the socialists. Having assumed the correctness of the formula, they charged the practice with contradiction to the theory and appealed to bourgeois society to realize in practice the conclusions which were supposed to follow from its theoretical principles. That was at least the way in which the English socialists turned Ricardo's formula of exchange value against political economy. It remained for Mr. Proudhon not only to proclaim the fundamental principle of old society as the principle of the new, but also to declare himself the discoverer of the formula in which Ricardo summed up the combined results of classical English political economy. It has been proven that the utopian interpretation of the Ricardian formula was about forgotten in England when Mr. Proudhon "discovered" it on the other side of the Canal. (Cf. my work: "Misère de la Philosophie," etc., Paris, 1847, paragraph on la valeur constituée.)

38.   True, Aristotle sees that the exchange value of commodities underlies their prices: "ὅτι ἡ ἀλλαγὴ ἦν πρὶν τὸ νόμισμα εἶναι, δῆλον· διαφέρει γὰρ οὐδὲν ἢ εἰ κλίναι πέντε ἀντὶ οἰκίας, ἢ ὅσου αἱ πέντε κλῖναι." ("It is clear that exchange existed before coin. For it does not make any difference whether you give five beds for a house, or as much money as five beds are worth"). On the other hand, since commodities acquire only in price the form of exchange value with respect to one another, he makes them commensurable through money. "Διὸ δεῖ πάντα τετιμῆσθαι· οὕτω γὰρ ἀεὶ ἔσται ἀλλαγή, εἰ δὲ τοῦτο, κοινωνία. Τὸ δὴ νόμισμα ὥσπερ μέτρον σύμμετρα ποιῆσαν ἰσάζει, οὔτε γὰρ ἂν μὴ οὔσης ἀλλαγῆς κοινωνία ἦν, οὔτ᾽ ἀλλαγὴ ἰσότητος μὴ οὔτ᾽ ἰσότης, μὴ οὔσης συμμετρίας." ("Therefore all has to be appraised. In that way exchange may always take place, and, with it, society can exist. Coin, like measure, makes everything commensurable and equal, for without exchange there would be no society, without equality there would be no exchange, and without commensurability, no equality.") He does not conceal from himself that these different objects measured by money are entirely incommensurable quantities. What he is after is the common unit of commodities as exchange values, which as an ancient Greek he was unable to find. He gets out of the difficulty by making commensurable through money what is in itself incommensurable, so far as it is necessary for practical purposes. "Τῇ μὲν οὖν ἀληθείᾳ ἀδύνατον τὰ τοσοῦτον διαφέροντα σύμμετρα γενέσθαι, πρὸς δὲ τὴν χρείαν ἐνδέχεται ἱκανῶς." ("In truth it is impossible to make things that are so different, commensurable, but for practical purposes it is permissible.") Aristotle, Ethica Nicomachea. l. 5, c. 8, edit. Bekkeri. Oxonii, 1837.

39.   The peculiar circumstance that, while the ounce of gold serves in England as the unit of the standard of money, it is not divided into aliquot parts has been explained as follows: "Our coinage was originally adapted to the employment of silver only-hence an ounce of silver can always be divided into a certain adequate number of pieces of coin; but as gold was introduced at a later period into a coinage adapted only to silver, an ounce of gold cannot be coined into an adequate number of pieces." Maclaren: "A Sketch of the History of the Currency," p. 16, London, 1858.

40.   "Money may continually vary in value and yet be as good a measure of value as if it remained perfectly stationary. Suppose, for instance, it is reduced in value....Before the reduction, a guinea would purchase three bushels of wheat or 6 days' labour; subsequently it would purchase only 2 bushels of wheat, or 4 days 'labour. In both cases, the relations of wheat and labour to money being given, their mutual relations can be inferred; in other words, we can ascertain that a bushel of wheat is worth 2 days

'labour. This, which is all that measuring value implies, is as readily done after the reduction as before. The excellence of a thing as a measure of value is altogether independent of its own variableness in value" (p. 11, Bailey, "Money and its Vicissitudes." London, 1837).

41.   "Le monete lequali oggi sono ideali sono le piu antiche d'ogni nazione, e tutte furono un tempo reali (the latter assertion is too sweeping), e perchè erano reali con esse si contava." Galiani, "Della Moneta," l. c., p. 153 ("Coins which are ideal to-day [i. e., whose names no longer correspond to their value] are among the more ancient with every nation; at one time they were all real, and for that reason served for the purpose of counting.")

42.   The romantic A. Müller says: "According to our idea every independent sovereign has the right to name the metal money, and to give it a nominal social value, rank, standing and title (p. 276, v. II., A. H. Müller, "Die Elemente der Staatskunst," Berlin, 1809). As far as title is concerned the Hon. Hofrath is right; but he forgets the *substance*. How confused his "ideas" were, may be seen, e. g., from the following passage: "Everybody understands how much depends upon the right determination of the mint-price, especially in a country like England, where the government with *magnificent liberality* coins money gratuitously (Herr Müller seems to think that the members of the English government defray the mint expenses out of their own pockets), where it does not charge any mintage, etc., and thus if the mint-price of gold were set considerably above its market price, if instead of paying as now £3 17s. 10-1/2d. per 1 oz. of gold, it would set the price of an ounce of gold at £3 19s., all money would flow into the mint and exchanging for the silver contained there bring it into the market to be exchanged there for the cheaper gold; the latter would in the same manner be brought again to the mint and the entire coinage system would be upset" (l. c., p. 280-281). To preserve order in English coinage, Müller falls back on "disorder." While shilling and pence are mere names of certain parts of an ounce of gold represented by signs of silver and copper, he imagines that an ounce of gold is estimated in gold, silver and copper and thus confers upon the Englishmen the blessing of a triple standard of value. Silver as a measure of money, next to gold, was formally abolished only in 1816 by 56 George III., c. 68. As a matter of fact, it was legally abolished as early as 1734 by 14 George II., c. 42, and still earlier by actual practice. There were two circumstances that made A. Müller capable of a so-called higher conception of political economy: first, his wide ignorance of economic facts; second, his dilettanti-like visionary attitude toward philosophy.

43.   "Ἀνάχαρσις, πυνθανομένου τινὸς, πρὸς τί οἱ Ἕλληνες χρῶνται τῷ ἀργυρίῳ εἶπε πρὸς τὸ ἀριθμεῖν." (Athen. Deipn. l. IV. 49. v. 2, ed. Schweighäuser, 1802.) (When Anacharsis was asked for what purpose the Greeks used money, he replied, "For reckoning.")

44.   G. Garnier, one of the early French translators of Adam Smith, conceived the queer notion of fixing a proportion between the use of money of account and that of actual money. His proportion is 10 to 1. (G. Garnier, "Histoire de la Monnaie depuis les temps de la plus haute antiquité," etc., t. 1, p. 78.)

45.   The act of Maryland in 1723 by which tobacco was made the legal standard, but its value reduced to terms of English gold money, namely one penny equal to one pound of tobacco, reminds of the "leges barbarorum," in which, inversely, certain sums of money were expressed in terms of oxen, cows, etc. In that case neither gold nor silver, but the ox and the cow were the actual material of the money of account.

46.   Thus, we read, e. g., in the "Familiar Words" of Mr. David Urquhart: "The value of gold is to be measured by itself; how can any substance be the measure of its own worth in other things? The worth of gold is to be established by its own weight, under a false denomination of that weight-and an ounce is to be worth so many pounds and fractions of pounds. This is falsifying a measure, not establishing a standard."

47.   "Money is the measure of Commerce, and of the rate of everything, and therefore ought to be kept (as all other measures) as steady and invariable as may be. But this cannot be, if your money be made of two Metals, whose proportion ... constantly varies in respect of one another." John Locke: Some Considerations on the Lowering of Interest, etc., 1691 (p. 166, p. 65 in his Works 7 ed., London, 1768, vol. III.)

48.   Locke says among other things: " ... call that a Crown now, which before ... was but a part of a Crown.... An equal quantity of Silver is always the same Value with an equal quantity of Silver.... For if the abating 1-20 of the quantity of Silver of any Coin does not lessen its Value, the abating 19-20 of the quantity of the Silver of any Coin will not abate its Value. And so a single Penny, being called a Crown, will buy as much Spice, or Silk, or any other Commodity, as a Crown-Piece, which contains 20 times as much Silver.... Now [all that may be done] is giving a less quantity of Silver the Stamp and Denomination of a greater.... But 'tis Silver and not Names that pay Debts and purchase Commodities" (l. c., p. 135-145 passim). If to raise the value of money means nothing but to give any desired name to an aliquot part of a silver coin, e. g., to call an eighth part of an ounce of silver a penny, then money may really be rated as high as you please. At the same time, Locke answered Lowndes that the rise of the market price above the mint price was due not to the rise of the value of silver, but to the lighter silver coins. Seventy-seven clipped shillings do not weigh a particle more than 62 full-weighted ones. Finally he pointed out with perfect right that, aside from the loss of weight in the circulating coin, the market price of silver bullion in England could rise to some extent above its mint price, since the export of silver bullion was allowed while that of silver coin was prohibited (l. c., p. 54-116 passim). Locke was exceedingly careful not to touch upon the burning question of public debts, and no less carefully avoided the discussion of the delicate economic question, viz., the depreciation of the currency out of proportion to its real loss of silver, as was shown by the rate of exchange and the ratio of silver bullion to silver coin. We shall return to this question in its general form in the chapter on the Medium of Circulation. Nicholas Barbon in "A Discourse Concerning Coining the New Money Lighter, in Answer to Mr. Locke's Considerations, etc.," London, 1696, tried in vain to entice Locke to difficult ground.

49.   Steuart, l. c., v. II., p. 154.

50.   The Querist, l. c., (p. 5-6-7.) The "Queries on Money" are generally clever. Among other things Berkeley is perfectly right in saying that by their progress the North American colonies "make it plain as daylight, that gold and silver are not so necessary for the wealth of a nation, as the vulgar of all ranks imagine."

51.   Price means here real equivalent in the sense commonly employed by English economic writers in the seventeenth century.

52.   Steuart, l. c., v. II., p. 154, 299 [1st London edition, of 1767, v. I., p. 526-531. Transl.].

53.   On the occasion of the last commercial crisis the ideal African money received loud praise from certain English quarters, after its seat was this time moved from the coast to the heart of Barbary. The freedom of the Berbers from commercial and industrial crises was ascribed to the ideal unit of measure of their bars. Would it not have been

simpler to say that trade and industry are the *conditio sine qua non* of commercial and industrial crises?

54.   The Currency Question, The Gemini Letters, London, 1844, p. 260-272, passim.

55.   John Gray: "The Social System. A Treatise on the Principle of Exchange, Edinburgh, 1831." Compare with "Lectures on the Nature and Use of Money, Edinburgh, 1848," by the same author. After the February revolution Gray sent a memorial to the provisional French government, in which he instructs the latter that France is not in need of an "organization of labour," but of an "organization of exchange" of which the plan is fully worked out in his money system. Honest John did not suspect that sixteen years after the appearance of his "Social System" a patent for the same discovery would be taken out by the ingenious Proudhon.

56.   Gray, "The Social System," etc., p. 63: "Money should be merely a receipt, an evidence that the holder of it has either contributed certain value to the national stock of wealth or that he has acquired a right to the same value from some one who has contributed to it."

57.   An estimated value being previously put upon produce, let it be lodged in a bank, and drawn out again, whenever it is required, merely stipulating, by common consent, that he who lodges any kind of property in the proposed National Bank, may take out of it an equal value of whatever it may contain, instead of being obliged to draw out the self-same thing that he put in." L. c., p. 68.

58.   L. c., p. 16.

59.   Gray: "Lectures on Money, etc.," p. 182.

60.   L. c., p. 169.

61.   "The business of every country ought to be conducted on a national capital." John Gray, "The Social System," etc., p. 171.

62.   "The land to be transformed into national property." L. c., p. 298.

63.   See e. g. W. Thompson: "An Inquiry into the Distribution of Wealth, etc.," London, 1827. Bray, "Labour's Wrongs and Labour's Remedy," Leeds, 1839.

64.   Alfred Darimont's "De la Reforme des banques," Paris, 1856, may be considered as a compendium of this melodramatic theory of money.

65.   "Di due sorte è la moneta, ideale e reale; e a dui diversi usi è adoperata, a valutare le cose e a comperarle. Per valutare è buona la moneta ideale, cosi come la reale e forse anche più. L'altro uso della moneta è di comperare quelle cose istesse, ch'ella apprezza ... i prezzi e i contratti si valutano in moneta ideale e si eseguiscono in moneta reale." Galiani, l. c., p. 112 sq. ("Money is of two kinds, ideal and real; and is adapted to two different uses: to determine the value of things and to buy them. For the purpose of valuation ideal money is as good as real and perhaps even better. The other use of money is to buy the same things which it appraises ... prices and contracts are determined in ideal money and are executed in real money.")

66.   This, of course, does not prevent the market price of commodities to be above or below their value. However, this consideration is foreign to simple circulation and belongs to quite another sphere to be considered later, when we shall investigate the relation between value and market price.

67.   How deeply some beautiful souls are wounded by the merely superficial aspect of the antagonism which asserts itself in buying and selling, may be seen from the following abstract from M. Isaac Pereire's: "Leçons sur l'industrie et les finances," Paris, 1832. The fact that the same Isaac in his capacity of inventor and dictator of the "Credit mobilier" has acquired the reputation of the wolf of the Paris Bourse shows what lurks behind the sentimental criticism of economics. Says Mr. Pereire at the time an apostle of St. Simons: "C'est parceque tous les individus sont isolés, séparés les uns des autres, soit dans leur travaux, soit pour la consommation, qu'il y a echange entre eux des produits de leur industrie respective. De la necessité de l'échange est derivée la necessité de determiner la valeur relative des objets. Les idées de la valeur et de l'échange sont donc intimement liées, et toutes deux dans leur forme actuelle exprime l'individualisme et l'antagonisme....Il n'y a lieu à fixer la valeur des produits que parcequ'il y a vente at achat, en d'autres termes, antagonisme entre les divers membres de la societé. Il n'y a lieu à s'occuper du prix, de valeur que là oú il y avait vente et echat, c'est à dire, oú chaque individu était obligé de lutter, pour se procurer les object nécessaires a l'entretien de son existence" (l. c., p. 2, 3 passim). ("Since individuals are isolated and separated from one another both in their labors and in consumption, exchange takes place between them in the products of their respective industries. From the necessity of exchange arises the necessity of determining the relative value of things. The ideas of value and exchange are thus intimately connected and both express in their actual form individualism and antagonism....The determination of values of products takes place only because there are sales and purchases, or, to put it differently, because there is an antagonism between different members of society. One has to occupy himself with price and value only where there is sale and purchase, that is to say, where every individual is obliged to struggle to procure for himself the objects necessary for the maintenance of his existence.")

68.   "L'argent n'est que le moyen et l'acheminement, au lieu que les denrées utiles à la vie sont la fin et le but." ("Money is but the ways and means, while the things useful in life are the end and object.") Boisguillebert: "Le Détail de la France," 1697, in Eugene Daires "Economistes financiers du XVIIIieme siècle, vol. I., Paris, 1843, p. 210.

69.   In November, 1807, William Spence published a pamphlet in England under the title: "Britain Independent of Commerce." The principle set forth in this pamphlet was further elaborated by William Cobbet in his "Political Register" under the virulent title, "Perish Commerce." To this James Mill replied in 1808 in his "Defence of Commerce" which contains the passage quoted above from his "Elements of Political Economy" (p. 190-193, Transl.). In his controversy with Sismondi and Malthus on commercial crises, J. B. Say appropriated this clever device, and as it would be difficult to point out with what new idea this comical "prince de la science" had enriched political economy, his continental admirers have trumpeted him as the man who had unearthed the treasure of the metaphysical balance of purchases and sales; as a matter of fact, his merits consisted rather of the impartiality with which he equally misunderstood his contemporaries, Malthus, Sismondi and Ricardo.

70.   The manner in which economists explain the different aspects of the commodity may be seen from the following examples:
"With money in possession, we have but one exchange to make in order to secure the object of desire, while with other surplus products we have two, the first of which (procuring the money) is infinitely more difficult than the second." (G. Opdyke, "A Treatise on Political Economy," New York, 1851, p. 277-278.)
"The superior saleableness of money is the exact effect or natural consequence of the less saleableness of commodities." (Th. Corbet, "An Inquiry into the Causes and Modes of the Wealth of Individuals." etc., London, 1841, p. 117.)

"Money has the quality of being always exchangeable for what it measures." (Bosanquet, "Metallic, Paper and Credit Currency," etc., London, 1842, p. 100.)

"Money can always buy other commodities, whereas other commodities can not always buy money." (Th. Tooke, "An Inquiry into the Currency Principle," 2d ed., London, 1844, p. 10.)

71. The same commodity can be bought and resold many times. It circulates, then, not merely as a commodity, but in a capacity which does not exist from the point of view of simple circulation, of the simple contrast of commodity and money.

72. The quantity of money is immaterial "pourvu qu'il y en ait assez pour maintenir les prix contractés par les denrées" (as long as it is sufficient to maintain the existing prices of commodities). Boisguillebert, l. c. p. 210. "If the circulation of commodities of four hundred millions required a currency of forty millions, and ... this proportion of one-tenth was the due level, estimating both currency and commodities in gold; then, if the value of commodities to be circulated increased to four hundred and fifty millions, from natural causes ... I should say the currency, in order to continue at its level, must be increased to forty-five millions." (William Blake, "Observations on the Effects Produced by the Expenditure of Government, etc.," London, 1823, p. 80.)

73. "E la velocità del giro del danaro, non la quantità dei metalli che fa apparir molto a poco il danaro." (Galiani, l. c. p. 99.) ("It is the rapidity of the circulation of money and not the quantity of metals that causes a greater or smaller amount of money to appear.")

74. An example of an extraordinary decline of metallic circulation from its average level was furnished by England in 1858, as may be seen from the following extract from the London Economist: "From the nature of the case (namely, the isolated nature of simple circulation) very exact data cannot be procured as to the amount of cash that is fluctuating in the market, and in the hands of the not banking classes. But, perhaps, the activity or the inactivity of the mints of the great commercial nations is one of the most likely indications in the variations of that amount. Much will be manufactured when it is wanted; and little when little is wanted.... At the English mint the coinage was in 1855 £9,245,000; 1856, £6,476,000; 1857, £5,293,855. During 1858 the mint had scarcely anything to do." (Economist, July 10, 1858.) But at the same time about eighteen million pounds sterling were lying in the bank vaults.

75. Dodd, "Curiosities of Industry," etc., London, 1854.

76. "The Currency Question Reviewed, etc., by a Banker." (Edinburgh, 1845, p. 69.) "Si un écu un peu usé etait reputé valoir quelque chose de moins qu'un écu tout neuf, la circulation se trouverait continuellement arrêtée, et il n'y aurait pas un seul payement qui ne fut matière à contestation." (G. Garnier, l. c. t. I., p. 24.) ("If an ecu slightly used would pass for a little less than an entirely new ecu, circulation would be continually interfered with, and not a payment would take place that would not give rise to controversy.")

77. W. Jacob, "An Inquiry Into the Production and Consumption of the Precious Metals." (London, 1831, vol. II., ch. XXVI.)

78. David Buchanan, "Observations on the Subjects Treated of in Dr. Smith's Inquiry on the Wealth of Nations," etc. (Edinburgh, 1841, p. 3.)

79. Henry Storch, "Cours d'Economic Politique." etc., avec des notes par J. B Say. Paris, 1823, tom. IV., p. 179. Storch published his work in French at St. Petersburg. J. B. Say immediately issued a Parisian reprint, supplemented with alleged "notes," which as a matter of fact contain nothing but commonplaces. Storch (see his "Considerations

sur la Nature du Revenue National," Paris, 1824) took by no means kindly to this annexation of his work by the "prince de la science."

80. Plato de Rep. L. II *"νόμισμα ξύμβολον τῆς ἀλλαγῆς."* ("Money symbol of exchange.") Opera omnia, etc., ed. G. Stallbumius, London, 1850, p. 304. Plato develops money only in two capacities-as a measure of value and a token of value, but demands, in addition to the token of value serving for home circulation, another one for trade between Greece and foreign countries. (See also Book V of his Laws.)

81. Aristotle, Ethic. Nicom, l. 5., ch. 8, l. c.: *οἷον δ᾽ ὑπάλλαγμα τῆς χρείας τὸ νόμισμα γέγονου κατὰ συνθήκην καὶ διὰ τοῦτο τοὔνομα ἔχει νόμισμα. ὅτι οὐ φύσει ἀλλὰ νόμῳ, καὶ ἐφ᾽ ἡμῖν μεταβαλεῖν καὶ ποιῆσαι ἄχρηστον."* ("In the satisfaction of wants money became the medium of exchange by agreement. And for that reason it bears the name *νόμισμα*, because it owes its existence, not to nature, but to law (*νόμῳ*), and it is in our power to change it and make it void.") Aristotle had a far more comprehensive and deep view of money than Plato. In the following passage he beautifully shows how barter between different communities creates the necessity of assigning the character of money to a specific commodity, i. e., one which has itself an intrinsic value. *"Ξενικωτέρας γὰρ γενομένης τῆς βοηθείας τῷ εἰσάγεσθαι ὧν ἐνδεεῖς καὶ ἐκπέμπειν ὧν ἐπλεόναζον, ἐξ ἀνάγκης ἡ τοῦ νομίσματος ἐπορίσθη χρῆσις· διὸ πρὸς τὰς ἀλλαγας τοιοῦτόν τι συνέθεντο πρὸς σφᾶς αὐτοὺς διδόναι καὶ λαμβάνειν, ὃ τῶν χρησίμων αὐτὸ ὂν εἶχε τὴν χρείαν εὐμεταχείριστον ... οἷον σίδηρος καὶ ἄργυρος κἂν εἴ τι τοιοῦτον ἕτερον".* (Arist. De Republica, l. i. p. 9, [secs. 7, 8] l. c.) ("When the inhabitants of one country became more dependent on those of another, and they imported what they needed and exported the surplus, money necessarily came into use ... and hence men agreed to employ in their dealings with each other something which was intrinsically useful and easily applicable to the purposes of life, for example, iron, silver and the like." Trans, by B. Jowett, "The Politics of Aristotle, Oxford, 1885, p. 16). This passage is quoted by Michel Chevalier, who either has not read Aristotle or did not understand him, to prove that in Aristotle's opinion currency must consist of a substance having intrinsic value. On the contrary, Aristotle says expressly that money as a mere medium of circulation seems to owe its existence to agreement or law, as is shown by its name *νόμισμα*, and that in reality it owes its utility as coin to its function and not to any intrinsic use-value of its own. *λῆρος εἶναι δοκεῖ τὸ νόμισμα καὶ νόμος παντάπασι, φύσει δ᾽ οὐδὲν ὅτι μεταθεμένων τε τῶν χρωμένων οὐδενὸς ἄξιον οὐδὲ χρήσιμον πρὸς οὐδὲν τῶν ἀναγκαίων ἐστί.* ("Others maintain that coined money is a mere sham, a thing not natural, but conventional only, which would have no value or use for any of the purposes of daily life if another commodity were substituted by the users." (l. c. sec. 11.)

82. Mandeville, Sir John, "Voyages and Travels," London, 1705, p. 105: "This Emperor (of Cattay or China) may dispende ols muche as he wile withouten estymacion. For he despendethe not, nor makethe no money, but of lether empredeth, or of papyre. And when that money bathe ronne so longe that it begynethe to waste, than men beren it to the Emperoure Tresorye, and then they taken newe Money for the old. And that money gothe thorghe out all the contree, and thorge out all his Provynces.... They make no money neither of Gold nor of Sylver," and "therefore," thinks Mandeville, "he may despende ynew and outrageously."

83. Benjamin Franklin, "Remarks and Facts Relative to the American Paper Money," 1764, p. 348, l. c. "At this very time, even the silver money in England is obliged to the legal tender for part of its value; that part which is the difference between its real weight and its denomination. Great part of the shillings and sixpences now current are by wearing become 5, 10, 20, and some of the sixpences even 50 per cent., too light. For this difference between the *real* and the *nominal* you have no intrinsic value. You have

not so much as paper, you have nothing. It is the legal tender, with the knowledge that it can easily be repassed for the same value, that makes three-pennyworth of silver pass for a sixpence."

84.   Berkeley, l. c., p. 5-6. "Whether the denominations being retained, although the bullion were gone … might not nevertheless … a circulation of commerce (be) maintained?"

85.   "Non solo i metalli ricchi son segni delle cose …; ma vicendevolmente le cose … sono segni dell'oro e dell'argento." (A. Genovesi, "Lezioni di Economia Civile," 1765. p. 281 in Custodi, Parte Mod. 1. VIII.) ("Not only are precious metals tokens of things, but vice versa, things are tokens of gold and silver.")

86.   Petty. "Gold and silver are universal wealth." (Political Arithmetic, l. c., p. 242.)

87.   E. Misselden. "Free Trade, or the Means to Make Trade Flourish," etc., London, 1622. "The natural matter of Commerce is Merchandise, which Merchants from the end of Trade have stiled Commodities. The Artificiall matter of Commerce is Money, which hath obtained the title of sinewes of warre and of State.… Money, though it be in nature and time after Merchandise, yet forasmuch as it is now in use become the chiefe." (p. 7.) He compares his own treatment of merchandise and money with the manner of "Old Jacob, who, blessing his Grandchildren, crost his hands, and laide his right hand on the yonger, and his left hand on the elder." (l. c.) Boisguillebert, "Dissert. sur la Nature Des Richesses," etc. "Voilà donc l'esclave du commerce devenu son maître.… La misère des peuples ne vient que de ce qu'on a fait un maître, ou plutôt un tyran de ce qui était un esclave." (p. 395, 399.)

88.   Boisguillebert, l. c. "On a fait une idole de ces métaux (l'or et l'argent) et laissant là, l'objet et l'intention pour lesquels ils avaient été appelés dans le commerce, savoir, pour y servir de gages dans l'échange et la tradition réciproque, on les a presque quittés de ce service pour en former des divinités, aux quelles on a sacrifié et sacrifie toujours plus de biens et de besoins précieux et même d'hommes, que jamais l'aveugle antiquité n'en immola à ces fausses divinités," etc. (l. c., p. 395.)

89.   In the first halt of the perpetuum mobile, i. e., in the suspension of the function of money as a medium of circulation, Boisguillebert at once suspects its independent existence from commodities. Money, he says, must be "in constant motion, it can be money only by being mobile, but as soon as it becomes motionless all is lost." ("Dans un mouvement continuel, ce qui ne peut être que tant qu'il est meuble, mais sitôt qu'il devient immeuble tout est perdu." ("Le Détail de la France," p. 231.) What he overlooks is that this halt constitutes the condition of its movement. What he really wants is that the value form of commodities should appear merely in the transitory form of their change of matter, but should never become an end in itself.

90.   " … The more the stock … is … encreased in wares, the more it decreaseth in treasure." (E. Misselden, l. c., p. 23.)

91.   l. c., p. 11-13 passim.

92.   Petty, "Political Arith.," l. c., p. 196 (1899 edition, v. I, p. 269. Transl.)

93.   Francois Bernier, "Voyage contenant la description des états du Grand Mogul." (Paris edition, 1830, t. l., conf., p. 312-314.

94.   Dr. Martin Luther, "Bücher vom Kaufhandel und Wucher," 1524. In the same passage Luther says: "Gott hat uns Deutsche dahin geschleidert, dass wir unser gold und silber müssen in fremde Länder stossen, alle Welt reich machen und selbst Bettler Bleiben. England sollte wohl weniger Goldes haben, wenn Deutschland ihm sein

Tuch liesse, und der König von Portugal sollte auch weniger haben, wenn wir ihm die Würze liessen. Rechne Du, wie viel eine Messe zu Frankfurt aus Deutschen Landen gefürt wird, ohne Not und Ursache: so wirst Du Dich wundern, wie es zugehe, dass noch ein heller in Deutschen Landen sei. Frankfurt ist das Silber- und Goldloch, dadurch aus Deutschem Lande fleisst, was nur guillet und wächst, gemünzt oder geschlagen wird bei uns; wäre das Loch zuegestopft, so dürft man itzt der Klage nicht hören, die allethalben eitel Schuld und kein Geld, alle Land und Städte ausgewuchert sind. Aber lass gehen, es will doch also gehen; wir Deutsche müssen Deutsche bleiben! wir lassen nicht ab, wir müssen denn." In the work quoted above Misselden wishes to retain the gold and silver at least within the confines of Christendom: "The other forreine remote causes of the want of money, are the Trades maintained out of Christendome to Turky, Persia and the East Indies, which trades are maintained for the most part with ready money, yet in a different manner from the trades of Christendome within itselfe. For although the trades within Christendome are driven with ready monies, yet those monies are still contained and continued within the bounds of Christendome. There is indeede a fluxus and refluxus, a flood and ebbe of the monies of Christendome traded within it selfe; for sometimes there is more in one part of Christendome, sometimes there is lesse in another, as one Country wanteth and another aboundeth: It cometh and goeth, and whirleth about the Circle of Christendome, but is still contained within the compasse thereof. But the money that is traded out of Christendome into the parts aforesaid is continually issued out and never returneth againe." (p. 19-20.)

95. "A nummo prima origo avaritiae … haec paulatim exarsit rabie quadam, non jam avaritia, sed fames auris." (Plin., Hist. Nat., l. XXXIII., c. XIV.) ("From money first springs avarice … the latter gradually grows into a kind of madness, which is no more avarice, but a thirst for gold.")

96. Horace thus understands nothing of the philosophy of hoarding when he says (Satir. l. II., Satir. III): "Siquis emat citharas, emptas comportat in unum, Nec studio citharae nec musae deditus ulli; Si scalpra et formas non sutor; nautica vela Aversus mercaturis; delirus et amens, Undique dicatur merito. Qui discrepat istis, Qui nummos aurunque recondit nescius uti Compositis metuensque velut contingere sacrum?"
"If one buys fiddles, hoards them up when bought,
Though music's study ne'er engaged his thought,
One lasts and awls, unversed in cobbler's craft,
One sails for ships, not knowing fore from aft,
You'd call them mad: but tell me, if you please,
How that man's case is different from these,
Who as he gets it, stows away his gain,
And thinks to touch a farthing were profane?"
(Transl. by John Covington, London, 1874, p. 60.)
Mr. Senior understands the question much better: "L'argent paraît etre la seule chose dont le désir est universel, et il en est ainsi parceque l'argent est *une richesse abstraite* et parceque les hommes, en la possédant peuvent satisfaire à tous leur besoins de quelque nature qu'ils soient." ("Principes Fondamentaux de l'Economie Politique, tirés de leçons edites et inedites de N. W. Senior, par Comte Jean Arrivabene," Paris, 1836, p. 221. (The corresponding passage in the English edition of his Political Economy, London, 1863, is to be found on p. 27. Translator.) So does Storch: "Since money represents all other forms of wealth, it is only necessary to accumulate it to provide for oneself all kinds of wealth existing in the world." (l. c., v. 2, p. 134.)

97. To what extent the inner man of the commodity owner remains unchanged, even when he has become civilized and has developed into a capitalist, is shown by the example

of a London representative of a cosmopolitan banking house who adopted as a fitting coat of arms for his family a £100,000 bank note, which he had hung up in a glass frame. The point here is in the mocking contempt of the note for circulation.

98. See the passage from Xenophon, quoted below.

99. Jacob, l. c., v. 2, ch. 25 and 26.

100. "In times of great agitation and insecurity, especially during internal commotions or invasions, gold and silver articles are rapidly converted into money; whilst during periods of tranquility and prosperity, money is converted into plate and jewelry." (l. c., v. 2, p. 357.)

101. In the following passage Xenophon develops money in its specific forms of money and hoard: "ἐν μόνῳ τούτῳ ὧν ἐγὼ οἶδα ἔργων οὐδὲ φθονεῖ οὐδεὶς τοῖς ἐπισκευαζομένοις ... ἀργυρῖτις δὲ ὅσῳ ἂν πλείων φαίνηται, καὶ ἀργύριον πλεῖον γίγνηται, τοσούτῳ πλείονες ἐπὶ τὸ ἔργον τοῦτο ἔρχονται ...καὶ γὰρ δὴ ἔπιπλα μὲν ἐπειδὰν ἱκανά τις κτήσηται τῇ οἰκίᾳ, οὐ μάλα ἔτι προσωνοῦνται· ἀργύριον δὲ οὐδεὶς πω οὕτω πολὺ ἐκτήσατο ὥστε μὴ ἔτι προσθεῖσθαι, ἀλλ᾽ ἤν τισι γένηται παμπληθές, τὸ περιττεῦον κατορύττοντες οὐδὲν ἧττον ἥδονται ἢ χρώμενοι αὐτῷ· καὶ μὲν ὅταν γε εὖ πράττωσιν αἱ πόλεις ἰσχυρῶς, οἱ ἄνθρωποι ἀργυρίου δέονται. Οἱ μὲν γὰρ ἄνδρες ἀμφὶ ὅπλα τε καλὰ καὶ ἵππους ἀγαθοὺς καὶ οἰκίας καὶ κατασκευὰς μεγαλοπρεπεῖς βούλονται δαπανᾶν, αἱ δὲ γυναῖκες εἰς ἐσθῆτα πολυτελῆ καὶ χρυσοῦν κόσμον τρέπονται· ὅταν δὲ αὖ νοσήσωσι πόλεις ἢ ἀφορίαις καρπῶν ἢ πολέμῳ ἔτι καὶ πολὺ μᾶλλον τῆς γῆς ἀργοῦ γιγνομένης καὶ εἰς ἐπιτήδεια καὶ εἰς ἐπικουροὺς νομίσματος δέονται." (Xen. de Vectigalibus, c. IV.) ("Of all operations with which I am acquainted, this is the only one in which no sort of jealousy is felt at a further development of the industry ... the larger the quantity of ore discovered and the greater the amount of silver extracted, the greater the number of persons ready to engage in the operation.... No one when he has got sufficient furniture for his house dreams of making further purchases on this head, but of silver no one ever yet possessed so much that he was forced to cry "Enough." On the contrary, if ever anybody does become possessed of an immoderate amount he finds as much pleasure in digging a hole in the ground and hoarding it as an actual employment of it.... When a state is prosperous there is nothing which people so much desire as silver. The men want money to expend on beautiful armor and fine horses, and houses and sumptuous paraphernalia of all sorts. The women betake themselves to expensive apparel and ornaments of gold. Or when states are sick, either through barrenness of corn and other fruits, or through war, the demand for current coin is even more imperative (whilst the ground lies unproductive), to pay for necessaries or military aid." (Transl. by H. G. Dakyns, London, 1892, v. 2, Revenues, p. 335-336.) Aristotle develops in Book I., ch. 9 of his Politics the two opposite movements of circulation. C-M-C and M-C-M, calling them "economics" and "chrematistics" respectively. The two forms are represented by the Greek tragedian Euripides as Sikn (right) and Keodos (profit).

102. Of course, capital also is advanced in the shape of money, and the money thus advanced may be advanced capital, but this point of view does not fall within the horizon of simple circulation.

103. "The difference between the means of purchase and the means of payment" is emphasized by Luther.

104. Mr. MacLeod, in spite of his doctrinaire conceit about definitions, fails so utterly to grasp the most elementary economic relations that he tries to deduce the very origin of money from its crowning form, viz., that of a means of payment. He says among other things that since people do not always need each other's services at the same time, and not to the same extent, "there would remain over a certain difference or

amount of service due from the first to the second-debt." The owner of this debt needs the services of a third person, who does not directly need those of the second, and "transfers to the third the debt due to him from the first. Evidence of debts changes so hands-currency....When a person received an obligation expressed by metallic currency, he is able to command the services not only of the original debtor, but of the whole of the industrious community." (MacLeod, "Theory and Practice of Banking," etc., London, 1855, v. I., ch. I.)

105. Bailey, l. c., p. 3. "Money is the general commodity of contracts, or that in which the majority of bargains about property, to be completed at a future time, are made."

106. Says Senior (in his Lectures, published by Comte Arrivabene, l. c., p. 117): "Since the value of everything changes within a certain period of time, people select as a means of payment an article whose value changes least and which retains longest a given average ability to buy things. Thus, money becomes the expression or representative of values." On the contrary: just because gold, silver, etc., have become money, i. e., the embodiment of independently existing exchange value, they become the universal means of payment. When the consideration as to the stability of the value of money mentioned by Mr. Senior comes into play, i. e., in periods when money asserts itself as the universal means of payment through the force of circumstances, then is just the time when fluctuations in the value of money are discovered. Such was the time of Elizabeth in England, when Lord Burleigh and Sir Thomas Smith, in view of the manifest depreciation of the precious metals, put through an act of parliament which obliged the universities of Oxford and Cambridge to stipulate the payment of one-third of their ground rents in wheat and malt.

107. Boisguillebert, who would stem the development of bourgeois relations of production and violently attacks the bourgeois personally, has a soft heart for those forms of money in which it appears only ideally or transiently. Thus he speaks first of the medium of circulation and next of the means of payment. What he does not see is the direct transition of money from its ideal to the material form, since the hard cash is latently present in the ideal measure of value. That money is but another form of commodities, he says, is shown by wholesale trade, in which exchange takes place without the intervention of money, after "les marchandises sont appreciés." ("Le Detail de la France," l. c. p. 210.)

108. Locke, l. c., p. 17, 18.

109. "Il danaro ammassato supplisce a quella somma, che per essere attualmente in circolazione, per l'eventuale promiscuità de 'commerci si allontana *e sorte della sfera della circolazione medesima.*" ("The accumulated money supplements that amount which, in order to be actually in circulation and to meet all possible perturbations of trade, retires from that sphere of circulation." (G. R. Carli, note to Berri's "Meditazioni sulla Economia Politica," p. 196, t. XV. of Custodi's l. c.)

110. Montanari, "Della Moneta," 1683, l. c., p. 40. "È cosi fattamente diffusa per tutto il globo terrestre la communicazione de 'populi insieme, che puo quasi dirsi esser il mondo tutto divinuto una sola citta in cui si fa perpetua fiera d'ogni mercanzia, e dove ogni uomo di tutto cio che la terra, gli animali e l'umana industria altrove producono, puo mediante il danaro stando in sua casa provedersi e godere. Maravigliosa invenzione." ("The communication of nations among themselves is so widely extended all over the globe that it may be almost said that the entire world has become one city in which a perpetual fair of merchandise is held and where every man may by means of money acquire and enjoy, while staying at home, all that the earth, the animals and human industry produce elsewhere. Marvelous invention.")

111. I metalli han questo di proprio e singulare che in essi soli tutte le ragioni si riducono ad una che è la loro quantità, non avendo ricevuto delle natura diversa qualità nè nell'interna loro constituzione nè nell'externa forma e fattura." (Galiani, l. c., p. 130.) ("Metals have this singular property, that everything in them is reduced to one consideration, viz., that of quantity, since they are not endowed by nature with any differences in quality either in their internal structure or in their external form and shape.")

112. De Orbe Novo. "O, happy coin, which furnishes mankind with a pleasant and useful beverage and keeps its possessors immune from the hell-born pest of avarice, since it can not be either buried or preserved long."

113. In 760 a multitude of poor people emigrated to the south of Prague to wash the gold sand found there, and three men were able to extract three marks of gold a day. As a result of that the run on the "diggings" and the number of hands taken away from agriculture became so great that the country was visited by a famine the following year. See M. G. Körner, "Abhandlung von dem Alterthum des Böhmischen Bergwerks," Schneeberg, 1758.

114. So far the Australian and other discoveries have not affected the ratio of the values of gold and silver. The assertions to the contrary of Michel Chevalier are worth as much as the Socialism of this ex-St. Simonist. The quotations of silver on the London market prove, however, that the average gold price of silver during 1850-1858 is not quite 3 per cent. higher than the price during 1830-1850. But this rise in price is accounted for simply by the Asiatic demand for silver. In the course of the years 1852-1858 the price of silver was changing in certain years and months only with a change in this demand, and in no case with the importation of gold from the newly discovered sources. The following is a summary of the gold prices of silver on the London market.
PRICE OF SILVER PER OUNCE.
Year —
March.
July.
November.
1852
60-1/8 pence
60-1/4 pence
61-7/8 pence
1853
61-3/8 pence
61-1/2 pence
61-7/8 pence
1854
61-7/8 pence
61-3/4 pence
61-1/2 pence
1855
60-7/8 pence
61-1/2 pence
60-7/8 pence
1856
60-7/8pence
61-1/4 pence
62-1/8 pence
1857

61-3/4 pence
61-5/8 pence
61-1/2 pence
1858
61-5/8 pence

115. "Gold is a wonderful thing! Whoever possesses it, is master of all that he desires. By means of gold even admission to Heaven may be gained for souls." (Columbus in a letter from Jamaica in 1503).

116. The slowness of the process was admitted by Hume, although it but little agrees with his principle. See David Hume "Essays and Treatises on several subjects." London, 1777, v. I, p. 300.

117. Conf. Steuart, l. c. v. I, p. 394-400.

118. David Hume, l. c. p. 300.

119. David Hume, l. c. p. 303.

120. David Hume, l. c. p. 303.

121. David Hume, l. c. p. 307, 308, 303: "It is evident, that the prices do not so much depend on the absolute quantity of commodities, and that of money, which are in a nation, as on that of the commodities, which can or may come to market, and of the money which circulates. If the coin be locked up in chests, it is the same thing with regard to prices, as if it were annihilated; if the commodities be hoarded in magazines and granaries, a like effect follows. As the money and commodities in these cases, never meet, they cannot affect each other. The whole (of prices) at last reaches *a just proportion with the new quantity of specie which is in the kingdom.*"

122. See *Law* and *Franklin* about surplus value which gold and silver are supposed to acquire from their function of money. Also *Forbonnais*.

123. This fiction is literally advanced by Montesquieu. [The passage from Montesquieu is quoted by Marx in his Capital, v. I. Part 1, Ch. III, section 2, b, foot-note. Note by K. Kautsky to 2nd German edition].

124. Steuart, l. c. v. I., p. 394 seq.

125. Steuart, l. c., v. 2. p. 377-379 passim (not found in the 1767 London edition. Translator).

126. Steuart, l. c., p. 379-380 passim (London, 1767 edition, v. l. p. 400. Transl.).

127. "The additional coin will be locked up, or converted into plate....As for the paper money, so soon as it has served the first purpose of supplying the demand of him who borrowed it, it will return upon the debtor in it and become realized....Let the specie of a country, therefore, be augmented or diminished in ever so great a proportion, commodities will still rise and fall according to the principles of demand and competition, and these will constantly depend upon the inclinations of those who have property or any kind of equivalent whatsoever to give, but never upon the quantity of coin they are possessed of....Let it (namely, the quantity of specie in a country) be ever so low, while there is real property of any denomination in the country, a competition to consume in those who possess it, prices will be high, by the means of barter, symbolical money, mutual prestations and a thousand other inventions....If this country has a communication with other nations, there must be a proportion between the prices of many kinds of merchandize there and elsewhere, and a sudden augmentation

or diminution of the specie, supposing it could of itself operate the effects of raising or sinking prices, would be restrained in its operation by foreign competition." l. c. v. 1, p. 400-402. "The circulation of every country must be in proportion to the industry of the inhabitants producing the commodities which come to market.... If the coin of a country, therefore, falls below the proportion of the price of industry offered to sale, inventions, like symbolical money, will be fallen upon, to provide for an equivalent for it. But if the specie be found above the proportion of industry, it will have no effect in raising prices, nor will it enter into circulation: it will be hoarded up in treasures.... Whatsoever be the quantity of money in a nation, in correspondence with the rest of the world, there never can remain in circulation, but the quantity nearly proportional to the consumption of the rich and to the labour and industry of the poor inhabitants," and this proportion is not determined "by the quantity of money actually in the country" (l. c. p. 403-408 passim.) "All nations will endeavor to throw their ready money, not necessary for their own circulation, into that country where the interest of money is high with respect to their own." (l. c. v. 2. p. 5). "The richest nation in Europe may be the poorest in circulating specie." l. c., v. 2, p. 6. For the polemics against Steuart see Arthur Young. [In his foot-note in Capital, v. 1, Part 1, ch. III., section 2, b. p. 62, Humboldt ed., Marx says: The theory of Hume was defended against the attacks of J. Steuart and others, by A. Young, in his "Political Arithmetic," London, 1774, in which work there is a special chapter entitled "Prices depend on quantity of money." Note by K. Kautsky to 2nd German edition].

128. Steuart, l. e., v. 2, p. 370. Louis Blanc translates the expression "money of the society" which stands for home or national money, as socialist money, which is perfectly meaningless and makes a Socialist of John Law. (See the first volume of his History of the French Revolution).

129. Maclaren, l. c. p. 43 seq. Patriotism led Gustav Julius, a German writer who met with very early death, to hold up old Büsch as an authority as against the Ricardian school. Honest Büsch rendered Steuart's elegant English into Hamburg Platt and by trying to improve upon the original spoiled it as often as he could.

130. Note to the 2nd edition: This is not an exact statement. Adam Smith expresses the law correctly on many occasions. [See Capital, Humboldt edition, p. 62, ft-note 1, where writing seven years later, Marx makes the following qualification: "This statement applies only in so far as Adam Smith, ex officio, treats of money. Now and then, however, as in his criticism of the earlier systems of political economy, he takes the right view. 'The quantity of coin in every country is regulated by the value of the commodities which are to be circulated by it.... The value of the goods annually bought and sold in any country requires a certain quantity of money to circulate and distribute them to their proper consumers, and can give employment to no more. The channel of circulation necessarily draws to itself a sum sufficient to fill it, and never admits any more.' Wealth of Nations, Book iv., ch. I."

131. The distinction between currency and money is therefore not found in "Wealth of Nations." Deceived by the apparent impartiality of Adam Smith, who knew his Hume and Steuart very well, honest Maclaren remarks: "The theory of the dependence of prices on the extent of the currency had not as yet, attracted attention; and Doctor Smith, like Mr. Locke (Locke undergoes a change in his view), considers metallic money nothing but a commodity." Maclaren, l. c. p. 44.

132. David Ricardo, "The High Price of Bullion, a Proof of the Depreciation of Banknotes." 4th edition, London, 1811. (The first edition appeared in 1809). Further, "Reply to Mr. Bosanquet's Practical Observations on the Report of the Bullion Committee." London, 1811.

133. David Ricardo: "On the Principles of Political Economy, etc." p. 77. "Their value [of metals] [like that of all other commodities], depends on the total quantity of labour necessary to obtain the metal, and to bring it to market."

134. l. c. p. 77, 180, 181.

135. Ricardo, l. c. p. 421. "The quantity of money that can be employed in a country must depend on its value: if gold alone were employed for the circulation of commodities, a quantity would be required, one fifteenth only of what would be necessary, if silver were made use of for the same purpose." See also Ricardo's: "Proposals for an Economical and Secure Currency," London, 1816, p. 89, where he says: "The amount of notes in circulation depends on the amount required for the circulation of the country; which is regulated ... by the value of the standard [of money], the amount of payments, and the economy practised in effecting them."

136. Ricardo, "Principles of Political Economy", p. 432.

137. David Ricardo, "Reply to Mr. Bosanquet's Practical Observations, etc." p. 49. "That commodities would rise or fall in price, in proportion to the increase or diminution of money, *I assume as a fact which is incontrovertible.*"

138. David Ricardo, "The High Price of Bullion," etc. "Money would have the same value in all countries." p. 4. In his Political Economy Ricardo modified this statement, but not in a way to affect what has been said here.

139. l. c. p. 3-4.

140. l. c., p. 4.

141. Ricardo, l. c., p. 11-12.

142. Ricardo, l. c., p. 14.

143. l. c., p. 17.

144. Ricardo, l. c., p. 74-75. "England, in consequence of a bad harvest, would come under the case of a country having been deprived of a part of its commodities, and, therefore, requiring a diminished amount of circulating medium. The currency which was before equal to her payments would now become super-abundant and relatively cheap, in proportion ... of her diminished production; the exportation of this sum, therefore, would restore the value of her currency to the value of the currencies of other countries." His confusion of money and commodity, and of money and coin borders on the ludicrous in the following passage: "If we can suppose that after an unfavorable harvest, when England has occasion for an unusual importation of corn, another nation is possessed of a super-abundance of that article, but has no wants for any commodity whatever, it would unquestionably follow that such nation would not export its corn in exchange for commodities: *but neither would it export corn for money*, as that is a commodity which no nation ever wants absolutely, but relatively." l. c., p. 75. Pushkin in his hero poem makes the father of his hero incapable of comprehending that commodities are money. But that money is a commodity, the Russians have understood from times of yore as is proven not only by the English corn imports in 1838-1842, but by the entire history of their commerce.

145. Conf. Thomas Tooke, "History of Prices," and James Wilson, "Capital, Currency and Banking." (The latter work is a reprint of a series of articles which appeared in the London Economist in 1844, 1845 and 1847.)

146. James Deacon Hume: "Letters on the Corn Laws." London, 1834, p. 29-31. [Letter by H. B. T. on the Corn Laws and on the Rights of the Working Classes. Transl.]

147. Thomas Tooke, "History of Prices," etc. London, 1848, p. 110.

148. Conf. W. Blake's above quoted "Observations etc."

149. James Mill: "Elements of Political Economy." [London, 1821, p. 95-101 passim. Transl.]

150. A few months before the outbreak of the commercial crisis of 1857, a committee of the House of Commons was in session to inquire into the effect of the bank-laws of 1844 and 1845. Lord Overstone, the theoretical father of these laws, delivered himself of this boast in his testimony before the committee: "By strict and prompt adherence to the principles of the act of 1844, everything has passed off with regularity and ease; the monetary system is safe and unshaken, the prosperity of the country is undisputed, the public confidence in the wisdom of the act of 1844 is daily gaining strength; and if the committee wish for further practical illustration of the soundness of the principles on which it rests, or of the beneficial results which it has assured, the true and sufficient answer to the committee is, look around you; look at the present state of trade of the country, look at the contentment of the people; look at the wealth and prosperity which pervades every class of the community; and then, having done so, the committee may be fairly called upon to decide whether they will interfere with the continuance of an act under which these results have been developed." Thus did Overstone blow his own horn on the fourteenth of July, 1857; on the twelfth of November of the same year the Ministry had to suspend on its own responsibility the wonderful law of 1844.

151. Tooke was entirely ignorant of Steuart's work, as may be seen from his "History of Prices for 1839-1847," London, 1848. where he reviews the history of the theories of money.

152. Tooke's most important work besides the "History of Prices" which his co-worker Newmarch published in six volumes, is "An Inquiry into the Currency Principle, the Connection of the Currency with Prices" etc., 2nd edition, London, 1844. Wilson's book we have already quoted. Finally there is to be mentioned John Fullarton's "On the Regulation of Currencies," 2d edition, London, 1845.

153. "We ought to … distinguish … between gold … as merchandise, *i. e.* as capital, and gold … as currency" (Tooke, "An Inquiry into the Currency Principle, etc." p. 10). "Gold and silver may be counted upon to realize on their arrival nearly the exact sum required to be provided … gold and silver possess an infinite advantage over all other description of merchandize … from the circumstance of being universally in use as money.… It is not in tea, coffee, sugar or indigo that debts, whether foreign or domestic, are usually contracted to be paid, but in coin; and the remittance, therefore, either in the identical coin designated, or in bullion which can be promptly turned into that coin through the mint or market of the country to which it is sent, must always afford to the remitter, the most certain, immediate, and accurate means of affecting this object, without risk of disappointment from the failure of demand or fluctuation of price." (Fullerton, l. c. p. 132-133.) "Any other article (except gold or silver) might in quantity or kind be beyond the usual demand of the country to which it is sent." (Tooke: "An Inquiry, etc.")

154. The transformation of money into capital we shall consider in the third chapter which treats of capital and forms the end of the first book.

155. This introduction was first published in the Neue Zeit (see Translator's Preface, p. 5) of March 7, 14 and 21, 1903, by Karl Kautsky, with the following explanation:

"This article has been found among the posthumous papers of Karl Marx. It is a fragmentary sketch of a treatise that was to have served as an introduction to his main work, which he had been writing for many years and whose outline was clearly formed in his mind. The manuscript is dated August 23, 1857....As the idea is very often indicated only in fragmentary sentences, I have taken the liberty of introducing here and there changes in style, insertions of words, etc....A mere reprint of the original would have made it unintelligible....Not all the words in the manuscript are legible.... "Wherever there could be no doubt as to the necessity of corrections, I did so without indicating them in the text; in other cases I put all insertions in brackets. Wherever I am not certain as to whether I have deciphered a word correctly, I have put an interrogation point after it; other changes are specially noted. In all other respects this is an exact reprint of the original, whose fragmentary and incomplete passages serve to remind us only too painfully of the many treasures of thought which went down to the grave with Marx, treasures which would have sufficed for generations if Marx had not so anxiously avoided giving to the world any of his ideas until he had tested them repeatedly from every conceivable point of view and had given them a wording that would be incontrovertible. In spite of its fragmentary character it opens before us a wealth of new points of view."

156. The original reads "person."

157. The manuscript reads "production."

158. The manuscript reads "production."

159. The German text reads "instruktiv," which I take to be a misprint of "instinktiv." Translator.

160. Compare this with foot-note 1, on p. 34 of Capital, Humboldt edition, New York: "Truly comical is M. Bastiat, who imagines that the ancient Greeks and Romans lived by plunder alone. But when people plunder for centuries, there must always be something at hand for them to seize; the objects of plunder must be continually reproduced." K. Kautsky.

161. The English expression is used by Marx in his German original. Transl.

162. Marx evidently has in mind here a passage in Adam Smith's Wealth of Nations (vol. 2, ch. 2) in which he speaks of the circulation of a country as consisting of two distinct parts: circulation between dealers and dealers, and that between dealers and consumers. The word dealer signifies here not only a merchant or shopkeeper, but also a producer. K. Kautsky.

163. Here two words in the manuscript can not be deciphered. They look like "ausser sich" ("outside of itself"). K. Kautsky.

164. Distribution (Verkehr) is used here in the sense of physical distribution of goods and not in sense of economic distribution of the shares of the products between the different factors of production. Translator.

165. As the "notes" written down by Marx in the following eight paragraphs are extremely fragmentary, making translation in some cases impossible without a certain degree of interpretation, and as the original is not accessible in book-form, they are reproduced here in German for the benefit of the student who may feel interested in the original wording as it had been jotted down by Marx.

166. Im Original ist zu lesen Va

167. Im Original ist zu lesen egtl.

168.   The site of the "Times" building in London. K. K.

www.ingramcontent.com/pod-product-compliance
Lightning Source LLC
Chambersburg PA
CBHW060241030426
42335CB00014B/1557